Irish Political Documents, 1869-1916

IRISH
POLITICAL DOCUMENTS
1869-1916

WITHDRAWN

Edited by

Arthur Mitchell and Pádraig Ó Snodaigh

IRISH ACADEMIC PRESS

The typesetting for this book was
produced by Gilbert Gough Typesetting, Dublin, for
Irish Academic Press, Kill Lane, Blackrock, Co. Dublin

BRITISH LIBRARY CATALOGUING IN PUBLICATION DATA
Irish political documents 1869-1916.
1. Ireland, 1800-
I. Mitchell , A. (Arthur)   II. Ó Snodaigh,
P. (Pádraig)
941.5081

ISBN 0-7165-2422-8

Printed in Great Britain by A. Wheaton & Co. Ltd, Exeter

CONTENTS

INTRODUCTION

This collection of documents traces the emergence of the Irish nation and responses to that development. They represent an effort to present a broad spectrum of political and constitutional issues — all centered around the central question of national self-government. They are, in fact, a chronology of progress, with some diversions and set-backs, towards the attainment of the promised land of nationhood. Viewing that quest from the vantage point of the 1980s, we may find ourselves casting a pitying eye on what nationalist-minded people of the period from 1869 to 1916 expected self-government to achieve for Ireland. As well, we may wonder why so many people rejected the proposition that the Irish people should claim the right to demand this status. Our retrospective judgement, however, is irrelevant in terms of how politically-active people felt about this matter back then. Documents provide illumination concerning particular events. Their greatest value is in determining who said what at a particular time. They can also be of help in understanding how and why events took place. In our view, the documents included here tell their own story; hence, we have not provided introductory notes. Should the reader be unable to place a particular document in its historical context, he should turn to a narrative history of the period, probably the best of which is F.S.L. Lyons, *Ireland Since the Famine*. This collection is designed as a supplement, not a substitute, for such narratives.

This is the second collection of documents we have edited. The first traced the political evolution of Ireland from 1916 to 1949, from one republic to another. In this work we have had the advantage of drawing on the models of other collections of documents, particularly those of Edmund Curtis and R.B. McDowell, *Irish historical documents, 1172-1922* (Dublin, 1943), who were the first scholars to produce such a collection; James Carty, *Ireland from the great famine to the treaty* (Dublin, 1951); Patrick Buckland, *Irish unionism, 1885-1923* (Belfast, 1973); and Anthony C. Hepburn, *The conflict of nationality in modern Ireland* (New York, 1980).

In preparing both volumes we have received valuable assistance from a variety of persons and institutions, including Dr Chistopher J. Woods of the Royal Irish Academy, Prof. T.P. O'Neill, then of University College, Galway, and the staffs of the National Library of Ireland and the State Paper Office, Dublin. A special word of thanks is due to Milton W. Harden of of the University of South Carolina — Salkehatchie Campus for providing an excellent introduction to the world of word processing.

ARTHUR MITCHELL
PÁDRAIG Ó SNODAIGH

THE DOCUMENTS

1. Disestablishment of the Church of Ireland, 1869: preamble to the law
Acts parl. U.K., 1869 (32 & 33 Vict., c. 42)

An Act to put an end to the Establishment of the Church of Ireland, and to make provision in respect of the Temporalities thereof, and in respect of the Royal College of Maynooth. [26th July 1869]

Whereas it is expedient that the union created by Act of Parliament between the Churches of England and Ireland, as by law established, should be dissolved, and that the Church of Ireland, as so separated, should cease to be established by law, and that after satisfying, so far as possible, upon the principles of equality as between the several religious denominations in Ireland, all just and equitable claims, the property of the said Church of Ireland, or the proceeds thereof, should be applied in such manner as Parliament shall hereafter direct:

And whereas Her Majesty has been graciously pleased to signify that she has placed at the disposal of Parliament her interest in the several archbishoprics, bishoprics, benefices, cathedral preferments, and other ecclesiastical dignities and offices in Ireland:

Be it therefore enacted by the Queen's most Excellent Majesty, by and with the advice and consent of the Lords Spiritual and Temporal, and Commons, in this present Parliament assembled, and by the authority of the same, as follows:

1. This Act may be cited for all purposes as 'The Irish Church Act, 1869.'

2. On and after the first day of January one thousand eight hundred and seventy-one the said union created by Act of Parliament between the Churches of England and Ireland shall be dissolved, and the said Church of Ireland, hereinafter referred to as 'the said Church,' shall cease to be established by law.

2. Opposition to disestablishment: report of a protest meeting in Dublin
Irish Times, 16 April 1869

Last evening . . . an aggregate meeting convened by the Committee of the Central Protestant Association, was held in the Metropolitan Hall. . . .

Major Gun Cunninghame . . . said . . . he was sure that the House of Lords would not allow Her Majesty to be insulted by allowing such a nefarious Bill as that proposed by Mr Gladstone to become Law.

15

(Applause.) No matter how the bill was amended they would not accept it and in this country they were determined to give such a shout of 'No Surrender' — (cheers) — that every true Protestant would rally round the Queen when she felt it necessary to unfurl once more the banner that William III unfurled — (cheers and Kentish fire) — for the Protestant religion and the liberties of England. (Cheers.)

3. The land act, 1870
Acts parl. U.K., 1870 (33 & 34 Vict., c. 46)

An Act to amend the Law relating to the Occupation and Ownership of Land in Ireland [1st August 1870.]

Whereas it is expedient to amend the law relating to the occupation and ownership of land in Ireland:

Be it enacted by the Queen's most Excellent Majesty, by and with the advice and consent of the Lords Spiritual and Temporal, and Commons, in this present Parliament assembled, and by the authority of the same, as follows:

PART I

Law of Compensation to Tenants

Claim to Compensation
1. The usages prevalent in the province of Ulster, which are known as, and in this Act intended to be included under, the denomination of the Ulster tenant-right custom, are hereby declared to be legal, and shall, in the case of any holding in the province of Ulster proved to be subject thereto, be enforced in manner provided by this Act.

Where the landlord has purchased or acquired or shall hereafter purchase or acquire from the tenant the Ulster tenant-right custom to which his holding is subject, such holding shall thenceforth cease to be subject to the Ulster tenant-right custom.

A tenant of a holding subject to the Ulster tenant-right custom, and who claims the benefit of such custom, shall not be entitled to compensation under any other section of this Act; but a tenant of a holding subject to such custom, but not claiming under the same, shall not be barred from making a claim for compensation, with the consent of the Court, under any of the other sections of this Act, except the section relating to compensation in respect of payment to incoming tenant; and where such last-mentioned claim has been made, and allowed, such holding shall not be again subject to the Ulster tenant-right custom.

2. If, in the case of any holding not situate within the province of

16

Ulster, it shall appear that an usage prevails which in all essential particulars corresponds with the Ulster tenant-right custom, it shall in like manner, and subject to the like conditions, be deemed legal, and shall be enforced in manner provided by this Act.

Where the landlord has purchased or acquired or shall hereafter purchase or acquire from the tenant the benefit of such usage as aforesaid to which his holding is subject, such holding shall henceforth cease to be subject to such usage.

A tenant of any holding subject to such usage as aforesaid, and who claims the benefit of the same, shall not be entitled to claim compensation under any other section of this Act; but a tenant of a holding not claiming the benefit of such usage shall not be barred from making a claim for compensation with the consent of the Court under any of the other sections of this Act, and where such last-mentioned claim has been made and allowed, such holding shall not be again subject to such usage as aforesaid.

3. Where the tenant of any holding held by him under a tenancy created after the passing of this Act is not entitled to compensation under sections one and two of this Act, or either of such sections or if entitled does not seek compensation under said sections or either of them, and is disturbed in his holding by the Act of the landlord, he shall be entitled to such compensation for the loss which the Court shall find to be sustained by him by reason of quitting his holding, to be paid by the landlord, as the Court may think just, so that the sum awarded does not exceed the scale following; that is to say,

In the case of holdings valued under the Acts relating to the valuation of rateable property in Ireland at an annual value of —

(1) £10 and under, a sum which shall in no case exceed seven years rent;

(2) Above £10 and not exceeding £30, a sum which shall in no case exceed five years rent;

(3) Above £30 and not exceeding £40, a sum which shall in no case exceed four years rent;

(4) Above £40 and not exceeding £50, a sum which shall in no case exceed three years rent;

(5) Above £50 and not exceeding £100, a sum which shall in no case exceed two years rent;

(6) Above £100, a sum which shall in no case exceed one year's rent;

But in no case shall the compensation exceed the sum of £250.

Any tenant in a higher class of the scale may, at his option, claim compensation under a lower class, provided such compensation shall not exceed the sum to which he would be entitled under such lower class on the assumption that the annual value of his holding is reduced to the sum (or where two sums are mentioned, the highest sum) stated in such lower class, and that his rent is proportionally reduced.

Provided that no tenant of a holding valued at a yearly sum exceeding £10, and claiming under this section more than four years rent, and no tenant of a holding valued at a yearly sum not exceeding £10, and claiming as aforesaid more than five years rent, shall be entitled to make a separate or additional claim for improvements other than permanent buildings and reclamation of waste land.

Provided that —

(1) Out of any moneys payable to the tenant under this section all sums due to the landlord from the tenant or his predecessors in title in respect of rent, or in respect of any deterioration of a holding arising from non-observance on the part of the tenant of any express or implied covenant or agreement, may be deducted by the landlord, and also any taxes payable by the tenant due in respect of the holding, and not recoverable by him from the landlord:

(2) A tenant of a holding who at any time after the passing of this Act subdivides such holding, or sublets the same or any part thereof without the consent of the landlord in writing, or, after he has been prohibited in writing by the landlord or his agent from so doing, lets the same or any part thereof in conacre, save for the purpose of being solely used and which shall be solely used for the growing of potatoes or other green crops, the land being properly manured, shall not, nor shall any sub-tenant of or under any such tenant as last aforesaid, be entitled to any compensation under this section:

(3) A tenant of a holding under a lease made after the passing of this Act, and granted for a term certain of not less than thirty-one years, shall not be entitled to any compensation under this section, but he may claim compensation under section four of this Act.

The tenant of any holding valued under the Acts relating to the valuation of rateable property in Ireland at an annual value of not more than one hundred pounds, and held by him under a tenancy from year to year existing at the time of the passing of this Act, shall, if disturbed by the Act of his immediate landlord, be entitled to compensation under and subject to the provisions of this section.

Any contract made by a tenant by virtue of which he is deprived of his right to make any claim which he would otherwise be entitled to make under this section shall, so far as relates to such claim, be void, both at law and in equity; this provision shall be subject to the enactment contained in the section of this Act relating to the partial exemption of certain tenancies, and remain in force for twenty years from the first day of January one thousand eight hundred and seventy-one, and no longer, unless Parliament shall otherwise determine.

4. Any tenant of a holding who is not entitled to compensate under sections one and two of this Act, or either of such sections, or if entitled does not make any claim under the said sections, or either of them, may on quitting his holding, and subject to the provisions of section three of this Act, claim compensation to be paid by the landlord under this section in respect of all improvements on his holding made by him or his predecessors in title.

Provided that —

(1) A tenant shall not be entitled to any compensation in respect of any of the improvements following; that is to say, —

(a) In respect of any improvement made before the passing of this Act, and twenty years before the claim of such compensation shall have been made, except permanent buildings and reclamation of waste land; or,

(b) In respect of any improvement prohibited in writing by the landlord as being and appearing to the Court to be calculated to diminish the general value of the landlord's estate, and made within two years after the passing of this Act, or made during the unexpired residue of a lease granted before the passing of this Act. . . .

4. Home Government Association founded
Evening Mail, 7 October 1870

Mr Butt, Q.C. said . . . They formed themselves — first, into a committee, and afterwards an association — not a public organization, but a society composed of a number of gentlemen who had joined together to impress upon the public mind of Ireland their own opinions, and to carry them out. They had obtained, up to the present, in that quiet and unobtrusive way, over 500 members; and he might truly say that those gentlemen represented all shades of political opinion, and were not by any means confined to one religious creed (hear, hear). He wished to draw attention to an incident in their proceedings which he had witnessed with great satisfaction. They had elected a committee of 61 gentlemen to manage the affairs of the association and the votes of the members were so given that it was plain that no favouritism for either Protestants or Roman Catholics was entertained. There was no feeling displayed but an earnest desire to represent upon that committee all shades of political opinion. He did not dispute the fact that, in point of religious opinion, the Roman

Catholics had a majority — though a very small one — upon the committee; and, in point of politics, the Liberals, as compared with the Conservatives, numbered only three to two. . . . They had great difficulties to meet with; they had old dissensions and old distrusts and enmities to break down; all that could not be the work of a day or of a year — it would take time to effect it. . . . Then they might organize into one Irish Legislature the whole nation (hear,hear). . . .

5. Principles of the Home Government Association
Home Government Association, *First report passed at a meeting at the Rotunda, Dublin,* 26 June 1871

I. This Association is formed for the purpose of obtaining for Ireland the right of Self-Government by means of a National Parliament.

II. It is hereby declared, as the essential principle of this Association, that the objects, and THE ONLY OBJECTS, contemplated by its organization are:

To obtain for our country the right and privilege of managing our own affairs, by a Parliament assembled in Ireland, composed of Her Majesty the Sovereign, and her successors, and the Lords and Commons of Ireland:

To secure for that Parliament, under a Federal arrangement, the right of legislating for and regulating all matters relating to the internal affairs of Ireland, and control over Irish resources and revenues, subject to the obligation of contributing our just proportion of the Imperial expenditure:

To leave to an Imperial Parliament the power of dealing with all questions affecting the Imperial Crown and government, legislation regarding the Colonies and other dependencies of the Crown, the relations of the United Empire with foreign states, and all matters appertaining to the defence and the stability of the Empire at large:

To attain such an adjustment of the relations between the two countries, without any interference with the prerogatives of the Crown, or any disturbances of the principles of the constitution.

III. The Association invites the co-operation of all Irishmen who are willing to join in seeking for Ireland a Federal arrangement based upon these general principles.

IV. The Association will endeavour to forward the object it has in view, by using all legitimate means of influencing public sentiment, both in Ireland and Great Britain, by taking all opportunities of instructing and informing public opinion, and by seeking to unite Irishmen of all creeds and classes in one national movement, in support of the great national object hereby contemplated.

V. It is declared to be an essential principle of the Association, that while every member is understood by joining it to concur in its general object and plan of action, no person so joining is committed to any political opinion, except the advisability of seeking for Ireland the amount of Self-Government contemplated in the objects of the Association.

6. Proclamation of the mayor of Belfast during sectarian riots in August 1872
Northern Whig, 20 August 1872

Whereas for several days past riots have taken place in the Borough of Belfast, whereby great injury has been done to property and the lives of peaceable inhabitants endangered:

And whereas I have received sworn information that riotous mobs still continue to do injury to life and property:

Now, take notice, that I hereby require the following regulations to be observed: —

That peaceable inhabitants residing in or about the disturbed districts are to keep within their houses. Those found in the streets in mobs and obstructing the thoroughfares will be treated as rioters.

That all public houses shall close and keep closed until Friday next at twelve o'clock.

That any publican found selling spirits, etc., after this notice shall be prosecuted according to law.

That all persons selling firearms shall forthwith close, and keep closed until further orders.

That the military have authority to disperse, by force, all mobs and assemblies of people on the public streets.

They have also instructions to enter all houses from which fire-arms shall be discharged, and arrest all persons found within.

Take notice, the military and police have positive orders to fire upon riotous mobs.

John Savage,Knt.,
Mayor of Belfast
Dated this 19th August, 1872.

7. Constitution of revived Irish Republican Brotherhood
Adopted 17 March 1873. *National Museum of Ireland*, EW 1358

WHEREAS The Irish People have never ceased to struggle for the recovery of their Independence since the date of its destruction, and WHEREAS It has, on this seventeenth Day of March (the Day of our Patron Saint, Saint Patrick) 1873, been resolved by a Convention of Irish Patriots, held in Dublin, and representing associations of Irishmen existing in various parts of Ireland, England and Scotland, to amend the Constitution of the present Irish Revolutionary Organisation for the purpose of overthrowing English Power in Ireland, and of establishing an Independent Irish Republic. Said organisation being known as The Irish Republican Brotherhood, and governed by a Council entitled the Supreme Council of the Irish Republican Brotherhood and Government of the Irish Republic. The following is declared to be and promulgated as the Amended Constitution of the Irish Republican Brotherhood and of the Supreme Council of the Irish Republican Brotherhood and Government of the Irish Republic.

Constitution of the Irish Republican Brotherhood

1. The I.R.B. is and shall be composed of Irishmen, irrespective of class or creed, resident in Ireland, England, Scotland, America, Australia, and in all other lands where Irishmen live, who are willing to labour for the establishment of a free and independent Republican Government in Ireland.
2. The I.R.B. whilst labouring to prepare Ireland for the task of recovering her independence by force of arms, shall confine itself in times of peace to the exercise of moral influences - - - the cultivation of union and brotherly love amongst Irishmen - - - the propagation of Republican principles and the spreading of a knowledge of the national rights of Ireland.
3. The I.R.B. shall await the decision of the Irish Nation, as expressed by a majority of the Irish people, as to the fit hour of inaugurating a war against England, and shall, pending such an emergency, lend its support to every movement calculated to advance the cause of Irish Independence consistently with the preservation of its own integrity.
4. The mode of initiating members into the I.R.B. shall be the rendering of the following oath of Allegiance to its Government: —
    'In the Presence of God, I, - - - - - -, do solemnly swear that I will do my utmost to establish the National Independence of Ireland,

and that I will bear true allegiance to the Supreme Council of the Irish Republican Brotherhood and Government of the Irish Republic, and implicitly obey the Constitution of the Irish Republican Brotherhood, and all my superior officers and that I will preserve inviolable the secrets of the Organisation.'

5. No one shall be inducted into the I.R.B. whose character for sobriety, truth, valour and obedience to Authority cannot bear scrutiny.

6. Each member of the I.R.B. shall contribute according to his means for the production of war materials, and also towards the expense of keeping up communication in the different divisions of the I.R.B., and for maintaining the efficiency of the Supreme Council.

7. In every case where arms are lost through negligence, the department through the neglect of which the loss occurred shall be responsible for the value of the arms.

8. The members of the I.R.B. resident in towns or parishes shall be directed and governed by an Officer to be entitled a Centre and to be elected by the members of the I.R.B., each body of members electing the Centre for their own town or parish.

9. The members and centres of the I.R.B. shall be directed and governed by an Officer to be entitled a County Centre, and to be elected by the Centres of the respective counties, and in England and Scotland the towns shall be grouped into districts corresponding in population to the counties in Ireland and each District shall be directed and governed by a District Centre, who shall be elected by the Centres of his district.

10. The I.R.B. shall be divided into Seven Electoral Divisions, to wit - - - Leinster, Munster,Ulster, Connaught,North of England, South of England, and Scotland and in each division one Civil and one Military Secretary shall be elected by the County or District Centres and the duty of the Civil Secretary shall be to act in all respects as deputy of the member of the Supreme Council of his division, and in the event of the removal of said member by the act of the enemy, disability, or death the Civil Secretary shall exercise authority in the division until a new member of the Supreme Council shall have been elected in the manner provided for the Constitution of the Supreme Council; and the duties of the Military Secretary shall be to execute all orders received by him in relation to the procuring, distributing and safe keeping of arms and ammunition. . . .

Amended Constitution of the Supreme Council of the I.R.B. and Government of the Irish Republic

1. The Supreme Council of the Irish Republican Brotherhood and

Government of the Irish Republic is and shall be composed of seven [eleven] members; seven of said members shall be elected by the seven electoral divisions as marked out in the Constitution of the Irish Republican Brotherhood, and the remaining four shall be honorary members, and shall be elected by the seven, to whom alone their names shall be known and enactments of the Government so constituted shall be the laws of the Irish Republic until the territory thereof shall have been recovered from the English enemy and a permanent Government established.

2. The manner of the election of the before-mentioned seven members of the Supreme Council shall be as follows: The County or District Centres shall be assembled in convention and shall elect a Committee of five of their number who under seal of an oath of secrecy shall elect the member of the Supreme Council for the division whereunto they belong.

3. The term of office of the Supreme Council shall be two years, but any member may be removed at any time by a two-thirds vote of his constituents or a two-thirds vote of the Supreme Council, and any member of the S.C. wishing to resign will give a month's notice to his constituents and to the S.C.

4. There shall be an Executive of the Supreme Council, composed of the President, Secretary and Treasurer of that body, the decision of any two of whom shall be binding to all.

5. The duty of the President of the Supreme Council shall be to direct the working of the Irish Republican Brotherhood in all its departments, subject to the control of the Supreme Council.

6. The appointment, suspension and removal of all departmental officers shall be vested in the executive subject to the approval of the Supreme Council.

7. No member of the Supreme Council or officers in the employment thereof shall be in receipt of any salary from the funds of the Supreme Council of the Irish Republican Brotherhood.

8. The authority of the Supreme Council shall be unquestioned by those who have become, or may hereafter become members of the I.R.B., and the Supreme Council is hereby declared in fact, as well as by right, the sole Government of the Irish Republic, and has authority to levy taxes, negotiate loans, make war and peace, and do all other acts necessary for the protection of the Irish Republic; and the members of the Supreme Council shall be bound to this constitution and to one another by an oath of fidelity and inviolable secrecy; and every act or attempted act of any member of the I.R.B. to subvert the authority of the Supreme Council shall, in time of peace, be a grave misdemeanour and

punishable accordingly; and in time of war every such act or attempted act shall be treason and punishable with death.

9. The Supreme Council reserves to itself the right of dealing with all friendly powers on all matters concerning the welfare of Ireland and the advancement of the cause of Irish Independence.

10. Executive power shall never be vested in one man, but shall be vested in the President, Secretary and Treasurer of the Supreme Council.

11. Each member of the I.R.B. and every member of the Supreme Council owes civil and military obedience to the Executive of the Supreme Council, and the President thereof is in fact, as well as by right, President of the Irish Republic.

12. In the event of the Supreme Council being inavoidably reduced in number, the member or remaining members shall exercise the authority of the Supreme Council until such time as the vacancies shall have been filled up, which shall be done as soon as possible and the same for the Executive.

13. The military authority shall at all times be and remain subject to the civil Government, and shall never be permitted to arrogate to itself the power of legislating or of restraining in any way the Constitution of the Irish Republic as promulgated by the Supreme Council.

14. At each meeting of the Supreme Council the members thereof shall hand in a summarised statement of the receipts and expenditure of the respective divisions.

15. The Supreme Council shall have power to award Capital Punishment only in cases of treason, and the crime of treason is hereby defined as any wilful act or word on the part of any member of the I.R.B. or of the Supreme Council calculated to betray the cause of Irish Independence and subserve the interest of the British or any foreign Government in Ireland, to the detriment of Irish Independence.

16. The Supreme Council shall appoint a Secret Court in each of the seven divisions of the I.R.B. for the trial of all members charged with the commission of treason or grave misdemeanours.

17. The Supreme Council shall undertake the punishment of all minor offences committed by the members of the I.R.B. once the offending members have removed from the division whereunto they belonged; and in cases where members unlawfully appropriate moneys intrusted to them for national purposes, such members shall be expelled the I.R.B., and the Supreme Council shall draw up a list of the names of such members and circulate it through all parts of the I.R.B. and forward copies of it to representative Irishmen in every part of the world, in order that those who rob the treasury of their country may be held up to the execration of all honest men.

18. In the Irish Republic there shall be no State Religion but every citizen shall be free to worship God according to his conscience, and perfect freedom of worship shall be guaranteed as a right, and not granted as a privilege.

19. The Supreme Council shall have power to alter or revise the foregoing Constitution of the Irish Republican Brotherhood and of the Supreme Council of the Irish Republican Brotherhood and Government of the Irish Republic, but whenever it is contemplated to make any alterations it shall be necessary to give One Month's notice of the meeting of the Supreme Council at which such alteration is proposed to be effected; and it shall require a two-thirds vote of the Supreme Council to make the proposed change.

By Order of
THE SUPREME COUNCIL

8. Isaac Butt on home rule
Hansard 3 (Commons), 3rd series, ccxx, 702-17, 30 June 1874

The Resolutions he now submitted to the House were very clear, and if they were debated, it would be seen that they were quite sufficient to guide the House to a conclusion. In the next place, he would direct their attention to this fact — that they involved no change in the Constitution; and he was anxious that the House should clearly understand this. He proposed no change in the Imperial Parliament, and if his scheme were adopted, the House would meet next year just as it had done this; there would not be a single change in Members or constituencies; there would be the Members for Leeds, Glasgow, Dublin and Limerick — the only change would be to take from that Assembly some of the duties which it now discharged in reference to Irish business, and to relegate them to another. That being so, he was tempted to ask, whether the removal of the Irish business from the house would be regarded by the hon. Members as an intolerable grievance? Some might be of opinion that it would be no great grievance if the Irish Members were sent away; but the great majority, he believed, would be of opinion that if the Irish business were transacted elsewhere, more time would be left for the transaction of the legitimate business of the House. Now, he might be asked what he called Irish business; and further, if, should Irish Members go into a Parliament of their own to transact their own business, they would still claim the power and privilege of voting on English questions in this House? He would answer the second question by saying emphatically 'No'. . . .

The English parliament, including the Scotch Members — he would perhaps have a word to say on the last point presently — would meet to discuss purely English affairs, and when there was any question affecting the Empire at large, Irish members might be summoned to attend. He saw no difficulty in the matter. The English Parliament could manage English affairs as before the Union; but now the English Parliament undertook a duty it was unable to perform — namely, to manage the internal affairs of Ireland to the satisfaction of the Irish people. He did not seek to interfere with the right of taxing Ireland for Imperial purposes, providing always that Ireland had a voice in Imperial matters. He was only asking for a Constitutional Government, and the benefit of those free institutions which made England great. If he succeeded in showing that Ireland had not a Constitutional Government, then he thought he could rely on the justice and generosity of the English Parliament and of the Commons at large to give it to her. What was Constitutional Government? It consisted of adequate representation in Parliament — a control of the administration of affairs by a Representative Assembly of the people, so as to bring the Government of the country into harmony with the feeling, the wants, and the wishes of the people. Did the representation by 103 Irish Members in the English House of Commons amount to that? Could it be said that that House discharged the great function of Constitutional Government to Ireland? If it did not, then it followed that Ireland was deprived of that Constitutional Government which was its inherent right. He knew it might be said that this involved the question whether Ireland and England were not so blended into one nation, that the same House might discharge the duties of a representative assembly for both. That, again, was a matter of fact. The House might wish that they were all West Britons, but wishes would not alter facts. . . . The two countries were not blended together, because in every department in Ireland the distinction was marked. They had a separate Government, a separate Lord Lieutenant, separate Courts of Law; and exceptional laws were passed for Ireland which would never be tolerated for England. How then, could one Representative Assembly act for both? Was not the consequence that the weaker country had no Constitutional Government? In this country there was Constitutional Government. The House of Commons administered the affairs of the nation in harmony with the sentiments of the English people. Statesmen in that House breathed an atmosphere of English feeling; they discussed English questions in an English assembly; they were driven of necessity to mould the administration of the Government in accordance with the wants and wishes of the people. They asked the same for Ireland, and they asked for no more. . . .

As a matter of fact, the whole Government of Ireland was based upon distrust of all classes in the community. Stipendary magistrates were substituted for the resident gentry of the country, and a sub-inspector of constabulary was a more influential person than the lord-lieutenant of a county. The whole record of the legislation for Ireland since the Union was made up of successive Arms Acts, suspensions of the Habeas Corpus Act, to Party Processions Prevention Acts, and Coercion Acts, each one being more severe than its predecessor. And this record was the more gloomy because it was a record of the doings of well-intentioned Parliaments. Nowithstanding all that had been done, the curfew bell of the Norman conquerors was rung in many parts of the country, and in others blood money was exacted after the example of the Saxons. Even if it were true — which he denied — that such a course of legislation had been necessary, that very fact would be its most grievious condemnation. He was therefore justified in saying that up to now the Government of the country had failed, and in asking that the Irish people might have an opportunity of managing their own affairs. He was told that Parliament having passed the Land Act and the Church Act, the Irish people were ungrateful in coming forward and demanding Home Rule also. It was even said that such a course was an act of ingratitude towards the individual Minister who had been mainly instrumental in passing those Acts. All he could say was that such assertions showed the faultiness of the system under which they could be possible. Who ever spoke of the English people being grateful for the passing of a good Act? . . . Was there an Englishman in the House who would not be glad to get rid of the opprobriums attaching to the Government of Ireland? If the wish was really entertained, the way to get rid of it was by allowing the Irish people an opportunity of trying to govern themselves. If they succeeded, great and glorious would be the reward of those who gave the opportunity; if they failed, theirs alone would be the blame. And where was there to be found any valid objection to granting what they asked? The Imperial Parliament would hold the Army, the Navy, and all that was connected with affairs purely Imperial, and no difficulty would be found in separating from Imperial questions those with which an Irish Parliament might properly deal. The United States of America afforded an illustration of a successful Federal Government with independent State Legislatures, and in some of our own Colonies they found instances of people owning the Imperial sway of England, but at the same time managing their own internal affairs. Even supposing that there might be some disaffected Members of an Irish Parliament — and this he did not admit — they would be in a miserable minority, and the fact of their disaffection being open to the light would give the strongest assurance of its speedy extinction. In two English Colonies were to be found men who, driven out of Ireland because they could no longer endure the system of government existing there, had become Ministers under the British Crown, and were doing honour alike to the Colonies in which they served and to the Sovereign who had appointed them. Sir George Grey, the Governor of the Cape of Good Hope, wrote strongly in favour of giving a Federal Parliament to Ireland, and he believed in his soul that it would be the means of effecting a complete union with England. Wrong had driven a large proportion of the Irish people into the madness of insurrection or sympathy with insurrection. It was, indeed, the consciousness of this fact which made him set himself earnestly to work to devise a means of stopping this miserable series of abortive insurrections and revolts by which Ireland had been torn and some of the best and bravest of her sons driven into exile. He believed he had devised a plan which would satisfy the just demands of the people without producing a disintegration of the Empire; therefore, he had asked the people to give up the madness of revolt and join with him in constitutionally and peacefully making an appeal to England. Many of the people who supported this moderate proposal would waste their lives in useless struggles against England, if they saw no other redress for the sufferings of their country. . . . He believed the Irish people were essentially Conservative. It was only misgovernment that had driven them into revolt. Give them fair play, and there was no people on earth who would be more attached to true Conservative principles than the Irish nation. The geographical position of Ireland made it her interest to be united with England. They were allied to England by ties of kindred and ties of self-interest which bound them to maintain inviolate the connection with this country, and the way to maintain that connection was to give them justice in the manage- ment of their own internal affairs. . . . Give us . . . a full participation in your freedom, and make us sharers in those free institutions which have made England so great and glorious. Give us our share which we have not now in the greatest and best of all free institutions — a free Parliament, representing indifferently the whole people. Then, indeed, we might speak the words which were spoken before in this House.

'Non ego nec Teucris Italos parere jubebo
Nec nova regna peto: paribus se legibus ambae
Invictae gentes aeterna in foedera mittant.' . . .

9. John Mitchel's election address in his successful candidacy in a Tipperary by-election
The Nation, 6 February 1875

New York, Feb. 3, 1875

I solicit the high honour of being elected as your representative.

I am in favour of Home Rule — that is, the Sovereign Independence of Ireland.

I shall seek the total overthrow of the Established Church; Universal Tenant-Right, and the abolition of Ejectments; Free Education — that is, Denominational Education for those who like it, Secular Education for those who like that, with the express organic provision of law, that no person shall be taxed for the education of other person's children.

I am in favour of the immediate liberation of those prisoners of State whom the English Government keeps in prison as 'Fenians'.

Lastly, as well as firstly, I am for *Home Rule*.

Electors of Tipperary! Many of you, as I hope, know me by name and reputation. If you believe that all the strength and energy left in me would be faithfully, and perhaps usefully, dedicated to the service of our native land, then give me your suffrages, and believe that the honour of Tipperary will not suffer in my hands.

I shall immediately present myself to you in person, and ask Tipperary to confer upon me the highest honour that I can even conceive awarded to mortal man — that of being the representative of the Premier County.

John Mitchel

10. The ownership of Irish land
Report,'Owners of Land (Ireland)', *Parliamentary papers*, 1876 (422) lxxx, 25

	Number of Owners	Extent			Valuation	
		A.	R.	P.	£.	s.
Total Number of Owners of less than 1 acre	36,144	9,065	1	80	1,366,448	-
Total Number of Owners of 1 acre and under 10 acres	6,892	28,968	-	35	498,917	6
Total Number of Owners of 10 acres and under 50	7,746	195,525	3	4	480,181	12

	Number of Owners	Extent			Valuation	
		A.	R.	P.	£.	s.
Total Number of Owners of 50 acres and under 100	3,479	250,147	-	-	313,374	8
Total Number of Owners of 100 acres and under 500	7,989	1,955,536	1	2	1,772,570	19
Total Number of Owners of 500 acres and under 1,000	2,716	1,915,528	-	6	1,332,435	9
Total Number of Owners of 1,000 acres and under 2,000	1,803	2,514,743	-	36	1,452,982	19
Total Number of Owners of 2,000 acres and under 5,000	1,198	3,675,267	3	22	1,997,210	7
Total Number of Owners of 5,000 acres and under 10,000	452	3,154,628	1	11	1,583,472	18
Total Number of Owners of 10,000 acres and under 20,000	185	2,478,493	-	19	1,113,673	13
Total Number of Owners of 20,000 acres and under 50,000	90	2,558,850	-	30	1,071,616	12
Total Number of Owners of 50,000 acres and under 100,000	14	1,023,677	-	29	397,829	2
Total Number of Owners of 100,000 acres and under upwards	3	397,079	3	18	37,644	10
Total Number of Owners with no valuation	5	40	3	-	-	-
TOTAL	68,716	20,157,557	1	2	13,418,357	15
TOTAL in Printed Return (Summary of Ireland)	68,758	20,159,678	-	10	13,419,258	-
Add Errors in Totalling, Printing, etc., etc.	8	2,404	3	9	2,697	19
	68,766	20,162,082	3	19	13,421,955	19
Deduct Errors in Totalling, Printing, etc., etc.	50	4,525	2	17	3,598	4
TOTAL as Classified	68,716	20,157,557	1	2	13,418,357	15

11. Charles Kickham's oration at the grave of John O'Mahony
The Irishman, 10 March 1877

It has never been the custom in Ireland to eulogise the illustrious dead over their graves; and, for my own part, I have always thought that the grave of the patriot was not the fitting place for oratory, even for eloquence the most chaste or the most imposing, but rather for the prayer and the tear and the resolve. I have not forgotten the address read in Glasnevin cemetery upon a memorable occasion, when the ashes of Terence Bellew McManus, after being carried over two oceans and a continent, found a resting-place in his own land . . . nor do I forget the eloquent panegyrics more recently spoken in the cemetery of our southern capital . . .; but 'God's acre' seems to me like God's house; and for this reason alone I will venture to express a hope that public speaking at funerals may continue among us to be the exception and not the rule. You will easily understand from what I have just said, that it was with the utmost reluctance I consented to address a few words to you even here, rather than embarrass by my refusal the committee who have given so much time and labour to the organising of this most impressive and significant manifestation of a people's gratitude and a people's faith. But I am sure you will all agree with me that this is not the moment, nor is this the place to delineate or try to delineate the character of the perfect patriot, the earnest worker, the able and prudent leader, who lies dead in our midst to-day; or to speak at any length of his labours and sacrifices in the undying cause of this unhappy but unconquered nation. The name of John O'Mahony is a household word in Ireland, and in every clime where her scattered children have found a home. His whole life was given to his country. True, he was never in chains, never knew the cruelties, the insults, and untold horrors of a British convict prison, nor was he strangled upon a British scaffold. Yet was John O'Mahony a martyr for Ireland; and from my knowledge of the man — and I believe he showed me his whole heart — his tender, affectionate nature, his yearning love of home and kindred, his sensitive pride — it is my firm conviction that no patriot living or dead ever endured more intense or prolonged suffering for the sake of the land that bore him than was endured for Ireland's sake by him around whose lifeless clay we are now assembled, and whose name will live for ever in the affections of a generous people, who reject with loathing the cold hearted suggestion that honour should be accorded only to the successful and the victorious. . During the latter years of his life of sacrifice he had to struggle, and he did struggle long and courageously, against bodily disease. Yes, his constitution, if not his heart, was broken; and, feeling that his end was near, he reluctantly loosed his grasp of the old flag, and said, 'I'll go home to die.' Oh! it is a sad, sad story. Less happy than Mitchel, he was never again to see his beloved *Erin of the Streams* — never to rest his eyes on the fair hills of holy Ireland. It was hard; but when he saw even this last fond hope fade away, thank God he at least knew that his dust would be Irish earth; for in the knowledge he had the assurance that he had not lived in vain. When the head of Robert Emmet fell upon the scaffold in Thomas-street, from that moment the great organisation founded by Wolfe Tone was a memory; an inspiring memory, no doubt, a memory to enkindle and keep alive the aspirations for liberty in the hearts of after generations; but still only a memory. When the imprisoned leaders of '48 prohibited any attempt to rescue them, O'Mahony, his heart torn with disappointment and anguish, broke up his camp on Ahinna, and with a price upon his head, escaped to France. From that hour Young Ireland lived only in its songs. But in spite of denunciation and calumny, of dissension and disorder and derision, in spite of the dungeon and the gallows the movement, the foundations of which were laid by Doheny, O'Mahony, and Stephens more than twenty years ago, is not a memory; it is an existing thing. . Behold the proof in these precious relics borne to us over three thousand miles of ocean, in the ordered lines which followed them through the streets of the great city on that ocean's far-off shore, in the hosts of men, who, from the moment of their arrival in Cork harbour, have thronged round them as to a holy shrine. Behold the proof that his has been no wasted life in the abounding love that says to every man in Ireland nursed, 'Join with us in honouring the memory of the dead, share in our sorrow to-day, as we mean that you shall share in the priceless blessing for which he has taught us how to labour — which he has showed us the way to win'. And you who expect to obtain from an alien Parliament some semblance of self-government, some security for the tiller of the soil, some right to educate your children in a way of which your consciences can approve — why can you not see, why have you not the justice to acknowledge, that you dare not even speak with bated breath of these things, if the country had not been lifted out of the lower deep of hopelessness into which venality and condoned treachery had plunged her — by men who knew how to dare and to suffer, as their fathers before them had dared and suffered, and who have demonstrated to friend and foe that — thanks to the progress of education — our people are at length capable of earnest, persevering, intelligent, sacrificing endeavour for the attainment of a possibly remote end! . . . No, we have not failed! John O'Mahony has not laboured and lived in vain. And, oh, how he did love Ireland! She was his mother, his queen, his idol, his all the world! And in the long roll of her patriot martyrs and confessors no name will shine with purer lustre than his. . Let us dry our tears; and standing around the bier of our dead chief, let us resolve and watch and labour and unite, always trusting in the justice of God, who has implanted this immortal longing for Nationhood in the hearts of our people, and hopefully remmembering that —

> 'Freedom hath arisen
> Oft from prison bars,
> Oft from battle flashes,
> Oft from patriot's life
> Oftenest from his ashes.'

His troubles are all over. Lay him gently to sleep in the bosom of his adored motherland. And as that sun goes down, millions and millions of the Irish race, remembering that his last beams are resting upon the grave of John O'Mahony, will join in our prayer — 'God rest the soul of the faithful and the brave!'

12. Michael Davitt on parliamentarianism
Report of his lecture at Brooklyn, New York in the *Irish World* (New York), 26 October 1878

He said he had chosen a somewhat 'dry' subject for his lecture, and while he knew that here in America, as well as elsewhere, Nationalists believed in a total separation of Ireland from England and a complete self-dependence, he would give his views on this occasion upon 'Irish Representation in the British Parliament'. He said that for years the Irish people have been misrepresented in the British Parliament, through which the civilized nations of the world were told that by granting a few remedial measures the Irish people would be happy, contented and *loyal*. That idea was spread broadcast through the instrumentality of West Britons, who have mispresented Ireland by asserting her loyalty to the British Crown. In the Home Rule party he had no faith. *That* he regarded as being what a prominent gentlemen, in conversation with him in London, said it was, *viz.*, an *organized hypocrisy*. Issac Butt, the leader of the movement, has proved his incompetency for the position he assumed, but, notwithstanding that fact, there is an effort being made at the present time to again put him forward as the champion representative of the Irish people. One thing, unfortunately, continues characteristic of the Irish race. In former ages the Irish people held in veneration and respect their chieftains and leaders, to whose support they always held themselves in readiness to rally. Even did those chieftains and leaders show incompetency or lack of judgment in their positions, they continued, notwithstanding unfitness, the recipients of the veneration, respect, and support of the people. From age to age up to the present that feature of the Irish has continued and is illustrated in the case of Mr. Butt. The people are inclined to think that because he is an able and learned lawyer who defended or rather pleaded for Fenian prisoners, advocated Home Rule measures, etc., he should still continue a[s] leader and represent them in the British Parliament, where he has already *misrepresented* them by asserting their loyalty to English domination. He had no faith in Parliamentary representation through the Home Rule party, the repeal party, or the disruption party. There is not, he said, a single Irish nationalist in the British Parliament, there to represent and proclaim to the world the views of the Irish people. There was a time when it was certain eviction for the Irish tenant to vote for any Parliamentary candidate except the one supported by his landlord. Now, however, that the ballot bill has been enacted as a law, the peasant can vote for any man without his landlord knowing how he voted. He (the speaker) was in favour of sending representatives imbued with nationalist ideas to the British Parliament — men who would not there fear to give expression to the feelings and demands of their constituency, and give the world to understand what the Irish people want. He was in favor of sending Nationalists to Parliament as well as electing them to every office possible from that down to town commissioners or poor law guardians. He was in favor of asserting and implanting the national spirit everywhere, in the representative assembly as well as in the individual's breast, be it under the peasant's cloak or the robe of the clergyman. He would regret very much if cunning England should succeed in her plans to get the Catholic hierarchy to try and crush out the national spirit. England knew full well the influence the priesthood has with the peasantry, and in her making concessions and courting Catholic favor through measures and appropriations calculated to secure such, she is endeavoring to create hostile feelings between the priests and the people, knowing full well that if she can succeed again at her old trick to create a disunion she can handle the Irish people at pleasure. Beaconsfield, who succeeded in getting Isaac Butt as an ally to imperialize Ireland, is now, as England's negotiator, willing to grant measures to the Catholic hierarchy, which, a few years since, would be regarded as treason, and are now offered with the view to control the people through their priests. It is to be hoped, however, that he will not succeed in arraying the priesthood in the English service and against the interests of the peasantry — a peasantry many of whom shed their heart's blood to protect the priest while celebrating Mass in the mountain from the bayonet of the English assassin. The lecturer reviewed the records of the Home Rule members of Parliament, and regards Mr. Parnell, the Obstructionist, as the best Irish representative in the British Parliament. While he did not think Mr. Biggar possessed as much ability, he had the honesty and fearlessness of Mr. Parnell, whom he acknowledged as his leader. He referred to Mr. O'Connor Power, and his visit to this country, and also to Mr. O'Donnell, who so disgracefully betrayed the trust of the Irish people. The lecturer then sketched a platform of principles, to which every Parliamentary candidate should pledge himself in order to get the support of Nationalists. Among other things, it demanded the establishment of small landed proprietorship, such as are in France and Belguim.

13. Charles Stewart Parnell and the land war
Connaught Telegraph, 14 June 1879

Mr. Parnell, M.P., who was loudly cheered, proposing the second resolution, said he wished to refer to the letter of his Grace the Archbishop of Tuam, which had appeared in the *Freeman's Journal*. He need not tell them that it would ill- become him, or anybody else, to treat anything proceeding from a man who had stood, as his Grace had, between the Irish people and the exterminator, with anything but the highest respect. This meeting had been placarded throughout the county Mayo for some six or seven weeks, announcing that he (the speaker) and other public men would address it. During all these weeks not a single person in Mayo or out of it, no clergyman ever intimated to him that the Archbishop was opposed to this meeting.

A Voice — It was never him who wrote the letter.

Mr. Parnell — It was only when leaving my home yesterday to come here that I, for the first time, became acquainted, by reading that letter, that his Grace was opposed to the meeting. I am sure 'John of Tuam' would not wish me to dishonour myself by breaking my word to this meeting and by remaining away from it (applause). The resolution I have to propose is this —

'That, whereas many landlords by successfully asserting in the courts of law their power to arbitrarily increase their rents, irrespective of the value of the holdings on their estates, have rendered worthless the Land Act of 1870 as a means of protection to the Irish tenants, we hereby declare that not only political expediency, but justice, and the vital interests of Ireland, demand such a readjustment of the land tenure — a readjustment based upon the principle that the occupier of the land shall be the owner thereof — as will prevent further confiscation of the tenant's property by unscrupulous landlords, and will secure to the people of Ireland their natural right to the soil of their country'.

I am one of those who believe the landlord institution is not a natural institution in any country. I believe that the maintenance of the class of landlords in a country is not for the greatest benefit of the greatest number. Ireland has, perhaps, suffered more than any other country in the world from the maintenance of such a class. England has, perhaps, assimilated itself better than any other country to the landlord system; but in almost every other country in the world where the system has been tried it has been given up. In Belgium, in Prussia, in France, and in Russia, the land has been given to the people — to the occupiers of the land. In some cases the landlords have been deprived of their property in the soil by the iron hand of revolution; in other cases, as in Prussia, the landlords have been purchased out. If such an arrangement could be made without injuring the landlord, so as to enable the tenant to have his land as his own, and to cultivate it as it ought to be cultivated, it would be for the benefit and prosperity of the country. I look to this as the final settlement of this question; but, in the meanwhile, it is necessary to ensure that as long as the tenant pays a fair rent he shall be left to enjoy the fruits of his industry. A fair rent is a rent the tenant can reasonably pay according to the times, but in bad times a tenant cannot be expected to pay as much as he did in good times, three or four years ago (applause). If such rents are insisted upon a repetition of the scenes of 1847 and 1848 will be witnessed. Now what must we do in order to induce the landlords to see the position? You must show the landlords that you intend to hold a firm grip of your homesteads and lands (applause). You must not allow yourselves to be dispossessed, as you were dispossessed in 1847. You must not allow your small holdings to be turned into large ones. I am supposing that the landlords will remain deaf to the voice of reason, but I hope they may not, and that on those properties which the rents are out of all proportion to the times, that a reduction may be made, and that immediately. If not, you must help yourselves, and the public opinion will stand by you and support in your struggle to defend your homesteads (applause). I shall be deceiving you if I told you that there was any use in relying upon the exertions of the Irish members of Parliament in your behalf. I think that if your members were determined and resolute they could help you, but I am afraid they won't. I hope that I may be wrong, and that you may rely upon the constitutional action of your Parliamentary representative in this the sore time of your need and trial, but above all things remember that God helps him who helps himself, and that by showing such a public spirit as you have shown here to-day, by coming in your thousands in the face of every difficulty, you will do more to show the landlords the necessity of dealing justly with you than if you had 150 Irish members in the House of Commons (applause). Perhaps I may be permitted for a moment to refer to the great question of self-government for Ireland. You will say, perhaps, that many men have said that this struggling for concessions in the House of Commons is a demoralising thing. Now I am confident as I am of my own existence that if you had men of determination, of some sort of courage and energy, representing you that you could obtain concessions (hear, hear). We are not likely to get them of such importance and amount as to run the risk of being demoralised by them; and also there is really no reason why we should permit ourselves to be demoralised by the greatest concession of all. If you obtain concessions on right principles, such as the Irish Church Act and the Land Act, you run no risk of demoralising yourselves. I have always noticed that the breaking down of barriers between different classes has increased their self-respect and increased the spirit of nationality amongst our people. I am convinced that nothing would more effectually promote the cause of self-government for Ireland than the breaking down of those barriers between different classes. Nothing would be more effectual for that than the obtaining of a good land bill — the planting of the people in the soil. If we had the farmers of Ireland the owners of the soil to-morrow we would not be long without getting an Irish Parliament (applause). I don't intend to be demoralised myself by any concessions. While we are getting a concession we may show the Government a little consideration for the time being, and give them a *quid pro quo*; but after that the bargain ceases, and when we have returned them a fitting return for what we have got we are quite [*sic.* quit] again, and are free to use such measures as may be necessary according to the times and according to the circumstances. You have a great country to struggle for — a great country before you. It is worth a little exertion on your part — it is worth a little time. Do your best, and your country will thank you for it, and your children hereafter (loud applause).

14. The National Land League of Mayo
Connaught Telegraph, 23 August 1879

An influential and representative meeting of Tenant-farmers, merchants, and traders of Mayo was held at Daly's Hotel [Castlebar] this day....

The Chairman read the following manifesto: — This body shall be known a[s]

THE NATIONAL LAND LEAGUE OF MAYO

and shall consist of farmers and others who will agree to labour for the objects here set forth and subscribe to the conditions of membership, principles and rules specified below —

OBJECTS

The objects for which this body is organised are —

1. To watch over the interests of the people it represents; protect the same, as far as may be in its power to do so, from an unjust or capricious exercise of power or privilege on the part of landlords or any other class of the community.

2. To resort to every means compatible with justice, morality and right reason which shall not clash defiantly with the Constitution upheld by the power of the British Empire in this country for the abolition of the present land laws of Ireland, and the substitution in their place of such a system as shall be in accord with the social rights and necessities of our people, the traditions and moral sentiments of our race, and which the contentment and prosperity of our country imperitively [*sic*] demand.

3. Pending a final and satisfactory settlement of the Land Question, the duty of this body will be to expose the injustice, wrong, or injury which may be inflicted upon any farmer in Mayo, either by rack-renting, eviction, or other arbitrary exercise of power which the existing laws enables the landlords to exercise over their tenantry, by giving all such arbitrary acts the widest possible publicity, and meeting their perpetration with all the opposition which the laws for the preservation of the peace will permit of, in furtherance of which the following plans will be adopted: —

a. Returns to be obtained, printed, and circulated, of the number of landlords in this county; the amount of acreage in possession of same, and the means by which such land was obtained; farms let by each, with the conditions under which they are held by their tenants, and excess of rent paid by same over Government valuation.

b. To publish by placard, or otherwise, notice of contemplated evictions for non-payment of exorbitant rent, or other unjust cause, and the convening of a public meeting, if deemed necessary or expedient, as near the scene of such eviction, as circumstances will allow, and on the day fixed upon for the same.

c. The publication of a list of evictions carried out, together with ca[u]ses of eviction, giving full particulars of same, names of landlords, agents, etc. concerned, and number of people affected by such acts.

d. The publication of the names of all persons who shall rent or occupy land or farms, from which others have been dispossessed for non-payment of exorbitant rent, or who shall offer a higher rent for land or farms than that paid by the occupiers.

e. The publication of reductions of rent and acts of justice or kindness performed by landlords in this county.

4. This body to undertake the defence of such of its members, or those of local clubs affiliated with it, who may be required to resist by law the actions of landlords or their agents who may purpose doing them injury, wrong, or injustice in connection with their land or farms.

5. To render assistance when possible to such farmer-members as may be evicted or otherwise wronged by landlords or their agents.

6. To undertake the organising of Local Clubs or Defence Associations in the baronies, towns and parishes of the county, the holding of public meetings on the land question, and the printing of pamphlets on that and other subjects for the information of the farming classes.

7. And finally to act as a Vigilance Committee in Mayo, note the conduct of its Grand Jury, Poor Law Guardians, Town Commissioners, and members of Parliament and pronounce upon the manner in which their respective functions are performed wherever the interests, social or political, of the people represented by this body renders it necessary or expedient to do so.

CONDITIONS OF MEMBERSHIP

1. To be a member of any Local Club or Defence Association in the county, and be selected by such club or association to represent the same on this central or county association.

2. A desire to co-operate in the carrying out of the foregoing objects and subscribing to the principles here enunciated with the view of propagating the same and labouring for their successful application in Ireland will qualify non-representative farmers or others for membership of this body, subject to the subscription and Rules laid down for same.

3. To pay any sum not under five shillings a year towards the carrying out of the foregoing objects and the end for which this body is created — the obtaining of the soil of Ireland for the people of Ireland who cultivate it.

The land of Ireland belongs to the people of Ireland to be held and cultivated for the sustenance of those whom God decreed to be the inhabitants thereof. Land being created to supply the necessaries of existence, those who cultivate it to that end have a higher claim to its absolute possession than those who make it an article of barter to be used or disposed of for purposes of profit or pleasure.

The end for which the land of a country is created requires an equitable distribution of the same among the people who are to live upon the fruits of their labour in its cultivation; any restriction, therefore, upon such a distribution by a feudal system embodying laws of primogeniture and entail, the ammassing [sic] of large estates, the claiming of proprietorship under penal obligations from occupiers, and preventing the same from developing the full resources of the land, must necessarily be opposed to the Divine purpose for which it was created, and to the social rights, security, and happiness of the people. . . .

If the land in the possession of 744 landlords in this country were divided into 20 acre farms it would support in ease and comparative independence over two millions and a half of our people.

To substitute for such an unjust and anomalous system as the present land code — one that would show an equal protection and solicitude for the social rights and well-being of the labouring millions as for those of the wealthy but non-operative few — is the principle upon which enlightened statesmanship aims at following in modern times to meet the growing necessities of that popular intelligence and awakening civilization which demands the sweeping away of those feudal laws opposed to the social progress and ideas of the age. Sacraficing [sic] the interests of the few to the welfare of the many by the abolition of feudal land codes, has laid the foundations of solid governments and secured the contentment of peoples in most European countries.

The interests of the landlords of Ireland are pecuniary and can be compensated, but the interest of the people of Ireland, dependent upon the produce of the soil, is their very existence.

In denouncing the existing land laws and demanding in their place such a system as will recognise and establish the cultivator of the soil as its proprietor, we neither purpose nor demand the confiscation of the interest which the landlords now hold in the land, but ask that compensation be given them for loss of said rights when the State, for the peace, benefit and happiness of the people, shall decree the abolition of the present system.

We appeal to the farmers of Ireland to be up and doing at once and organise themselves forthwith in order that their full strength may be put forth in behalf of themselves and their country in efforts to obtain what has brought security and comparative plenty to the farming classes of continental [*sic*] countries. Without an evidence of earnestness and practical determination being shown now by the farmers of Ireland and their friends in a demand for a small proprietory system, which alone can fully satisfy the Irish people or finally settle the great land question of the country, the tribunal of public opinion will neither credit the urgent necessity for such a change nor lend its influence in ameliorating the condition or redressing the social and political wrongs of which we complain.

Let us remember, in the words of one of Ireland's greatest sons, that 'the land is the fund whence we all ultimately draw; and if the terms on which the land is cultivated be unfair — if the agricultural system of a country be unsound, then the entire structure is rotten and will inevitably come down [']. Let us never forget that mere appeals to the public to encourage native industry in other departments must be utterly futile so long as the great and paramount native industry of the farmer is neglected.

In vain shall we try to rouse national spirit if the very men who make the nation sink into paupers before our face. Paupers have no country, no rights, no duties; and, in short, if we permit the small farmers to be reduced to pauperism — if we see them compelled to give up their land and throw themselves on public relief, there is an end of Ireland.

The f[m]anifesto was unanimously adopted.

The Chairman reminded the delegates that on them depended the organisation and encouragement of their weaker-hearted brethren. He trusted that before many months every part of Ireland would be organised. He trusted that those differences, those political or polemical differences, which had for so long kept Irishmen asunder, would disappear for ever from their ranks (hear, hear), and that on the platform which had been erected in Mayo would be found men of all shades of opinion in Ireland — the Home Ruler and the Nationalist, the devout Catholic and the sturdy Orangeman — and he trusted that they would know each other for the future only as Irishmen (hear, hear). . . .

15. Objectives of the Irish National Land League
Poster collection, National Library of Ireland

The Irish National Land League was formed for the following objects:—

First — To put an end to Rack-renting, Eviction,and Landlord Oppression.

Second — To effect such a radical change in the Land System of Ireland as will put it in the power of every Irish Farmer to become the owner, on fair terms, of the land he tills.

The means proposed to effect these objects are: —

(1) Organisation amongst the people and Tenant Farmers for the purpose of self-defence, and inculcating the absolute necessity of their refusing to take any Farm from which another may be evicted, or from purchasing any Cattle or Goods which may be seized on for non-payment of impossible rent.

(2) The cultivation of public opinion by persistent exposure, in the Press and by Public Meetings, of the monstrous injustice of the present system, and of its ruinous results.

(3) A resolute demand for the reduction of the excessive rents which have brought the Irish People to a state of starvation.

(4) Temperate but firm resistance to oppression and injustice.

16. Land war manifesto of the Land League
Poster collection, National Library of Ireland

TO ALL FARMERS OF IRELAND AND ALL INTERESTED IN THE
SETTLEMENT OF THE LAND QUESTION

Having addressed the exiled of our race in behalf of the investment which has been initiated for the redress of the land evils of our country, we now venture to appeal to you for practical assistance in the efforts we are making towards securing the soil of Ireland for those who cultivate it.

No more favourable opportunity has ever presented itself to our people for the settlement of a momentous national question than that which is now offered by circumstances, the most propitious for a radical reform, existing in conjunction with an extraordinary popular agitation demanding the justice of its concession.

The first industry of our people is paralysed. Foreign competition has supplemented the disastrous effects of bad harvests and produced a crisis which renders it almost impossible for farmers to meet their rent obligations. Agitation has had to be evoked to demand reduction of rents which could not be paid. The price of land has also fallen in consequence of the lowering of farm produce and the stand which the farming classes have been compelled to make for reduced rents.

Both will continue to be lowered until rents are brought to a proper level and land to its fair value.

Will the people of Ireland lay a firm hold on this land question at the tide that is now approaching and which will inevitably lead to a peasant proprietary, and thus ensure for our country that prosperity and contentment which a free soil has produced in countries where landlordism has been abolished.

We earnestly hope that those whom we address will prove themselves equal to the occasion. We at least are resolved to do our duty but if our efforts are not seconded by Farmer and Labourer, Trader and Mechanic, and all others whom a system must benefit, that would create and foster an industry which is the mainspring of a people's wealth and would prove the panacea for the social evils arising from unemployed masses, we are hopeless of success.

The best arguments for obtaining help from our exiled countrymen and other sympathisers will be the practical efforts we at home will make to show our earnestness in the cause for which we solicit their generous support.

We call upon all who desire the success of this movement to aid us by their subscription and assistance. We ask only for what will show the sympathy of those whose helping hands are required in the work.

The agitation for reduction of excessive rents must be sustained so that the operation of natural causes may be assisted in bringing land to a fair valuation, in order to enable its cultivators to become the owners of their own farms upon terms within the means of every occupier.

For this and other purposes beneficial to the farming classes, organisation is required among them and to sustain this land movement and encourage such organisation as well as to render assistance when necessary, to victims of Landlord oppression, we have appealed for money to our banished kindred and for these purposes and these alone, we now appeal to you for whatever aid you can afford to render.

This is no sectarian movement but one which affecting alike the social well-being of Catholic and Protestant should invite their emulative co-operation in efforts to achieve its success; nor is it exclusively concerned in ameliorating the condition of the farmer and agricultural labourer, but has for its scope the general advancement of every commerical interest and the encouragement of every occupation in the industrial ranks of our people.

The attention of the civilised world will be directed on Ireland to observe how she will work out the great social problem for the un-fettering of land and labour and the removal of those legal restrictions which prevent the soil of the country from producing the good for which it was created, thus making a struggle with poverty, through life, the penalty which the mass of mankind have to pay to evil laws for being born poor. Will Ireland be true to herself and equal to the task?

Signed,   Charles S. Parnell
Joseph G. Biggar
W.H. O'Sullivan
Patrick Egan
A.J. Kettle
Michael Davitt
Thomas Brennan
Executive, Irish National Land League

Committee Rooms, 62 Middle Abbey Street,
Dublin, 5th November, 1879

17. Clan na Gael circular concerning the 'New Departure', 1880
John Devoy papers, National Library of Ireland

TO S.G's AND BROTHERS OF V.C.

Office of 'X', F.C.,
January 5th, 1880

Brothers:

Messrs. PARNELL and DILLON have arrived. It is very important that they receive prompt and substanial support for the *political* purposes of the Land League they represent. It is, therefore, respectfully re-commended, that wherever practicable they shall be invited to address the people, and that it be specified in the invitation sent them, that the receipts, whether from sale of tickets or subscriptions, will be placed at their disposal for the political objects of the League.

Letters or telegrams may be sent for them, through your S.G's, to this office, or direct to themselves.

Respectfully and fraternally,
'X', F.C., of V.C.

18. Parnell on the land question.

Address in Ennis, Co. Clare, 1880, reported in the *Cork Examiner*, 20 September 1880

. . .Depend upon it that the measure of the Land Bill of next session will be the measure of your activity and energy this winter (cheers). It will be the measure of your determination not to pay unjust rent (cheers). It will be the measure of your determination to keep a firm grip of your homesteads. It will be the measure of your determination not to bid for farms from which others have been evicted, and to use the strong force of public opinion to deter any unjust men amongst yourselves, and there are many such . . . from bidding for such farms. If you refuse to pay unjust rents, if you refuse to take farms from which others have been evicted, the land question must be settled (cheers), and settled in a way that will be satisfactory to you. . . . It depends, therefore, upon yourselves, and not upon any commissions or any Governments. When you have made this question ripe for settlement, then, and not till then, will it be settled. It is very nearly ripe already in many parts of Ireland. It is ripe in Mayo, Galway, Roscommon, Sligo, and portions of the county Cork, but I regret to say that the tenant farmers of the county Clare have been backward in organisation up to the present time. . . .

You must then band yourselves together into Land Leagues. Every town and village must have its own branch. You must know the circumstances of all the holdings, and of all the tenures within the district over which the League has jurisdiction. . . . You must see that the principles of the Land League are included, and when you have done this in Clare, Clare will take her rank with the other Irish counties, and you will be included in the next Land Bill that will be brought forward by the Government (cheers). Now, what are you to do to a tenant who bids for a farm from which his neighbour has been evicted?

A Voice — Shoot him (cheers, and cries of 'shoot him')

Mr. Parnell — Now, I think I heard some boy say shoot him . . . but I wish to point out to you a very much better way — a more Christian and a more charitable way — it will give the lost sinner an opportunity of repenting (laughter, and cheers). When a man takes a farm from which another has been evicted, you must show him on the roadside when you meet him — you must show him in the streets of the town, you must show him at the shop counter, you must show him in the fair and in the market place, and even in the house of worship — by leaving him individually alone, by putting him into a moral coventry, by isolating him from the rest of his kind as if he was a leper of old — you must show him your detestation of the crime he has committed, and you may depend on it . . . there will be no man so full of avarice, or lost to shame, as to dare the public opinion of all the right-thinking men within the county and transgress your unwritten code of laws. . . .

But I stand here to-day to express my conviction that no settlement can be satisfactory or permanent which does not ensure the uprooting of that system of feudalism which has brought the country three times within the century to famine. . . . The feudal system of land tenure has been tried in almost every European country and it has been found wanting everywhere, but nowhere has it wrought more evil, produced more suffering, crime and destitution than in Ireland (cheers). . . . It was abolished in Prussia by the transfer of the lands from the landlords to the occupiers. . . . Let the English government give the landlords their paper to-morrow as compensation. We want no money, not a single penny of hard coin would be necessary. Why, if they gave the Irish landlords or the bad section of them, the four or five millions a year they spend on the police and the military (groans) in helping . . . to collect their rents, that would be a solution of it . . . and a very cheap solution of it too; but, perhaps, as with every reform they will try a little patchwork and tinkering for a while until they learn better. Well, let them patch and tinker if they wish; but in my opinion the longer the landlords wait, the worse will be the settlement that they will get (cheers). Now is the time for them to settle before the people learn the power of com-bination. We have been accused of preaching Communistic doctrines when we tell the people not to pay an unjust rent, and following out that advice not a few of the Irish counties had shown the English government the necessity for a radical alteration in the land laws. . . . But how would they like it if we tell the people some day or other not to pay any rent until this question is settled (cheers). We have not told them that yet. . . . I hope it may never be necessary for us to speak in that way. I hope the question will be settled peacefully, fairly, and justly to all parties. . . . But if it should not be settled we cannot continue to allow this mill stone to hang round the neck of our country . . . throttling its industries and preventing its progress (cheers). It will be for the consideration of wiser heads than mine . . . whether, if the landlords continue obdurate, and refuse all just concessions, we shall not be obliged to tell the people of Ireland to strike against all rent until this question has been settled (cheers) and if the five hundred thousand tenant farmers of Ireland strike against the ten thousand landlords, I would like to see where they would get police and soldiers enough to protect them. . . .

19. Report on rural distress

Preliminary report of the Royal Commission . . . on agriculture, *Parliamentary papers*, 1881 [c. 2778] xv,6-9

The evidence submitted to us upon the conditions of agriculture and the existing system of land tenure in Ireland has been directed to subjects which may be conveniently divided into several heads. Many of the witnesses who have appeared before us have pressed upon us their remedies for the relief of Irish distress, regarding which we would venture to repeat the remark of Your Majesty's former Commission (of which the Earl of Devon was the chairman) that 'Substantial and permanent relief can only be hoped for from a combination of measures adapting themselves to the varying circumstances under which the owners and occupiers of land are placed in different parts of the country.' The very nature of the soil and the geographic attributes of the country vary so much that remedies which would serve in one locality might be inapplicable or of little value elsewhere.

General Condition.

In common with the rest of the United Kingdom the agricultural depression of the years 1877, '78, and '79 has greatly affected Ireland, and has been to some extent increased in that country by the absence of manufacturing industries and other sources of employment. There is no doubt that the depression has fallen with extreme severity upon the smaller farmers.

We have, therefore, reason to fear that a very large proportion of these farmers are insolvent, and it is stated that the bountiful harvest of this year has alone prevented their entire collapse.

With respect to the very small holders in the western districts of Ireland we are satisfied that with the slightest failure of their crops they would be unable to exist upon the produce of their farms, even if they paid no rent. Many of them plant their potatoes, cut their turf, go to Great Britain to earn money, return home to dig their roots and stack their fuel, and pass the winter, often without occupation, in most miserable hovels. Employment at a distance, always precarious, has largely failed them during the late calamitous season.

The causes of depression, seriously aggravated by unfavourable seasons, and especially by that of 1879, must be sought in the peculiar circumstances and conditions of the country, as well as in defects in the Land Laws, and they may be briefly stated as follows: —

1. Inclemency of the seasons, and consequent failure of the potato crop.

2. Foreign competition.

3. An undue inflation of credit, partly produced by the security afforded by the Land Act of 1870, and partly by a series of prosperous seasons.

4. Excessive competition for land. The excessive competition is owing mainly to the fact that apart from the land there are few, if any, other means of subsistence for the population, and it has led to serious abuses, which have come before your Commissioners in the evidence they have taken, such as —

(a) Unreasonable payments for tenant right.

(b) Arbitrary increase of rents.

(c) Over-crowding of the population in certain districts.

(d) Minute subdivision of farms.

To meet these the following remedies have been suggested: —

Emigration and Migration.

It is proved by the evidence that in some parts of Ireland agricultural depression arises from the population upon the soil being larger than can be profitably employed in the cultivation of the land, or than can be sustained by its produce. This has arisen from various causes, chiefly from the subdivision of holdings into lots too small to sustain the tenant and his family; and partly from the laying down of arable into pasture land, which renders less labour needful. The remedies which have been suggested are emigration and migration.

Emigration is a subject too familiar to need explanation here, but it must be noticed that all the witnesses lay a particular stress upon two conditions for its success in Ireland — the one, that whole families should be taken; and the other, that the emigrants should be accompanied by those in whom they have confidence, such as their clergy, and that the places of their future settlement should be allotted to them for their new homes before they leave their old ones.

There is reason to suppose that some of our colonial possessions would co-operate in the necessary arrangements.

Your Commissioners are convinced that emigration under a properly organised scheme, and the voluntary act of the people, would materially tend to relieve the congestion of population wherever it now exists, and would conduce to the social, moral, and material welfare of the emigrants and of the population remaining behind.

Migration, as it is proposed by some witnesses, assumes the existence of large tracts of land which could be profitably brought into cultivation; and it has been stated in evidence by competent witnesses that there are thousands of acres, irrespective of bog, that might under judicious management be made remunerative to the capital and labour needed for their development. Migration would involve the acquisition of such tracts, and the transfer to them of a part of the population from other districts.

Statutory powers would probably be necessary for acquiring from those transferees their interest in their existing holdings with a view to consolidation.

That advantage has been derived from migration when voluntarily carried out may be admitted, and it is hardly to be doubted that similar advantages would arise from such a system if furthered by legislation; but it is open to serious question whether Parliament, even if the money were forthcoming from local sources, could be asked on behalf of the Irish peasant to confer upon the Crown, or its nominees, compulsory powers of purchase for this purpose.

Public Works.

The employment of capital and labour upon the development of the country by arterial drainage, the construction of railways and other public works, and the encouragement of fisheries has also been urged upon us by witnesses as one of the best remedies for the present depression, and to prevent a recurrence of the existing distress. It will be seen in evidence that from want of regular and continous employment the condition of this class, except on some large estates and well managed farms, is deplorable, and the sufferings and privations which they and their families have periodically to endure demand, we venture to think, the serious attention of Your Majesty's Government and of Parliament; and here we cannot forbear to express our opinion that the improvement of dwellings and farm buildings, and the extension of scientific agricultural teaching, with the view of an improved cultivation of the soil, are indispensable measures to secure general prosperity and an improved condition of the people.

Tenure.

The tenure of land, using the term with the limited definition placed upon it by Your Majesty's former Commissioners, viz.,'the interest which an occupying tenant has in his farm', has engaged a considerable portion of our attention. The difficulty of dealing with the subject appears to be increased by the change of ownership which has taken place in a large portion of the soil of Ireland under the provisions of the

Encumbered Estates Act. The sales under this Act, which gave a Parliamentary title, were, it is alleged, made without regard, and therefore without any protection, to the occupying tenant, the fee simple of whose farm frequently passed into the hands of a speculator, who too often sought to obtain an increase of profit from his investment by raising the tenant's rent.

Difficulties have been raised regarding the assessment made by the late Sir R. Griffith, called 'Griffith's Valuation', by the endeavour to set up this valuation, which was based on the prices current 30 years ago, as a standard of rent at the present day.

The circumstances under which the valuation was made are set forth in the evidence of several witnesses; and it is conclusively proved that the annual value, as set forth in that document, was not intended to represent, and did not represent at the date when the valuation was made, the rental value of the property.

The increase which has taken place in the prices of all kinds of agricultural produce by the introduction of railways, steam, and other developments, since the valuation was made is so great, that even after making allowance for the increased cost of production, we are led to the conclusion that the valuation is not a trustworthy guide to the present rental value.

Difficulty also arises affecting the relationship of landlord and tenant from the undefined nature of the Ulster and other tenant right usages or customs to which legal validity is given by the Act of 1870. These usages or customs have, in many instances, to be investigated and established upon oral and other evidence in a court of law, a difficulty which is aggravated by the fact that these customs are shown by the witnesses examined before us to differ not only in the same county or district, but even upon the same estate. Hence, incipient controversy exists in too many tenancies, endangering the friendly relationship which would otherwise control the conduct of both landlord and tenant.

Great stress has been laid upon the want of security felt by an improving tenant, which, it is alleged, limits not only the number of persons employed in agriculture, but also the quantity of food produced for the benefit of the general community.

Bearing in mind the system by which the improvements and equipments of a farm are very generally the work of the tenant, and the fact that a yearly tenant is at any time liable to have his rent raised in consequence of the increased value that has been given to his holding by the expenditure of his own capital and labour, the desire for legislative interference to protect him from an arbitrary increase of rent does not seem unnatural; and we are inclined to think that by the majority of landowners legislation, properly framed to accomplish this end, would not be objected to.

With a view of affording such security, 'fair rents', 'fixity of tenure', and 'free sale', popularly known as the 'three F's', have been strongly advocated by many witnesses, but none have been able to support these propositions in their integrity without admitting consequences that would, in our opinion, involve an injustice to the landlord.

It is only fair to add that the evidence which has been brought before us shows that there are very many estates which are well-managed, and upon which the tenants have no just ground of complaint.

In laying before Your Majesty this Preliminary Report we think it right to state that, as our inquiries into the causes of the recent distress in Ireland have not yet been completed, and as we are waiting the receipt of reports from some of our Assistant Commissioners with reference to peasant proprietors in Belgium and elsewhere, we do not feel ourselves to be in a position to offer any observations of a more definite character than those now submitted.

All which we humbly certify to Your Majesty.

RICHMOND AND GORDON.
BUCCLEUCH.
VERNON.
WILLIAM H. STEPHENSON.
NIGEL KINGSCOTE.
HENRY CHAPLIN.
JAMES L. NAPER.
ROBERT PATERSON.
BONAMY PRICE.
C.T. RITCHIE.
B.B. HUNTER RODWELL.
WILLIAM STRATTON.
JACOB WILSON.

January 14th, 1881.   W.A.Peel, *Secretary*

20. The land act of 1881 explained
Denis B. Sullivan, *The land law (Ireland) act, 1881* (Dublin 1881), 3-5

To explain in plain and simple terms, divested of cumbrous or technical phraseology, the nature and effect of the Land Act which has just passed into law — the Act which has placed the relation of landlord and tenant in Ireland on a new basis, and which is likely for an indefinite period to regulate the rights and obligations of the tenant-farmers of Ireland — appears to me to be an undertaking likely to be attended with some benefit to the large classes affected by that measure. After a prolonged struggle this last effort to deal with the Irish land question has taken its final shape. For good or ill its influence on the lives and fortunes of the tillers of our soil must be of national importance; and whatever may prove to be its ultimate value, a correct appreciation of its provisions must now be a matter of consequence to the large body of Irishmen with whose interests it deals. The Act itself is a long one, by no means free of complexity, involved in many of its details, and not easily apprehended in many of its branches by casual readers. It will, moreover, be necessary to take prompt advantage of some of the benefits it confers, and I do not think that the Irish peasantry can too quickly be made acquainted with the true circumstances of their new position. Of the policy or sufficiency of this statute I do not intend to offer any opinion. It may be, as some will assert, of little permanent advantage. It may be that its aim is rather the perpetuation of landlordism on a somewhat less intolerable position than before, rather than the extension to the Irish tenantry of those reforms to which they have fully established their title. As a final solution of the great question which has convulsed this island during the past few years, and on which, after a lengthened period of comparative apathy and unequalled suffering, the attention of our countrymen has at length been concentrated, it will hardly be accepted by anyone. But, viewed in any light, it is still a measure of great importance, vitally affecting the daily life, the welfare, and prospects of the bulk of the Irish population.

That it is an enormous improvement on the legislation embodied in the Landlord and Tenant Act of 1860 and the Land Act of 1870 few, I think, will be disposed to doubt. Judges have more than once questioned from the bench the propriety of the title of the first of these statutes. It was not a Landlord and Tenant Act; it was a Landlord Act pure and simple, designed almost solely to facilitate the lords of the soil in this country in the exercise of their so-called rights, in the recovery of their exorbitant rents, and in the expulsion of the Irish tenants from their homes. The Act of 1870 was framed with a far different intention; but as a protection against landlord rapacity and injustice, as a barrier against heartless rackrenting and cruel evictions, it was a signal and almost contemptible failure. Some of its glaring shortcomings and mischievous operations will be referred to later on; but the contrast between that wretched piece of legislation and the statute with which I propose to deal affords a most striking illustration of the extent to which the tenant-farmers of Ireland in ten short years in their struggle for justice have won their way. To-day, at any rate, we stand on the threshold of a new departure, the herald perhaps of still more extensive reform; but whatever the future may bring, nothing can be lost, but there is much to be gained, by correctly understanding the situation in which the tenant-farmers of Ireland have now been placed. To be of some assistance to them in realising their position, their rights, and their duties under the altered circumstances of land law in Ireland is the object with which the following pages are written.

TENANCIES TO WHICH THE ACT DOES NOT APPLY.

Speaking generally, the new Act enlarges the rights of the whole body of the Irish tenant-farmers. While conferring the largest measure of benefits upon tenants from year to year of holdings existing at the passage of the Act, it directly affects the position of leaseholders of yearly tenancies created after the passing of the Act, of tenants-at-will, and tenants for a year certain. There are, however, a few classes of holdings entirely outside its scope, all of which were also excluded from the far less important advantages conferred by the Act of 1870. The first in order is any holding which is not agricultural or pastoral in its character, or partly agricultural and partly pastoral. This excludes buildings and houses in towns or villages, villa residences, and all lettings of land attached to a dwelling-house, provided such land is merely let for the greater convenience of the inhabitants of the house, and is not what is properly designated a farm. Thus a public house with an acre of land attached, the rent of the entire holding being £17, and the valuation of the land £1 5s, was held to be excluded by the similar terms in the 71st section of the Act of 1870. The next exception is of demesne lands, or town parks in the occupation of persons living in an adjacent town and possessing an extra value as accommodation lands. This exception is not of extensive application. Demesne lands are defined by Mr. Justice Fitzgerald as lands within the ambit of the demesne reserved with the mansion house, and used for purposes of pleasure, or sometimes let to dairymen during the minority of an owner. Town park is an English expression, and there are very few holdings to which it is properly applicable in Ireland. It means, according to the judgment of Baron Fitzgerald, land that not only bears an increased value in consequence of its proximity to a town, but which is also taken by persons living in that town for the convenience of their own residences — a definition which has also been adopted by the Chief Baron of the Court of Exchequer, and may be regarded as the settled legal construction of the term.

The third and fourth exceptions are easily understood. They exempt grazing farms valued at £50 a year and over, and also grazing farms, whatever be their valuation, if the tenants do not actually reside on them, unless they adjoin or are ordinarily used with the holdings on which the tenants live.

The next class of tenancies excluded from the operation of the statute comprise holdings which the tenant occupies by reason of his being a hired labourer or a hired servant. On the corresponding provision in the Act of 1870 there have been many decisions. The mere fact that the tenant pays his rent not in cash but in labour will not deprive him of the rights of an ordinary farmer; and to bring a case within this exception it must be shown that the premises are merely occupied by a servant or labourer by virtue of his position as such, and for the more convenient discharge of his duties.

The sixth exception is of any letting in conacre, or for grazing the cattle of others for pay, or for supplying temporary pasturage for the cattle of the person to whom the letting is made.

The seventh subsection of this 60th Clause, to which I am referring, excludes any holding let by written contract, and therein expressed to be let to the tenant during his continuance in some defined office or employment, or let for some temporary convenience, or to meet some temporary necessity of either landlord or tenant; and the eighth sub-section excludes cottage allotments not exceeding half an acre.

With the above exceptions — which, as it will be seen, are of a very limited character — the new Act applies, though in very different degrees, to all classes of tenancies which have been or may be created in Ireland.

Agricultural tenancies in Ireland are divisible into: —

1. Leasehold interests.
2. Tenancies from year to year.
3. Tenancies less than tenancies from year to year, including tenancies-at-will.
4. Tenancies for a year certain.

Of tenancies of the 3rd class there are few existing in Ireland, except as come within the 5th and 7th descriptions of exempted holdings. The reason for this is easily understood. The framers of the Act of 1870, having given under certain circumstances the right of compensation for disturbance and for improvements to tenants holding from year to year, and fearing that these provisions might be rendered nugatory by the action of Irish landlords in creating a smaller class of tenancies — say, for one year certain, or for shorter determinate periods, or by the establishment of tenancies at-will — enacted that the tenants of all such holdings created after the 1st of August, 1870, should have all the rights and privileges of yearly tenants, except where the relation sprung *bona fide* from motives of temporary convenience or necessity. The result, of course, was that outside the exception few lettings of that description have since been made, while those previously created have by their very nature long passed out of existence. One loophole legal ingenuity did discover in the barrier. Tenants holding for one year certain were not specifically mentioned, and the Court of Exchequer Chamber, in the case of Wright *v.* Tracy, to the astonishment of all unaccustomed to legal refinement, decided that a tenancy for a year certain was *not* less than a tenancy from year to year. The result of this somewhat startling decision was that a landlord who after the 1st of August, 1870, let land (not for the purpose of temporary convenience) for nine months, for ten months, or eleven months, could not turn out his tenant without a notice to quit and compensation for disturbance; but he had only to make the letting for exactly a year in order to escape all such penalties. Tenancies for a year certain have consequently been not unfrequently resorted to by a certain class of landlords during the last ten years, but their doom is now sealed, and the distinction between them and still smaller tenancies is swept away by the new Land Act, which places tenancies for one year only created after its passing on exactly the same footing as a yearly tenancy created at the same time. . . .

21.The Kilmainham manifesto, 1881
Poster collection, National Library of Ireland

TO THE IRISH PEOPLE,

Fellow Countrymen,

The hour has come to test whether the great organisation built up during years of patient labour and sacrifice, and consecrated by the allegiance of the whole Irish race the world over, is to disappear at the summons of a brutal tyranny.

The crisis with which we are face to face is not of our making. It has been deliberately forced upon the country, while the Land Act is as yet untested, in order to strike down the only power which might have exorted any solid benefits for the tenant-farmers of Ireland from the Act, and so leave them once more helplessly at the mercy of a law, invented to save landlordism, and administered by landlord minions. The Executive of the Irish National Land League, acting in the spirit of the resolutions of the National Convention — the most freely-elected representative body ever assembled in Ireland — was advancing steadily in the work of testing how far the administration of the Land Act might be trusted to eradicate from the rents of the Irish tenant-farmers the entire value of their own improvements, and to reduce these rents to such a figure as should for ever place our country beyond the peril of periodical famine. At the same time they took measures to secure, in the event of the Land Act proving a mere paltry mitigation of the horrors of land-lordism, in order to fasten it the more securely upon the necks of the people, that the tenant-farmers should not be delivered blind-folded into the hands of hostile law courts, but should be able to fall back upon the magnificent organisation which was crushing landlordism out of exis-tence, when Mr. Gladstone stepped to its rescue.

In either event the Irish tenant-farmers would have been in a position to exact the uttermost farthing of their just demands. It was this attitude of perfect self-command, impregnable while there remained a shadow of respect for law, and supported with unparalleled enthusiasm by the whole Irish race, that moved the rage of the disappointed English minister, upon the monstous pretext that the National Land League was forcing upon the Irish tenant-farmers an organisation which made them all-powerful, and was keeping them by intimidation from embracing an Act which offered them nothing except helplessness and uncertainty. The English Government has cast to the winds every shred of law and justice, and has plunged into an open reign of terror, in order to destroy by the foulest means an organisation which was confessedly too strong for it within the limits of its own English Constitution. Blow after blow has been struck at the Land League, in the mere wantoness [*sic*] of brute force.

In the face of provocation which turned men's blood to flame, the Executive of the Land League adhered calmly and steadily to the course traced out for them by the National Convention. Test cases of a varied and searching character were, with great labour, put in train for ad-judication in the Land Courts. Even the arrest of our president, Mr. Charles Stewart Parnell, and the excited state of popular feeling which it evoked, did not induce the Executive to swerve in the slightest from that course, for Mr. Parnell's arrest might have been accounted for by motives of personal malice, and his removal did not altogether derange the machinery for the preparation of the test cases, which he had been at much pains to perfect. But the events which have since occurred — the seizure or attempted seizure, of almost all the members of the Executive, and of the chief officials of the League, upon wild and preposterous pretences, and the violent suppression of free speech, put it beyond any possibility of doubt that the English Government, unable to declare the Land League an illegal association, defeated in the attempt to break its unity, and afraid to abide the results of test cases, watched over by a powerful popular organisation, has deliberately resolved to destroy the whole machinery of the Central League with a view to rendering an experimental trial of the Act impossible, and forcing it upon the Irish tenant-farmers, on the Government's own terms.

The brutal and arbitrary dispersion of the Central Executive has so far succeeded, that we are obliged to announce to our countrymen, that we no longer possess the machinery for adequately presenting the test cases in court, according to the policy prescribed by the National Convention.

Mr. Gladstone has, by a series of furious and wanton acts of despotism, driven the Irish tenant-farmers to choose between their own organisation and the mercy of his lawyers — between the power which has reduced landlordism to almost its last gasp, and the power which strives with all the ferocity of despotism to restore the detestable ascendancy from which the Land League has delivered the Irish people. One constitutional weapon alone now remains in the hands of the Irish National Land League; it is the strongest, the swiftest, the most irresistible of all. We hesitated to advise our fellow-countrymen to employ it until the savage lawlessness of the English Government provoked a cricis [sic], in which we must either consent to see the Irish tenant-farmers disarmed of their organisation and laid once more prostrate at the feet of the landlords, and every murmer [sic] of Irish public opinion suppressed with an armed hand, or appeal to our countrymen to at once resort to the only means now left in their hands of bringing this false and brutal government to its senses.

Fellow-countrymen! the hour to try your souls and to redeem your pledge has arrived. The Executive of the National Land League, forced to abandon the policy of testing the Land Act, feels bound to advise the tenant-farmers of Ireland from this forth to pay NO RENTS under any circumstances to their Landlords until the Government relinquishes the existing system of terrorism, and restores the constitutional rights of the people. Do not be daunted by the removal of your leaders. Your fathers abolished tithes by the same method without any leaders at all, and with scarcely a shadow of the magnificent organisation that covers every portion of Ireland to-day. Do not suffer yourselves to be intimidated by threats of military violence. It is as lawful to refuse to pay rents as it is to receive them. Against the passive resistance of an entire population, military power has no weapons. Do not be wheedled into compromise of any sort by the dread of eviction. If you only act together in the spirit to which, within the last two years, you have countless times solemnly pledged your vows, they can no more evict a whole nation than they can imprison them. The funds of the National Land League will be poured out unstintedly for the support of all who may endure eviction in the course of the struggle.

Our exiled brothers in America may be relied upon to contribute if necessary, as many millions of money as they have contributed thousands to starve out landlordism and bring English tyranny to its knees. You have only to show that you are not unworthy of their boundless sacrifices in your cause. No power on earth, except faint-heartedness on your part can defeat you, landlordism is already staggering under the blows which you have dealt it amidst the applause of the world. One more crowning struggle for your land, your homes, your lives — a struggle in which you have all the memories of your race, all the hopes of your children, all the sacrifices of your imprisoned brothers, all your cravings for rent-enfranchised land, for happy homes and national freedom to inspire you; — one more heroic effort to destroy landlordism at the very source and fount of its existence and the system which was and is the curse of your race and of your existence will have disappeared for ever. The world is watching to see whether all your splendid hopes and noble courage will crumble away at the first threat of a cowardly tyranny. You have to choose between throwing yourselves upon the mercy of England, and taking your stand by the organisation which has once before proved too strong for English despotism; you have to choose between all-powerful unity, and impotent disorganisation; between the land for the landlords, and the land for the people. We cannot doubt your choice. Every tenant-farmer of Ireland is to-day the standard-bearer of the flag unfurled at Irishtown, and can bear it to a glorious victory. Stand together in the face of the brutal and cowardly enemies of your race. Pay no rents under any pretext. Stand passively, firmly, fearlessly by while the armies of England may be engaged in their hopeless struggle against a spirit, which their weapons cannot touch. Act for yourselves if you are deprived of the counsels of those who have shown you how to act. No power of legalised violence can extort one penny from your purses against your will. If you are evicted you shall not suffer; the landlord who evicts will be a ruined pauper, and the Government which supports him with its bayonets, will learn in a single winter how powerless is armed force against the will of a united, determined and self-reliant nation.

Signed,

CHARLES S. PARNELL, President, Kilmainham Gaol.

A.J. KETTLE, Hon. Sec., Kilmainham Gaol.

MICHAEL DAVITT, Hon. Sec., Portland Prison.

THOMAS BRENNAN, Hon. Sec., Kilmainham Gaol.
JOHN DILLON, Head Organiser, Kilmainham Gaol.
THOMAS SEXTON, Head Organiser, Kilmainham Gaol.
PATRICK EGAN, Treasurer, Paris
18th October, 1881

22. Objectives of the Irish National League
Founded on 17 October 1882, a year after the Land League was declared an unlawful association. Poster collection, National Library of Ireland

THE IRISH NATIONAL LEAGUE

This League has been formed to attain for the Irish People the following objects: —
   1st. National Self-Government
   2nd. Land Law Reform
   3rd. Local Self-Government
   4th. Extension of the Parliamentary and Municipal Franchises.
   5th. The Development and Encouragement of the Labour and Industrial interests of Ireland.

23. Local industry, 1883
Poster collection, National Library of Ireland

LOCAL INDUSTRY, CARRAROE

There has been started, within the last six months, by Mr. Michael Davitt, among the evicted tenants of Carraroe, Connemara, an industry which ought to command the interest and support of Irishmen and women at home and abroad. It possesses special claims as being a means calculated to make our people in time independent alike of the mercy of the landlord and the charity of the world, on both of which they have been too long accustomed to rely. With adequate support, this Women's Cottage Industry, which first sprung into existence in the wilds of West Connaught, will grow and spread till it becomes a national institution. Already the national desire that it should be so is apparent; but of course this will depend on the success achieved by the parent company. Therefore, the generous support of all who desire to witness the industrial renaissance of Ireland, is most earnestly and hopefully solicited.

January, 1883.

24. Foundation of the Gaelic Athletic Association
Cork Examiner, 3 November 1884

GAELIC ASSOCIATION FOR NATIONAL PASTIMES

A meeting of athletes and friends of athletics was held on Saturday, at three o'clock, in Miss Hayes' Commercial Hotel, Thurles, for the purpose of forming an association for the preservation and cultivation of our national pastimes.

Mr. Michael Cusack, of Dublin, and Mr. Maurice Davin, Carrick-on-Suir, had the meeting convened. . . . Among those present at the preliminary meeting on Saturday were — Mr. Cusack, Mr. Davin, Mr. Bracken, Mr. O'Ryan (Thurles), Mr. Wise Power (Naas and Kildare Club), Mr. Ryan, sol., Callan; Mr. John McKey (Cork Athletic Club), &c . . . The following letter was read from Mr. Davitt: —

'London, October 30th,1884

My Dear Mr. Cusack, — Sorry I cannot attend the meeting which you announce for Thurles on Saturday. In any effort that may be made to revive a natural taste for games and pastimes, such as once developed the muscular power and manly bearing of our Gaelic ancestors, I shall be most happy to lend a hand. Why should we not have our athletic festivals like other peoples — I mean on a national scale? In this, as in so many other matters, we ought to cut ourselves adrift from English rules and patronage, and prevent the killing of those Celtic sports which have been threatened with the same fate, by the encroachment of Saxon custom, as that which menaces our nationality under alien rule. Why not make an effort for the revival of the Taltine games? A grand National Festival could be organised to come off at some historic spot, at which prizes could be awarded for merit, not only in the various athletic sports peculiar to the Celtic people (and in this expression I could include the Scotch, Welsh, and Manx), but in music, poetry, oratory, and other kindred accomplishments. To throw the prizes open to the Celtic race throughout the world, and give a couple of years in which to organise the first grand national competition, would, I am confident, ensure a great success. There are, of course, many other reasons why the physique of our people is not developing as it ought to be, but there is no doubt that one reason for the degenerate gait and bearing of most of our young men at home is to be found in the absence of such games and pastimes as formerly gave to Irishmen the reputation of a soldier-like and self-reliant race. — Yours, very truly,

Michael Davitt'.

On the motion of Mr. Cusack, seconded by Mr. Power, Archbishop Croke, Mr. Parnell, and Mr. Davitt were appointed patrons of the new association; and on the motion of the same gentlemen, the title of the new association was fixed as 'The Gaelic Association for the Preservation and Cultivation of National Pastimes'. . . .

25. Parnell and the national question
Speech at Cork, 21 January 1885, reported in the *Cork Examiner*, 22 January 1885

. . . I do not know how this great question will eventually be settled. I do not know whether England will be wise in time, and concede to constitutional arguments and methods the restitution of that which was stolen from us towards the close of the last century (cheers). It is given to none of us to forecast the future, and just as it is impossible for us to say in what way, or by what means the national question may be settled, in what way full justice may be done to Ireland, so it is impossible for us to say to what extent that justice shall be done. We cannot ask for less that the restitution of Grattan's Parliament (loud cheers), with its important privileges and wide and far-reaching Constitution. We cannot under the British Constitution ask for more than the restitution of Grattan's Parliament (renewed cheers). But no man has a right to fix the boundary to the march of a nation (great cheering). No man has a right to say to his country, 'thus far shalt thou go and no farther', and we never attempted to fix the *ne plus ultra* to the progress of Ireland's nationhood, and we never shall (cheers). But, gentlemen, while we leave those things to time, circumstances and the future we must each of us resolve in our hearts that we shall at all times do everything which within us lies to obtain for Ireland the fullest measure of her rights (applause). In this way we shall avoid difficulties and contentions amongst each other. In this way we shall not give up anything which the future may put in favour of our country, and while we struggle to-day for that which may seem possible for us with our combination, we must struggle for it with the proud consciousness that we shall not do anything to hinder or prevent better men who may come before us, from gaining better things than those for which we now contend (prolonged applause).

26. Parnell's address at Wicklow, October 1885
Irish Times, 6 October 1885

... When I last spoke in public in Ireland I expressed my conviction that in the new Parliament we should be able to form our platform of a single plank, and that plank the plank of Legislative Independence — (cheers) — and that we should carry that plank to a successful issue in the same way as during the last Parliament we have carried other subordinate planks, such as the extension of the franchise and so forth. (Cheers). My declaration has been received by the English Press and by some of — although not by all — the English leaders with a storm of disapproval, and they have told us that the yielding of an independent Parliament to Ireland is a matter of impossibility. But nothing that has been said in this interval has in the slightest degree diminished my confidence in the near success of our efforts (loud cheers). On the contrary, very much that has been said by our enemies in reference to this claim of ours has very much increased my confidence. (Cheers). They practically admit that things cannot be allowed to go on as they are; that it is impossible to keep an unwilling people and unwilling representatives in forced legislative connexion with the other two kingdoms. (Hear, hear). They admit that there must be some change, but the two conditions that they put forward in regard to this change, and as a condition of this change, are, firstly, that the separation of Ireland from England shall not be a consequence of the grant of legislative independence to Ireland; and, in the second place, they claim that we shall not be allowed to protect our manufactures at the cost of those of England. ... To take the last point first, and to deal with the question of the protection of Irish manufactures, I have claimed for Ireland a parliament that shall have power to protect these Irish manufactures — (cheers) — if it be the will of that Parliament and of the Irish people that they should be protected. (Cheers). But it is not for me to say beforehand what the action of such a freely-elected Irish assembly would be. I may have my own opinion as to the best course for that assembly to take; but I have claimed that no Parliamentary assembly will work satisfactorily which has not free power over Irish affairs — (applause) — which has not free power to raise a revenue for the purpose of government in Ireland as shall seem fit and best to that assembly. (Applause). I am of the opinion — an opinion that I had expressed before now — that it would be wise to protect certain Irish industries, at all events, for a time — (hear, hear) — that it is impossible for us to make up for the loss of the start in the manufacturing race which we have experienced owing to adverse legislation in times past against Irish industries by England, unless we do protect these industries, not many in number, which are capable of thriving in Ireland. (Applause). I am not of the opinion that it would be necessary for us to protect these industries very long. Possibly protection continued for two or three years would give us that start which we have lost, owing to the nefarious legislative action of England in times past. (Hear,hear). I can think also that Ireland could never be a manufacturing nation of such importance as to compete to any great extent with England. I believe there are several industries which would thrive and could be made to thrive in Ireland, but I think that as regards many other branches of manufacture of which we have now to seek our supply from the English markets, that we should still have to go to their markets for supply, on account of natural reasons, which I have not time to enter into at the present moment. But I claim this for Ireland, that if the Irish Parliament of the future considers that there are certain industries in Ireland which could be benefited by protection, which could be nursed by protection, and which could be placed in such a position as to enable them to compete with similar industries in other countries by a course of protection extending over a few years, that that Parliament ought to have power to carry out that policy. (Cheers). It is not for me to predict the extent to which that power should be used, but I tell English radicals and English liberals that it useless for them to talk of their desire to do justice to Ireland when, from notions of selfishness, they refused to repair that most manifest injustice of all — namely, the destruction of our manufactures by England in times past — when they refused to repair that injustice by giving us the power which we think would be sufficient to enable us to build up these comparatively few industries which Ireland is adapted by her circumstances to excel in. (Cheers). I will proceed a little further, and I will deal with the claim that has been put forward, that some guarantee should be given that the granting of legislative powers to Ireland should not lead to the separation of Ireland from England. This claim is one which at first sight may seem a fair one, it may appear preposterous, and it undoubtedly would be preposterous, to ask England to concede to us an engine which we announced an intention to use to bring about separation of the two countries, and which we accepted silently with the intention of so using it; but there is a great difference between having such an intention, or announcing such an intention, and giving counter guarantees against such an intention. It is not possible for human intelligence to forecast the future in these matters, but we can point to this — we can point to the fact that under 85 years of parliamentary connexion with England Ireland has become intensely disloyal and intensely disaffected; that notwithstanding the Whig policy of so-called conciliation, alternative conciliation and coercion, and ameliorative measures, that disaffection has hardened, deepened and intensified from day to day. (Cheers). Am I not, then entitled to assume that one of the roots of this disaffection — this feeling of disloyalty — is the assumption by England of the mangement of our affairs? (Cheers). It is admitted that the present system can't go on, and what are you going to put in its place? (Cries of 'Home Rule'.) My advice to English statesmen considering this question would be this — trust the Irish people altogether, or trust them not at all. (Cheers). Give with a full and open hand, give our people the power to legislate upon all domestic concerns, and you may depend upon one thing, that the desire for separation — the means of winning separation at least — will not be increased or intensified — (cheers) — that whatever chance the English rulers may have of drawing to themselves the affection of the Irish people lies in destroying the abominable system of legislative union between the two countries by conceding fully and freely to Ireland the right to manage her own affairs. It is impossible for us to give guarantees, but we can point to the past; we can show that the record of English rule is a constant series of steps from bad to worse — (cheers) — that the condition of English power is more insecure and more unstable at the present moment than it has ever been; we can point to the example of other countries, of Austria and Hungary, to the fact that Hungary having been conceded self-government became one of the strongest factors in the Austrian empire; we can show the powers that have been freely conceded to the colonies, to the greater colonies, including this very power to protect their own industries against and at the expense of those of England, we can show that disaffection has disappeared in all the greater English colonies: that while the Irishman who goes to the United States of America carries with him a burning hatred of English rule — (cheers) — that while that burning hatred constantly lives in his heart, never leaves him, and is bequeathed to his children; the Irishman coming from the same village, and from the same parish, and from the same townland, equally maltreated, cast out on the road by the relentless landlord, who goes to one of the colonies of Canada or one of the colonies of Australia, and finds there another and a different system of English rule to that which he has been accustomed to at home, becomes to a great extent a loyal citizen and a strength and a prop to the community amongst whom his lot has been cast, that he forgets the little memories of his experience of England at home, and that he no longer continues to look upon the name of England as a symbol of oppression, and the badge of the misfortunes of his country. (Cheers). I say that it is possible, and that it is the duty of English statesmen at the present day to inquire and examine into these facts for themselves with their eyes open, and to cease the impossible task, which they admit to be impossible, of going forward in the continued misgovernment of Ireland, and persisting in the government of our people by a people outside herself who know not her real wants. (Cheers). And, if these lessons be learned, I am convinced that English statesman who is great enough and who is powerful to carry out these teachings, to enforce them on the of his countrymen, to give to Ireland full legislative liberty, full power to manage her own domestic concerns, will be regarded in the future by his countrymen as one who has removed the greatest peril to the English Empire — (hear, hear) — a peril, I firmly believe, which, if not removed, will find some day — perhaps not in our time — some year, perhaps not for many years to come — but will certainly find, sooner or later, and it may be sooner than later, an opportunity of severing itself — (loud cheers) — to the destruction of that British empire for the misfortunes, the oppressions, and the misgovernment of our country. (Loud cheers).

27. Gladstone's speech introducing the home rule bill, 1886
Hansard 3 (Commons), 3rd series, cciv, 1036-81, 8 April 1886

I could have wished, Mr. Speaker, on several grounds, that it had been possible for me on this single occasion to open to the House the whole of the policy and intentions of the Government with respect to Ireland. The two questions of land and of Irish government are, in our view, closely and inseparably connected, for they are the two channels through which we hope to find access, and effectual access, to that question which is the most vital of all — namely the question of social order in Ireland. As I have said, those two questions are in our view — whatever they may be in that of anyone else — they are in our view, for reasons which I cannot now explain, inseparable the one from the other. But it is impossible for me to attempt such a task. . . .

Since the last half-century dawned, we have been steadily engaged in extending, as well as in consolidating, free institutions. I divide the period since the Act of Union with Ireland into two — the first from 1800 to 1832, the epoch of what is still justly called the great Reform Act; and secondly, from 1833 to 1885. I do not know whether it has been as widely observed as I think it deserves to be that, in the first of those periods — 32 years — there were no less than 11 years — it may seem not much to say, but wait for what is coming — there were no less than 11 of those 32 years in which our Statute Book was free throughout the whole year from repressive legislation of an exceptional kind against

Ireland. But in the 53 years since we advanced far in the career of Liberal principles and actions — in those 53 years, from 1833 to 1885 — there were but two years which were entirely free from the action of this special legislation for Ireland. Is not that of itself almost enough to prove we have arrived at the point where it is necessary that we should take a careful and searching survey of our position? . . .

Well, Sir, what are the results that have been produced? This result above all — and now I come to what I consider to be the basis of the whole mischief — that rightly or wrongly, yet in point of fact, law is discredited in Ireland, and discredited in Ireland upon this ground especially — that it comes to the people of that country with a foreign accent, and in a foreign garb. These Coercion Bills of ours, of course — for it has become a matter of course — I am speaking of the facts and not of the merits — these Coercion Bills are stiffly resisted by the Members who represent Ireland in Parliament. The English mind, by cases of this kind and by the tone of the press towards them, is estranged from the Irish people and the Irish mind is estranged from the people of England and Scotland. I will not speak of other circumstances attending the present state of Ireland, but I do think that I am not assuming too much when I say that I have shown enough in this comparatively brief review — and I wish it could have been briefer still — to prove that, if coercion is to be the basis for legislation, we must no longer be seeking, as we are always laudably seeking, to whittle it down almost to nothing at the very first moment we begin, but we must, like men, adopt it, hold by it, sternly enforce it, till its end has been completely attained — with what results to peace, good will and freedom I do not now stop to inquire. Our ineffectual and spurious coercion is morally worn out. . . .

Now, I enter upon another proposition to which I hardly expect broad exception can be taken. I will not assume, I will not beg, the question, whether the people of England and Scotland will ever administer that sort of effectual coercion which I have placed in contrast with our timid and hesitating repressive measures; but this I will say, that the people of England and Scotland will never resort to that alternative until they have tried every other. Have they tried every other? Well, some we have tried, to which I will refer. I have been concerned with some of them myself. But we have not yet tried every alternative, because there is one — not unknown to human experience — on the contrary, widely known to various countries in the world, where this dark and difficult problem has been solved by the comparatively natural and simple, though not always easy, expedient of stripping law of its foreign garb, and investing it with a domestic character. I am not saying that this will succeed; I by no means beg the question at this moment; but this I will say, that Ireland, as far as I know, and speaking of the great majority of the people of Ireland, believes it will succeed, and that experience elsewhere supports that conclusion. The case of Ireland, though she is represented here not less fully than England and Scotland, is not the same as that of England and Scotland. England, by her own strength, and by her vast majority in this House, makes her own laws just as independently as if she were not combined with two other countries. Scotland — a small country, smaller than Ireland, but a country endowed with a spirit so masculine that never in the long course of history, excepting for two brief periods, each of a few years, was the superior strength of England such as to enable her to put down the national freedom beyond the border — Scotland, wisely recognized by England, has been allowed and encouraged in this house to make her own laws as freely and as effectually as if she had a representation six times as strong. The consequence is that the mainspring of law in England is felt by the people to be English; the mainspring of law in Scotland is felt by the people to be Scotch; but the mainspring of law in Ireland is not felt by the people to be Irish; and I am bound to say — truth extorts from me the avowal — that it cannot be felt to be Irish in the same sense as it is English and Scotch. The net results of this statement which I have laid before the house, because it was necessary as the groundwork of my argument, are these — in the first place, I admit it to be a little less than a mockery to hold that the state of law and of facts conjointly, which I have endeavoured to describe, conduces to the real unity of this great, noble, and world-wide Empire. In the second place, something must be done, something is imperatively demanded from us to restore to Ireland the first conditions of civil life — the free course of law, the liberty of every individual in the exercise of every legal right, the confidence of the people in the law, apart from which no country can be called, in the full sense of the word, a civilized country, nor can there be given to that country the blessings which it is the object of civilized society to attain. Well, this is my introduction to the task I have to perform, and now I ask attention to the problem we have before us.

It is a problem not unknown in the history of the world; it is really this — there can be no secret about it as far as we are concerned — how to reconcile Imperial unity with diversity of legislation. Mr. Grattan not only held these purposes to be reconcilable, but he did not scruple to go the length of saying this — 'I demand the continued severance of the Parliaments with a view to the continued and everlasting unity of the Empire.' Was that a flight of rhetoric, an audacious paradox? No; it was the statement of a problem which other countries have solved; and under circumstances much more difficult than ours. We ourselves may be said to have solved it, for I do not think that anyone will question the fact that, out of the last six centuries, for five centuries at least Ireland has had a Parliament separate from ours. That is a fact undeniable. Did that separation of Parliament destroy the unity of the British Empire? Did it destroy it in the 18th century? Do not suppose that I mean that harmony always prevailed between Ireland and England. We know very well there were causes quite sufficient to account for a recurrence of discord. But I take the 18th century alone. Can I be told that there was no unity of Empire in the 18th century? Why, Sir, it was the century which witnessed the foundation of that great, gigantic manufacturing industry which now overshadows the whole world. It was, in a pre-eminent sense, the century of Empire, and it was in a sense, but too conspicuous, the century of wars. Those wars were carried on, that Empire was maintained and enormously enlarged, that trade was established, that Navy was brought to supremacy when England and Ireland had separate Parliaments. Am I to be told that there was no unity of empire in that state of things? Well, Sir, what has happened elsewhere? Have any other countries had to look this problem in the face? The last half-century — the last 60 or 70 years since the great war — has been particularly rich in its experience of this subject and in the lessons which it has afforded to us. There are many cases to which I might refer to show how practicable it is, or how practicable it has been found by others whom we are not accustomed to look upon as our political superiors — how practicable it has been found by others to bring into existence what is termed local autonomy, and yet not to sacrifice, but to confirm Imperial unity. . . .

What is the essence of the Union? That is the question. It is impossible to determine what is and what is not the repeal of the Union, until you settle what is the essence of the Union. Well, I define the essence of the Union to be this — that before the Act of Union there were two independent, separate, co-ordinate Parliaments; after the Act of Union there was but one. A supreme statutory authority of the Imperial Parliament over Great Britain, Scotland, and Ireland as one United Kingdom was established by the Act of Union. That supreme statutory authority it is not asked, so far as I am aware, and certainly it is not intended, in the slightest degree to impair. . . .

I will deviate from my path for a moment to say a word upon the state of opinion in that wealthy, intelligent, and energetic portion of the Irish community which, as I have said, predominates in a certain portion of Ulster. Our duty is to adhere to sound general principles, and to give the utmost consideration we can to the opinions of that energetic minority. The first thing of all, I should say, is that if, under any occasion, by any individual or section, violent measures have been threatened in certain emergencies, I think the best compliment I can pay to those who have threatened us is to take no notice whatever of the threats, but to treat them as momentary ebullitions, which will pass away with the fears from which they spring, and at the same time to adopt on our part every reasonable measure for disarming those fears. I cannot conceal the conviction that the voice of Ireland, as a whole, is at this moment clearly and constitutionally spoken. I cannot say it is otherwise when five-sixths of its lawfully-chosen Representatives are of one mind in this matter. There is a counter voice; and I wish to know what is the claim of those by whom that counter voice is spoken, and how much is the scope and allowance we can give them. Certainly, Sir, I cannot allow it to be said that a Protestant minority in Ulster, or elsewhere, is to rule the question at large for Ireland. I am aware of no constitutional doctrine tolerable on which such a conclusion could be adopted or justified. But I think that the Protestant minority should have its wishes considered to the utmost practicable extent in any form which they can assume.

Various schemes, short of refusing the demand of Ireland at large, have been proposed on behalf of Ulster. One scheme is, that Ulster itself, or, perhaps with more appearance of reason, a portion of Ulster, should be excluded from the operation of the bill we are about to introduce. Another scheme is, that certain rights with regard to certain subjects — such, for example, as education and some other subjects — should be reserved and should be placed, to a certain extent, under the control of Provincial Councils. These, I think, are the suggestions which reached me in different shapes; there may be others. But what I wish to say of them is this — there is no one of them which has appeared to us to be so completely justified, either upon its merits or by the weight of opinion supporting and recommending it, as to warrant our including it in the Bill and proposing it to Parliament upon our responsibility. What we think is that such suggestions deserve careful and unprejudiced consideration. It may be that free discussion, which I have no doubt will largely take place after a Bill such as we propose shall have been laid on the Table of the House, may give to one of these proposals, or to some other proposals, a practical form, and that some such plan may be found to be recommended by a general or predominating approval. If it should be so, it will, at our hands, have the most favourable consideration, with every disposition to do what equity may appear to recommend. . . .

. . . In 1782 there were difficulties that we have not now before us. At any time it might have been very fairly said that no one could tell how a separate Legislature would work unless it had under its control what is termed a responsible Government. We have no such difficulty and no such excuse now. The problem of responsible Government has been solved for us in our Colonies. It works very well there; and in, perhaps, a dozen cases in different quarters of the globe it works to our perfect satisfaction. It may be interesting to the House if I recount the fact that that responsible Government in the Colonies was, I think, first established by one of our distinguished statesmen, Earl Russell, when he held the Office of Colonial Secretary in the Government of Lord Melbourne. But it was a complete departure from established tradition; and, if I remember right, not more than two or three years before that generous and wise experiment was tried, Lord Russell had himself written a most able dispatch to show that it could not be done; that with responsible Government in the Colonies you would have two centres of gravity and two sources of motion in the Empire; while a United Empire absolutely required that there should be but one, and that consequently the proposition could not be entertained. . . .

There is only one subject more on which I feel it still necessary to detain the House. It is commonly said in England and Scotland — and in the main it is, I think, truly said — that we have for a great number of years been struggling to pass good laws for Ireland. We have sacrificed our time; we have neglected our own business; we have advanced our money — which I do not think at all a great favour conferred on her — and all this in the endeavour to give Ireland good laws. That is quite true in regard to the general course of legislation since 1829. But many of those laws have been passed under influences which can hardly be described otherwise than as influences of fear. Some of our laws have been passed in a spirit of grudging and of jealousy. . . .

But, Sir, I do not deny the general good intentions of Parliament on a variety of great and conspicuous occasions, and its desire to pass good laws for Ireland. But let me say that, in order to work out the purposes of government, there is something more in this world occasionally required than even the passing of good laws. It is sometimes requisite not only that good laws should be passed, but also that they should be passed by the proper persons. The passing of many good laws is not enough in cases where the strong permanent instincts of the people, their distinctive marks of character, the situation and history of the country require not only that these laws should be good, but that they should proceed from a congenial and native source, and besides being good laws should be their own laws. . . .

28. Irish unionist opposition to home rule

Extract from the report of the first annual general meeting of the Irish Loyal and Patriotic Union, in the *Irish Times*, 9 January 1886

The Union published and circulated 286,000 leaflets and pamphlets during the elections, irrespective of those put in circulation by the candidates themselves.

Special attention is directed to the Irish election returns, with details of voting in the contested elections, which were issued by the union at the close of the elections.

The following facts have been brought out by the action of the I.L.P.U.: —

Taking together all the contested elections in Ireland, the number of votes cast for Separation barely exceeded one-half of the electors; one quarter, roughly speaking, voted against Separation, and the remaining quarter abstained from voting.

If the representation of all Ireland were at all in proportion to the number of votes given, the Unionists would have 34 representatives, the Separatists 69.

As is already known, the operations of the Irish Loyal and Patriotic Union were confined to the three Southern provinces of Munster, Leinster, and Connaught.

For these three provinces 52 contests in all took place, and there were 18 uncontested elections.

The I.L.P.U. contributed to the expenses of the Unionist candidates in accordance with the circular issued to its supporters, subsidising candidates to an extent not less than the sheriff's nominating fees.

For the purpose of the association a considerable sum was subscribed, each subscriber receiving a formal receipt, with the undertaking that neither the name nor the amount of his subscription should be made public without the sanction of such.

For this reason no list of subscribers is published.

29. A description of boycotting
Special correspondent of *The Times, Letters from Ireland, 1886*
(London, 1887), 72-73

[14 September 1886]

I do not think I fully realized what boycotting meant till I met a large farmer at Newcastle Junction, in county Limerick, and asked him whether I could get a paper there. 'You may get one down the platform', was the answer, 'but they wouldn't sell me one'. When it comes to being unable to buy a penny paper, the system is perfect indeed. He was going into Limerick to buy supplies for the week, being unable to get anything nearer, and was taking in part of a hay-rake to be repaired, which any blacksmith could have done in half-an-hour. His butter merchant in Cork wrote to say that if he continued to do business for him all his other customers would leave and he has to sell his butter by strategy. He has a protection post in his yard and his daughter cannot go out without a revolver and an escort of police. His hay was maliciously burnt, and they endeavoured to prove that she had set fire to it. If he had not happened to be away from home himself at the time it was burnt, all the water in the Shannon, he said, would not have cleared him of it. His offence was the usual one — viz., taking a farm from which another had been evicted. . . .

30. Congested districts
Extract from report of royal commission on the land law, *Parliamentary papers*, 1887, c. 4969, xxvi, 11

Security through Local Authorities

26. We have found an all but unanimous opinion against the expectation that any satisfactory result could be obtained, by attempting to introduce local authorities as guarantors either for ordinary or congested districts. And the evidence shows that these authorities would decline such responsibility.

Congested Districts

27. Nothing hitherto has been effectual in bringing any improvement to the condition of the people inhabiting what are called 'congested districts'. It would, in our opinion, be a very grave mistake to deal with this class of people as if they were 'farmers', *i.e.*, people understood to

live altogether upon the produce of their holdings. That is not their position; it would therefore be mischievous to attempt to deal with them in this report, except as a class distinct and separate from 'farmers' properly so called. The inhabitants of these districts must be regarded as labourers, who occupy residences with portions of land attached, which assist them in support of themselves and of their families. Regarding them as such, we have to consider the conditions on which they occupy the holdings we have alluded to, and the labour or employment upon which they must largely depend.

28. It is well to define what we understand by a 'congested district'. We understand such a district as one where the land is of inferior quality, not good enough for pasturage, and not naturally adapted for profitable agriculture, occupied by a large number of poor people holding at small rents, and where each separate holding is not of itself capable of supporting the holder and a family. We desire to call attention to the evidence of the O'Conor Don on the subject, and to his description of these holdings of which he has much experience.

29. We found that the occupiers of such holdings supplemented their means of living by working as labourers during certain seasons of the year in England and Scotland, or for farmers at home, or, when they live near the coast, by fishing. In these congested districts a failure in any year of the potato crop, and of labour, means utter destitution, or public assistance. It is not their rent which reduces them to this condition, any more than the payment of rent affects other labourers. The liability to pay for house and home is an incident to the existence of all tenants. The inhabitants of these districts have this advantage, that the law of the land steps in to fix a 'fair rent' upon their holdings. Employment is the condition of their lives, but there is no field for it near their homes. The relief of people living in such a precarious position seems to demand the careful consideration, and prompt action of the State

30. The general introduction of mowing and reaping machines into England and Scotland has so greatly lessened the demand for Irish labour that these portions of the Kingdom can no longer be considered as offering a sufficient field for migratory labour of this kind. Under such circumstances, two remedies only have presented themselves; either employment must be found for these people at home, and we fear there is but little hope of this being practicable; or a considerable proportion of them must be enabled to move to some place where such employment exists.

31. We recommend that means should be found for affording technical education to those who remain in these districts, where knowledge as to the mode of earning a living is at present confined to a rude skill

in manual labour. The children are intelligent and quick-witted, and would, if afforded instruction, speedily attain a suffcient proficiency in any skilled employment to induce them to go out and take their place among the trained workers of the country.

32. Whether it is desirable that the occupiers of such holdings as we have been dealing with, should become purchasers under the Land Act of 1885, is a question on which we have heard a diversity of opinion. . . .

31. Randolph Churchill on the Irish question
Irish Times, 23 February 1888

Lord Randolph Churchill took part this evening (22nd) in the debate of the Oxford Union Society. . . . [He said] — those who had studied Irish history and Irish nature would come to the conclusion that all Irish Political Movements were essentially transient in their character. The great Repeal movement, which was far more passionately supported by the Irish than the Parnell movement, lasted but a few years, and had never been heard of since the day it disappeared. The Fenian movement had absolutely vanished into the past. Take the present condition of the Irish party. Did anybody who knew Ireland think that party likely to hold together until the month of August, 1893? He did not. He knew there were divisions of the deepest character in that party with difficulty bridged over. There was one section which believed in the efficacy of Parliamentary methods, and another section who did not believe in the efficacy of these methods. Depend upon it, as Home Rule receded further and further into the distance, those who did not believe in the efficacy of Parliamentary methods would assert their superiority, and the moment they succeeded in doing this the knell of the Irish party would have tolled (Cheers). As sure as they were here now, if this Parliament lasted five years, the Irish party as it was now would have gone to pieces. . . . If asked would home rule ever be granted? He would say yes, but he could not tell the time. He could only tell the epoch, and that would be when England had ceased to be a nation, when her wealth and manufactures and commerce had all departed; when the manly resolution and dogged determination of her sons had become a memory and a dream of the past — then only would Ireland obtain Home Rule. . . .

32. *The Nation* **on the views of the prime minister, Lord Salisbury**
The Nation, 27 April 1889

SWASHBUCKLE SALISBURY ON THE STUMP

Lord Salisbury, of Hottentot notoriety, is still true to his colours. He stood on a Bristol platform on last Tuesday evening and played the role of the apostle of hate and discord with a truculence quite peculiar to himself. His lordship trotted out once more his favourite hobby. He believed and hoped that with a good firm Government lasting for a number of years Ireland would improve.

They must, he said, retain a hold over Ireland, for Ireland under Home Rule would have to be retaken and reconquered. Having gone into ecstacies over the Ashbourne Act, the Premier was liberal enough to admit that there was a desire that Local Government should be extended to Ireland, although he qualified the admission by adding that it might not work so satisfactorily here as across the channel. He did not believe that Local Government would secure the final reconciliation of Ireland with England — a proposition which, as the song says, nobody can deny; but what Ireland wanted, he said, was a long spell of firmly and impartially administered law. When Irishmen respected their neighbour's rights, then Lord Salisbury would magnanimously admit them to the rights of civilised peoples. His generosity, it will be seen, knows no bounds. In conclusion, the Tory chief, rising to a climax of shrieking absurdity, observed that if England were to prove so feeble, so changeful, and so uncertain, as to give way on the Irish Question, the knell of the empire would be sounded and they would lose, alas! a far brighter gem in the Crown of their country. The speech is almost from beginning to end a tissue of flat, stale calumnies on the character of the Irish people. The old caricaturist displayed himself in his gibes and sneers on a long-tried and a suffering race, and he spoke with all the venom of a cowardly bully. The consciousness that the odious policy with which his name is associated is being condemned by all impartial Englishmen may have contributed to the stock of the right hon. gentleman's bile, and the acrimony of his abuse.

33. Evictions in Donegal
The Nation, 27 April 1889

FALCARRAGH IN A STATE OF SEIGE

Falcarragh is literally in a state of seige. On last Thursday week the Royal Irish banditti, accompanied by the Royal Rifles under Mr. Cameron, retook possession of all the remaining houses occupied by the evicted tenants. Some of the threatened buildings were barricaded, but any resistance that was offered proved ineffectual, and men and women were arrested and marched off to Falcarragh. On the same day a deputation from the Gladstone Liberal Club of Manchester waited on Dr. O'Donnell, Bishop of Raphoe, to ascertain his opinion as to the best means of affording relief in view of the impending distress in Donegal. His lordship suggested as a remedy that harbours and railways should be constructed and the fisheries developed. Meanwhile other members of the deputation, among whom was Mr. S. Norbury Williams, were passing through Derry for Falcarragh, accompanied by two professional photographers and the representatives of various Radical newspapers. The authorities having informed them that they could not address public meetings, they immediately drafted and had printed a circular for circulation among the tenants, in which they express the deepest sympathy with them in their sufferings. Mr. Williams brought with him on this occasion a letter from Mr. Gladstone, who thus refers to Father McFadden's case: 'The Government pointed out that they could not properly in the present state of things state the reasons of their conduct with regard to Father McFadden. This is true; but it is also true that, according to all appearances, they have incurred a very heavy responsibility, and I think you may properly say to the rev. gentleman that the proceedings will be carefully watched, and if ministers are eventually found to have no just reason for their conduct they will be severely called to account.'

POLICE BRUTALITY IN DONEGAL

The police in retaking possession of these houses in Falcarragh, displayed even more than their usual brutality. Among those put under arrest for the crime of having returned under the old rooftree was a woman with twin babes only a few weeks old. An old man of ninety winters was also pounced upon while an aged widow named Coyle was carried out on a chair and placed on the roadside. Father Boyle describes the situation only too faithfully when he says: — 'The land war here has reached a crisis unequalled even in the sickening history of the agrarian struggle in this country. On Saturday last over three hundred persons were evicted, and, having no prospect but the roadside or the hated workhouse, retook possession of their dismantled houses'. After recapitulating the recent incidents, including the arrest and commital of Mr. Harrison for supplying food to the besieged (and who are now the re-evicted tenants), Father Boyle says, as the *locum tenens* for Father Stephens, the duty devolves upon him of saving these poor people from starvation.

34. The fall of Parnell
Irish Times, 26 November 1890

MR. GLADSTONE AND MR. PARNELL
IMPORTANT LETTER TO MR. MORLEY
THE LIBERAL LEADER INSISTS ON RETIREMENT. . . .

We are authorised to state that the contents of the following letter from Mr. Gladstone to Mr. John Morley were communicated to Mr. Parnell in the course of this afternoon: —

'1 Carlton Gardens, November 24th, 1890.

My Dear Morley, — Having arrived at a certain conclusion with regard to the continuance at the present moment of Mr. Parnell's leadership of the Irish Party, I have seen Mr. McCarthy on my arrival in town, and have inquired from him whether I was likely to receive from Mr. Parnell himself any communication on the subject. Mr. McCarthy replied that he was unable to give me any information on the subject.

I mentioned to him that in 1882, after the terrible murder in the Phoenix Park, Mr. Parnell, although totally removed from any idea of responsibility, had spontaneously written to me and offered to take the Chiltern Hundreds, an offer much to his honour, but which I thought it my duty to decline.

While clinging to the hope of a communication from Mr. Parnell to whomsoever addressed, I thought it necessary, viewing the arrangements for the commencement of the Session tomorrow, to acquaint Mr. McCarthy with the conclusion to which, after using all the means of observation and reflection in my power, I had myself arrived. It was that, notwithstanding the spendid services rendered by Mr. Parnell to his country, his continuance at the present moment in the leadership would be productive of consequences disastrous in the highest degree to the cause of Ireland.

I think I may be warranted in asking you, so far, to expand the conclusion I have given above as to add that the continuance I speak of would not only place many hearty and effective friends of the Irish cause in a position of great embarrassment, but would render my retention of the leadership of the Liberal Party, based as it has been mainly upon the prosecution of the Irish cause, almost a nullity.

This expansion of my views I begged Mr. McCarthy to regard as confidential, and not intended for his colleagues generally, if he felt that Mr. Parnell contemplated spontaneous action; but I also begged that he would make known to the Irish Party at their meeting tomorrow afternoon that such was my conclusion, if he should find Mr. Parnell had not in contemplation any step of the nature indicated. . .'.

35. Report on distress and potato failure, 1891
Local Government Board for Ireland, *Report on the failure of the potato crop and the condition of the poorer classes in the west of Ireland* (Dublin, 1891), 1-2

. . . The districts in which the disease has appeared comprise about one-half of Ireland. On light dry soils with a limestone substratum and on well-drained lands the potato crop was in some places excellent and generally not very far short, but in cold wet inferior lands and in mountain districts the failure everywhere was very serious. In the eastern counties of Ulster the crop was generally a good one; in Leinster and part of Munster it was fair except in a few localities, but westward of an imaginary line drawn from Derry to Kinsale, and on to the shores of the Atlantic, the blight extended, spreading and increasing in severity until its worst effects were manifested along the whole extent of the seaboard from Donegal to west Cork. It would moreover appear from the Inspectors' reports that it is in those parts of the West where chronic poverty prevails and where the potato is the staple food of the people that the failure has been most complete.

Owing to the remarkable unevenness of the crop in every district the Inspectors have felt some difficulty in estimating the extent of the loss, but their reports appear to point to the conclusion that in the western unions the crop was from one-half to one-third of the average yield, while in some of the most congested districts, such as Kilcar in Donegal, Belmullet, Achill, and Louisburg in Mayo, Connemara, Galway, and parts of west Cork, the crop was hardly one-fourth of the usual return.

The same causes of failure are everywhere noted. The old champion seed, the disease-resisting properties of which have greatly weakened of late years, planted late in worn-out and badly cultivated lands made no growth against the heavy rains and want of sunshine. The young plants were killed, the stalks struck by the blight decayed into the ground, and the bulk of the tubers that escaped the disease failed to mature. In this respect the failure of the crop this year differs altogether from that of 1879. Contrasting the reports now received with those made by our Inspectors in 1879 we find that in 1879, while the disease injured nearly half the crop in every part of Ireland, the potatoes that were saved, though inferior in some districts, were usually saleable and fit for consumption. This year the failure was serious only in the western unions, and although the weight of the crop was not much below that of 1879, about one-third of the tubers raised was neither suitable for food nor saleable in the market, and, at the date of this report, latest advices to hand show that in the poorest districts the supply is nearly exhausted.

The reports received as to the corn crops are generally favourable; a good deal still remains unthreshed among the small holdings in the West, and the price is about fifteen per cent. higher than last year. In parts of Donegal and Limerick some damage was occasioned by the heavy rains. Green crops are everywhere reported to be fully equal to the average.

The occupiers of small holdings are stated to have in every district the usual quantity of cattle, sheep and fowl. Pigs are very scarce as they were disposed of before Christmas at reduced prices, the people having no prospect of being able to feed them. The migratory labourers returned with their earnings in November after a good season, and the other resources of the people, such as fishing, kelp making, and home industries, were last season productive of about the usual profit. Some of the Inspectors have noted that as the people had a succession of three prosperous years they are less indebted to shopkeepers than they have been for many years past.

In brief, the substance of the Inspectors' reports appears to be this: — that apart from the potato crop the small farmers are well circumstanced, but they are confronted with a greater scarcity of potatoes than they have experienced for over thirty years, and this fact will cause distress in each locality according to the extent to which the people rely for subsistence upon the potato.

The time when the people were entirely dependent on the potato has long gone by, and, in every part of the West, bread, tea, stirabout, milk and sometimes salt fish or eggs, form items of daily consumption. Some of the Inspectors estimate the loss of the potato crop to be equivalent to the loss of the mid-day meal and a portion of the supper for part of the year, and this estimate may probably be taken to apply to the greater part of all the western unions, where the small holders have other resources besides the land. But there are certain congested districts in the western counties where exceptional poverty prevails, and where the occupiers of land endeavour to live altogether on the produce of their small holdings, and in these localities, when life is a struggle at the best of times, the potato is the mainstay of the people, and its loss would mean a much more serious deprivation. In districts thus situated the people are usually able to obtain food on credit during the two or three months immediately preceding the harvest, but this year credit has been demanded at a much earlier period, and although the shopkeepers are willing to advance goods late in the season, when they are in a position to form some opinion as to the harvest prospects, they are reluctant to do so at present while uncertainty exists as to how the people will be situated when the present crisis is passed. . . .

36. Douglas Hyde on 'The necessity for de-anglicising Ireland'

Lecture to the Irish National Literary Society, Dublin, 25 November 1892, published in *The revival of Irish literature; addresses by Sir C. Gavan Duffy, Dr. George Sigerson and Dr. Douglas Hyde,* (Dublin, 1894), 117-69. The full text of this lecture appears in Hyde, *Language, Lore and Lyrics* edited by Breandán Ó Conaire (Dublin 1986), 153-170.

When we speak of 'The Necessity for De-Anglicising the Irish Nation', we mean it, not as a protest against imitating what is *best* in the English people, for that would be absurd, but rather to show the folly of neglecting what is Irish, and hastening to adopt, pell-mell, and indiscriminately, everything that is English, simply because it *is* English.

This is a question which most Irishmen will naturally look at from a National point of view, but it is one which ought also to claim the sympathies of every intelligent Unionist, and which, as I know, does claim the sympathy of many.

If we take a bird's-eye view of our island to-day, and compare it with what it used to be, we must be struck by the extraordinary fact that the nation which once was, as every one admits, one of the most classically learned and cultured nations in Europe, is now one of the least so; how one of the most reading and literary peoples has become one of the *least* studious and most *un*-literary, and how the present art products of one of the quickest, most sensitive, and most artistic races on earth are now only distinguished for their hideousness.

I shall endeavour to show that this failure of the Irish people in recent times has been largely brought about by the race diverging during this century from the right path, and ceasing to be Irish without becoming English. I shall attempt to show that with the bulk of the people this change took place quite recently, much more recently than most people imagine, and is, in fact, still going on. I should also like to call attention to the illogical position of men who drop their own language to speak English, of men who translate their euphonious Irish names into English monosyllables, of men who read English books, and know nothing about Gaelic literature, nevertheless protesting as a matter of sentiment that they hate the country which at every hand's turn they rush to imitate.

I wish to show you that in Anglicing ourselves wholesale we have thrown away with a light heart the best claim which we have upon the world's recognition of us as a separate nationality. What did Mazzini say? What is Goldwin Smith never tired of declaiming? What do the *Spectator* and *Saturday Review* harp on? That we ought to be content as an integral part of the United Kingdom because we have lost the notes of nationality, our language and customs.

It has always been very curious to me how Irish sentiment sticks in this half-way house — how it continues to apparently hate the English, and at the same time continues to imitate them; how it continues to clamour for recognition as a distinct nationality, and at the same time throws away with both hands what would make it so. If Irishmen only went a little farther they would become good Englishmen in sentiment also. But — illogical as it appears — there seems not the slightest sign or probability of their taking that step. It is the curious certainty that come what may Irishmen will continue to resist English rule, even though it should be for their good, which prevents many of our nation from becoming Unionists upon the spot. It is a fact, and we must face it as a fact, that although they adopt English habits and copy England in every way, the great bulk of Irishmen and Irishwomen over the whole world are known to be filled with a dull, ever-abiding animosity against her, and — right or wrong — to grieve when she prospers, and joy when she is hurt. Such movements as Young Irelandism, Fenianism, Land Leagueism, and Parliamentary obstruction seem always to gain their sympathy and support. It is just because there appears no earthly chance of their becoming good members of the Empire that I urge that they become the other; cultivate what they have rejected, and build up an Irish nation on Irish lines.

But you ask, why should we wish to make Ireland more Celtic than it is — why should we de-Anglicise it at all?

I answer because the Irish race is at present in a most anomalous position, imitating England and yet apparently hating it. How can it produce anything good in literature, art, or institutions as long as it is actuated by motives so contradictory? Besides, I believe it is our Gaelic past which, though the Irish race does not recognise it just at present, is really at the bottom of the Irish heart, and prevents us becoming citizens of the Empire, as, I think, can be easily proved.

To say that Ireland has not prospered under English rule is simply a truism; all the world admits it, England does not deny it. But the English retort is ready. You have not prospered, they say, because you would not settle down contentedly, like the Scotch, and form part of the Empire. 'Twenty years of good, resolute, grandfatherly government', said a well-known Englishman, will solve the Irish question. He possibly made the period too short, but let us suppose this. Let us suppose for a moment — which is impossible — that there were to arise a series of Cromwells in England for the space of one hundred years, able administrators of the Empire, careful rulers of Ireland, developing to the utmost our national resources, whilst they unremittingly stamped out every spark of national feeling, making Ireland a land of wealth and factories, whilst they extinguished every thought and every idea that was Irish, and left us, at last, after a hundred years of good government, fat, wealthy, and populous, but with all our characteristics gone, with every external that at present differentiates us from the English lost or dropped; all our Irish names of places and people turned into English names; the Irish language completely extinct; the O's and the Macs dropped; our Irish intonation changed, as far as possible by English schoolmasters into something English; our history no longer remembered or taught; the names of our rebels and martyrs blotted out; our battlefields and traditions forgotten; the fact that we were not of Saxon origin dropped out of sight and memory, and let me now put the question — How many Irishmen are there who would purchase material prosperity at such a price? It is exactly such a question as this and the answer to it that shows the difference between the English and Irish race. Nine Englishmen out of ten would jump to make the exchange, and I as firmly believe that nine Irishmen out of ten would indignantly refuse it.

And yet this awful idea of complete Anglicisation, which I have here put before you in all its crudity, is, and has been, making silent inroads upon us for nearly a century.

Its inroads have been silent, because, had the Gaelic race perceived what was being done, or had they been once warned of what was taking place in their own midst, they would, I think, never have allowed it. When the picture of complete Anglicisation is drawn for them in all its nakedness Irish sentimentality becomes suddenly a power and refuses to surrender it birthright. . . .

What we must endeavour to never forget is this, that the Ireland of to-day is the descendant of the Ireland of the seventh century, then the school of Europe and the torch of learning. It is true that Northmen made some minor settlements in it in the ninth and tenth centuries, it is true that the Normans made extensive settlements during the succeeding centuries, but none of those broke the continuity of the social life of the island. Dane and Norman drawn to the kindly Irish breast issued forth in a generation or two fully Irishised, and more Hibernian than the Hibernians themselves, and even after the Cromwellian plantation the children of numbers of the English soldiers who settled in the south and midlands were, after forty years' residence, and after marrying Irish wives, turned into good Irishmen, and unable to speak a word of English, while several Gaelic poets of the last century have, like Father English, the most unmistakably English names. In two points only was the continuity of the Irishism of Ireland damaged. First, in the north-east of Ulster, where the Gaelic race was expelled and the land planted with aliens, whom our dear mother Erin, assimilative as she is, has hitherto found it difficult to absorb, and in the ownership of the land, eight-ninths of which belongs to people many of whom always lived, or live, abroad, and not half of whom Ireland can be said to have assimilated.

During all this time the continuation of Erin's national life centred, according to our way of looking at it, not so much in the Cromwellian or Williamite landholders who sat in College Green, and governed the country, as in the mass of the people whom Dean Swift considered might be entirely neglected, and looked upon as hewers of wood and drawers of water; the men who, nevertheless, constituted the real working population, and who were living on in the hopes of better days; the men who have since made America, and have within the last ten years proved what an important factor they may be in wrecking or in building the British Empire. These are the men of whom our merchants, artisans, and farmers mostly consist, and in whose hands is to-day the making or marring of an Irish nation. But, alas, *quantum mutatus ab illo!* What the battleaxe of the Dane, the sword of the Norman, the wile of the Saxon was unable to perform, we have accomplished ourselves. We have at last broken the continuity of Irish life, and just at the moment when the Celtic race is presumably about to largely recover possession of its own country, it finds itself deprived and stript of its Celtic characteristics, cut off from the past, yet scarcely in touch with the present. It has lost since the beginning of this century almost all that connected it with the era of Cuchullain and of Ossian, that connected it with the Christianisers of

Europe, that connected it with Brian Boru and the heroes of Clontarf, with the O'Neills and O'Donnells, with Rory O'More, with the Wild Geese, and even to some extent with the men of '98. It has lost all that they had — language, traditions, music, genius, and ideas. Just when we should be starting to build up anew the Irish race and the Gaelic nation — as within our own recollection Greece has been built up anew — we find ourselves despoiled of the bricks of nationality. The old bricks that lasted eighteen hundred years are destroyed; we must now set to, to bake new ones, if we can, on other ground and of other clay. Imagine for a moment the restoration of a German-speaking Greece.

The bulk of the Irish race really lived in the closest contact with the tradition of the past and the national life of nearly eighteen hundred years, until the beginning of this century. Not only so, but during the whole of the dark Penal times they produced amongst themselves a most vigorous literary development. Their schoolmasters and wealthy farmers, unwearied scribes, produced innumerable manuscripts in beautiful writing, each letter separated from one another as in Greek, transcripts both of the ancient literature of their sires and of the more modern literature produced by themselves. Until the beginning of the present century there was no county, no barony, and, I may almost say, no townland which did not boast of an Irish poet, the people's representative of those ancient bards who died out with the extirpation of the great Milesian families. The literary activity of even the eighteenth century among the Gaels was very great, not in the South alone, but also in Ulster — the number of poets it produced was something astonishing. It did not, however, produce many works in Gaelic prose, but it propagated translations of many pieces from the French, Latin, Spanish, and English. Every well-to-do farmer could read and write Irish, and many of them could understand even archaic Irish. I have myself heard persons reciting the poems of Donogha More O'Daly, Abbot of Boyle, in Roscommon, who died sixty years before Chaucer was born. To this very day the people have a word for archaic Irish, which is much the same as though Chaucer's poems were handed down amongst the English peasantry, but required a special training to understand. This training, however, nearly every one of fair education during the Penal times possessed, nor did they begin to lose their Irish training and knowledge until after the establishment of Maynooth and the rise of O'Connell. These two events made an end of the Gaelicism of the Gaelic race, although a great number of poets and scribes existed even down to the forties and fifties of the present century, and a few may linger on yet in remote localities. But it may be said, roughly speaking, that the ancient Gaelic civilisation died with O'Connell, largely, I am afraid, owing to his example and his neglect of inculcating the necessity of keeping alive racial customs, language, and traditions, in which with the one notable exception of our scholarly idealist, Smith O'Brien, he has been followed until a year ago by almost every leader of the Irish race.

Thomas Davis and his brilliant band of Young Irelanders came just at the dividing of the line, and tried to give to Ireland a new literature in English to replace the literature which was just being discarded. It succeeded and it did not succeed. It was a most brilliant effort, but the old bark had been too recently stripped off the Irish tree, and the trunk could not take as it might have done to a fresh one. It was a new departure, and at first produced a violent effect. Yet in the long run it failed to properly leaven our peasantry who might, perhaps, have been reached upon other lines. I say they *might* have been reached upon other lines because it is quite certain that even well on into the beginning of this century Irish poor scholars and schoolmasters used to gain the greatest favour and applause by reading out manuscripts in the people's houses at night, some of which manuscripts had an antiquity of a couple of hundred years or more behind them, and which, when they got illegible from age, were always recopied. The Irish peasantry at that time were all to some extent cultured men, and many of the better off ones were scholars and poets. What have we now left of all that? Scarcely a trace. Many of them read newspapers indeed, but who reads, much less recites, an epic poem, or chants an elegiac or even a hymn?

Wherever Irish throughout Ireland continued to be spoken, there the ancient MSS. continued to be read, there the epics of Cuchullain, Conor MacNessa, Déirdre, Finn, Oscar, and Ossian continued to be told, there poetry and music held sway. . . .

. . . We must teach ourselves not to be ashamed of ourselves, because the Gaelic people can never produce its best before the world as long as it remains tied to the apron-strings of another race and another island, within for *it* to move before it will venture to take any step itself.

In conclusion, I would earnestly appeal to every one, whether Unionist or Nationalist, who wishes to see the Irish nation produce its best — and surely whatever our politics are we all wish that — to set his face against this constant running to England for our books, literature, music, games, fashions, and ideas. I appeal to every one whatever his politics — for this is no political matter — to do his best to help the Irish race to develop in future upon Irish lines, even at the risk of encouraging national aspirations, because upon Irish lines alone can the Irish race once more become what it was of yore — one of the most original, artistic, literary, and charming people of Europe.

37. The home rule bill, 1893
House of Commons, *Bills, public,* III,1893-94 (448) 327-32

. . . Whereas it is expedient that without impairing or restricting the supreme authority of Parliament, an Irish Legislature should be created for such purposes in Ireland as in this Act mentioned:

Be it therefore enacted by the Queen's most Excellent Majesty, by and with the advice and consent of the Lords Spiritual and Temporal, and Commons, in this present Parliament assembled, and by the authority of the same, as follows:

Legislative Authority

1. On and after the appointed day there shall be in Ireland a Legislature consisting of Her Majesty the Queen and of two Houses, the Legislative Council and the Legislative Assembly.

2. With the exceptions and subject to the restrictions in this Act mentioned, there shall be granted to the Irish Legislature power to make laws for the peace, order and good government of Ireland in respect of matters exclusively relating to Ireland or some part thereof. Provided that, notwithstanding anything in this Act contained, the supreme power and authority of the Parliament of the United Kingdom of Great Britain and Ireland shall remain unaffected and undiminished over all persons, matters, and things within the Queen's dominions.

3. The Irish Legislature shall not have power to make laws in respect of the following matters or any of them: —

(1) The Crown, or the succession to the Crown, or a Regency; or the Lord Lieutenant as representative of the Crown; or

(2) The making of peace or war or matters arising from a state of war; or the regulation of the conduct of any portion of Her Majesty's subjects during the existence of hostilities between foreign states with which Her Majesty is at peace, in respect of such hostilities; or

(3) Navy, army, militia, volunteers, and any other military forces, or the defence of the realm, or forts, permanent military camps, magazines, arsenals, dockyards, and other needful buildings, or any places purchased for the erection thereof; or

(4) Authorising either the carrying or using of arms for military purposes, or the formation of associations for drill or practice in the use of arms for military purposes; or

(5) Treaties or any relations with foreign States, or the relations between different parts of Her Majesty's dominions, or offences connected with such treaties or relations, or procedure connected with the extradition of criminals under any treaty; or

(6) Dignities or titles of honour; or

(7) Treason, treason-felony, alienage, aliens as such, or naturalization; or

(8) Trade with any place out of Ireland; or quarantine, or navigation, including merchant shipping (except as respects inland waters and local health or harbour regulations); or

(9) Lighthouses, buoys, or beacons within the meaning of the Merchant Shipping Act, 1854, and the Acts amending the same (except so far as they can consistently with any general Act of Parliament be constructed or maintained by a local harbour authority); or

(10) Coinage; legal tender; or any change in the standard of weights and measures; or

(11) Trade marks, designs, merchandize marks, copyright, or patent rights.

Provided always, that nothing in this section shall prevent the passing of any Irish Act to provide for any charges imposed by Act of Parliament, or to prescribe conditions regulating importation from any place outside Ireland for the sole purpose of preventing the introduction of any contagious disease.

It is hereby declared that the exceptions from the powers of the Irish Legislature contained in this section are set forth and enumerated for greater certainty, and not so as to restrict the generality of the limitation imposed in the previous section on the powers of the Irish Legislature.

Any law made in contravention of this section shall be void.

4. The powers of the Irish Legislature shall not extend to the making of any law —

(1) Respecting the establishment or endowment of religion, whether directly or indirectly, or prohibiting the free exercise thereof; or

(2) Imposing any disability, or conferring any privilege, advantage, or benefit, on account of religious belief, or raising or appropriating directly or indirectly, save as heretofore, any public revenue for any religious purpose, or for the benefit of the holder of any religious office as such; or

(3) Diverting the property or without its consent altering the constitution of any religious body; or

(4) Abrogating or prejudicially affecting the right to establish or maintain any place of denominational education or any denominational institution or charity; or

(5) Whereby there may be established and endowed out of public funds any theological professorship or any university or college in which the conditions set out in the University of Dublin Tests Act, 1873, are not observed; or

(6) Prejudicially affecting the right of any child to attend a school receiving public money, without attending the religious instruction at that school; or

(7) Directly or indirectly imposing any disability, or conferring any privilege, benefit, or advantage upon any subject of the Crown on account of his parentage or place of birth, or of the place where any part of his business is carried on, or upon any corporation or institution constituted or existing by virtue of the law of some part of the Queen's dominions, and carrying on operations in Ireland, on account of the persons by whom or in whose favour or the place in which any of its operations are carried on; or

(8) Whereby any person may be deprived of life, liberty, or property without due process of law in accordance with settled principles and precedents, or may be denied the equal protection of the laws, or whereby private property may be taken without just compensation; or

(9) Whereby any existing corporation incorporated by Royal Charter or by any local or general Act of Parliament may, unless it consents, or the leave of Her Majesty is first obtained on address from the two Houses of the Irish Legislature, be deprived of its rights, privileges, or property without due process of law in accordance with settled principles and precedents, and so far as respects property without just compensation. Provided nothing in this subsection shall prevent the Irish Legislature from dealing with any public department, municipal corporation, or local authority, or with any corporation administering for public purposes taxes, rates, cess, dues, or tolls, so far as concerns the same.

Any law made in contravention of this section shall be void.

Executive Authority

5.—(1) The executive power in Ireland shall continue vested in Her Majesty the Queen, and the Lord Lieutenant, or other chief executive officer or officers for the time being appointed in his place, on behalf of Her Majesty, shall exercise any prerogatives or other executive power of the Queen the exercise of which may be delegated to him by Her Majesty, and shall, in Her Majesty's name, summon, at least once in every year, prorogue, and dissolve the Irish Legislature; and every instrument conveying any such delegation of any prerogative or other executive power shall be presented to the two Houses of Parliament as soon as conveniently may be. Provided always that the lieutenants of counties shall be appointed by the Lord Lieutenant of Ireland as representing Her Majesty.

(2) There shall be an Executive Committee of the Privy Council of Ireland to aid and advise in the government of Ireland, being of such

numbers, and comprising persons holding such offices under the Crown as Her Majesty or, if so authorised, the Lord Lieutenant may think fit, save as may be otherwise directed by Irish Act.

(3) The Lord Lieutenant shall, on the advice of the said Executive Committee, give or withold the assent of Her Majesty to Bills passed by the two Houses of the Irish Legislature, subject nevertheless to any instructions given by Her Majesty in respect of any such Bill.

6. All the powers and jurisdiction to be exercised in accordance with the provisions of the Foreign Enlistment Act, 1870, and the Fugitive Offenders Act, 1881, by the Lord Lieutenant or Lord Justices, or other Chief Governor or Governors of Ireland, or the Chief Secretary of the Lord Lieutenant, shall be exercised by the Lord Lieutenant in pursuance of instructions given by Her Majesty.

Constitution of Legislature

7.—(1) The Irish Legislative Council shall consist of forty-eight councillors.

(2) Each of the constituencies mentioned in the First Schedule to this Act shall return the number of councillors named opposite thereto in that schedule.

(3) Every man shall be entitled to be registered as an elector, and when registered to vote at an election, of a councillor for a constituency, who owns or occupies any land or tenement in the constituency of a rateable value of more than twenty pounds, subject to the like conditions as a man is entitled at the passing of this Act to be registered and vote as a parliamentary elector in respect of an ownership qualification or of the qualification specified in section five of the Representation of the People Act, 1884, as the case may be: Provided that a man shall not be entitled to be registered, nor if registered to vote, at an election of a councillor in more than one constituency in the same year.

(4) The term of office of every councillor shall be eight years, and shall not be affected by a dissolution; and one half of the councillors shall retire in every fourth year, and their seats shall be filled by a new election.

8.—(1) The Irish Legislative Assembly shall consist of one hundred and three members, returned by the existing parliamentary constituencies in Ireland, or the existing divisions thereof, and elected by the parliamentary electors for the time being in those constituencies or divisions.

(2) The Irish Legislative Assembly when summoned may, unless sooner dissolved, have continuance for five years from the day on which the summons directs it to meet and no longer.

(3) After six years from the passing of this Act, the Irish Legislature may alter the qualifications of the electors, and the constituencies, and the distribution of the members among the constituencies, provided that in such distribution due regard is had to the population of the constituencies.

9. If a bill or any provision of a Bill adopted by the Legislative Assembly is lost by the disagreement of the Legislative Council, and after a dissolution, or the period of two years from such disagreement, such Bill, or a Bill for enacting the said provision, is again adopted by the Legislative Assembly and fails within three months afterwards to be adopted by the Legislative Council, the same shall forthwith be submitted to the members of the two Houses deliberating and voting together thereon, and shall be adopted or rejected according to the decision of the majority of those members present and voting on the question.

Irish Representation in House of Commons

10. Unless and until Parliament otherwise determines, the following provisions shall have effect —

(1) After the appointed day each of the constituencies named in the Second Schedule to this Act shall return to serve in Parliament the number of members named opposite thereto in that schedule, and no more, and Dublin University shall cease to return any member.

(2) The existing divisions of the constituencies shall, save as provided in that schedule, be abolished

(3) The election laws and the laws relating to the qualification of parliamentary electors shall not, so far as they relate to parliamentary elections, be altered by the Irish Legislature, but this enactment shall not prevent the Irish Legislature from dealing with any officers concerned with the issue of writs of election, and if any officers are so dealt with, it shall be lawful for Her Majesty by Order in Council to arrange for the issue of such writs, and the writs issued in pursuance of such Order shall be of the same effect as if issued in manner heretofore accustomed. . . .

38. The Parnellite party on Lord Rosebery's acceptance of the premiership
Cork Examiner, 9 March 1894

. . . The complacency with which the Liberal Leader received the rejection of Home Rule by the Lords was explained away in the speeches that promised an agitation against the very existence of the House of

Lords, when it extended its obstruction to English measures. That vain boast has ended in a miserable compromise with the Lords upon the English measures, and, as if in very mockery of the hopes that were excited in Ireland, the Prime Minister, whose continuance in office was the pledge of Home Rule, is cast aside, and a member of the House of Lords appointed in his stead. In Lord Rosebery and his present Cabinet we can have no confidence, and we warn our fellow-countrymen to have none. They will concede just as much to Ireland as she extorts by organisation among her people and absolute unfettered independence of English parties in her representatives. It is your duty, fellow-countrymen, to create and foster these National safeguards. The time has arrived not only for plain speaking, but for prompt action, and we call upon you to no longer tolerate a policy of National subserviency to English party interests. . . .

Signed on behalf of the Independent Party,
J.E. Redmond, T. Harrington, J. Kenny

39. Disenchantment of John Sweetman
United Ireland, 27 April 1895

TO THE ELECTORS OF EAST WICKLOW

Drumbaragh, Kells
April 6th, 1895

Gentlemen — When I accepted the offer to be a candidate at the last General Election, pledged to 'sit, act and vote with the Irish Parliamentary Party' I believed that the Party would act independently of all English parties when Irish interests were at stake; and I laid confidence not only in Mr. Gladstone's marvellous ability, but in his sincere desire to obtain Home Rule for Ireland, as it was a cause to this his reputation as a statesman was pledged.

When he retired last year from the leadership of the Liberal Party, for causes that we cannot at present fully know, I had little confidence in either the ability or the sincerity as a Home Ruler of his successor, Lord Rosebery.

More than a year ago I wrote to Mr. Justin McCarthy that I thought it was most necessary for the Home Rule cause that there should be a General Election as soon as possible. Mr. McCarthy replied that he did not think that time, or any time very near, would be opportune for a general election. I was also told that the Liberals were not then ready with their candidates. I therefore remained on last year voting with the Irish Party for British measures. Before the end of the Session when it was clear that the Government were determined to stick to office as long as they could, although able to do nothing for Ireland, another Irish member and myself tried to get the Irish Party to request the Government to dissolve Parliament at the beginning of the present Session which it was plain to everyone must prove barren as far as Irish legislation was concerned. The majority of the Irish Party were horrified at the idea of a dissolution. . . .

As that majority seems content with Lord Rosebery's policy of inaction, and is acting as if it were sacrificing the cause of Home Rule to keep a Government in office for the sake of obtaining some crumbs of Government patronage. . . and as the Party pledge. . . compels me to vote with them until I resign my seat, I have no course to take but to restore your trust back into your hands. This I have done by applying to the Chancellor of the Exchequer for the Chiltern Hundreds.

You will, therefore, now have an opportunity of electing a member in my place, if you so desire, to continue walking through the Government lobbies to keep Lord Rosebery in office while doing nothing for Ireland, which work I refuse to do any longer; or to elect a man who will do his best to force every Government that may be in power to put Irish measures before all British measures until we have been granted our right to self government. . . .

I now offer myself as a candidate for re-election on the above lines of policy — that is, as an Irish Nationalist, independent of all English parties. . . .

40. Object and programme of Irish Socialist Republican Party founded by James Connolly in 1896
Poster collection, National Library of Ireland

OBJECT.

Establishment of an IRISH SOCIALIST REPUBLIC based upon the public ownership, by the Irish people, of the Land, and Instruments of Production, Distribution and Exchange. Agriculture to be administered as a public function, under boards of management elected by the agricultural population and responsible to them and to the nation at large. All other forms of labour necessary to the wellbeing of the community to be conducted on the same principles.

As a means of organising the forces of the Democracy in preparation for any struggle which may precede the realisation of our ideal; of paving the way for its realisation; of restricting the tide of emigration by providing employment at home; and finally of palliating the evils of our present social system, we work by political means to secure the measures of our PROGRAMME here outlined: —

1. Nationalisation of railways and canals:

2. Abolition of private banks and money-lending institutions, and establishment of State Banks issuing loans at cost:

3. Establishment at public expense of rural depots for the most improved agricultural machinery, to be lent out to the agricultural population, at a rent covering cost and management alone:

4. Graduated Income Tax on all incomes over £400 per annum in order to provide funds for pensions to the aged, infirm, and widows and orphans:

5. Legislative restriction of Hours of Labour to 48 per week, and establishment of a Minimum Wage:

6. Free maintenance for all children:

7. Gradual extension of the principle of public ownership and supply to all the necessities of life:

8. Public control and management of National Schools by boards elected by popular ballot for that purpose alone:

9. Free Education up to the highest University grades:

10. Universal Suffrage.

41. Young Ireland, 1897
Irish Independent, 6 January 1897

REMEMBER '98
YOUNG IRELAND LEAGUE MEETING

A meeting of the Council of the Young Ireland League was held last evening at the Rooms of the League, 15 D'Olier Street, Dublin. Mr. Henry Dixon, jun., presided. . . .

The Chairman explained that the Council had had before them since the Vinegar Hill celebration in 1894, and had arranged last year that steps should be taken in 1897 to form a thoroughly representative committee formed for the purpose of carrying out the centenary celebration. The committee should be composed of persons (1) in sympathy with the principles of the United Irishmen, (2) representative of all sections of National opinion and (3) excluding any apologist for their principles or actions; for instance, those who are in the habit of using such phrases as 'they loved Ireland not wisely but too well'.

Mr. Lavelle proposed the following resolution — 'That a meeting be called for the 4th March (the next anniversary of Emmet's birth) for the purpose of having a committee formed to arrange for a proper celebration of the centenary of '98 and that the persons invited be selected from all existing National parties.'

42. The 1798 centenary celebration begins
Irish Independent, 5 March 1897

Last night a largely attended meeting was held in the Council Chamber, City Hall, for the purpose of making preliminary arrangements for the celebration on a National scale of the centenary of the insurrection of 1798. . . . On the motion of Mr. P. Gregan, T.C.,. . . the chair was taken by Mr. John O'Leary. . . .

The Chairman said that as it was his opinion that the business of the chairman was to listen to others rather than to say anything himself, and for that reason he would not trouble them at any length. They all knew, or ought to know, what he thought of the men of '98 (hear, hear). Nothing that he could say on this point would make them anything the wiser. He did not think it necessary to do more than barely allude to that brilliant and noble young Irishman — Robert Emmet (applause) — on whose anniversary they were fittingly met here to-night. He believed as strongly as he could that the movement which they now in a sense inaugurated should be, above all things, free from anything like exclusiveness or intolerance (hear, hear). They should be not only willing but anxious to receive the aid of any Irishman who by the mere fact of his adhesion proclaimed his belief that the men of '98 were true and brave men who fought and fell in what they at least believed to be the cause of Ireland (applause).

43. Foundation of the United Irish League
Connaught Telegraph, 29 January 1898

THE WESTPORT MEETING.

WEST MAYO UNITED IRISH LEAGUE ESTABLISHED

Last Sunday in the Octagon, Westport, was held a meeting that could compare favourably in numbers and enthusiasm with any held in West Mayo for years. Special trains were run from Achill, Newport, and Mulranny. The people came in from all the districts for miles around

Westport, marching in in processional order, four or five deep, headed by band[s], with banners, with banners bearing appropriate mottoes. Cavalcades of horsemen and long lines of vehicles came long distances to the meeting. The Newport, Kilmeena, Kilmaclasser and other contingents carried imitation pikes of the '98 pattern, which formed a special feature of the demonstration. . . .

On the motion of Mr. P.J. Kelly, seconded by Mr. Walter McEvilly, vice-chairman, Board of Guardians, the chair was taken amidst great cheering by the Very Rev. T. Healy, Adm.

The Chairman said it was indeed a very great honour to be called to preside at such a magnificent meeting as that. That meeting indeed proved beyond doubt that the spirit of Nationality was not yet dead in West Mayo (cheers, and a voice 'it never will be'). It proved beyond doubt that the spirit which animated the men of Mayo in the old Land League days was still alive. They knew that the object for which that great meeting was being held, in the first place, was to bring publicly under the notice of the Government the destitute condition of the districts around that neighbourhood (a voice, 'they are starving'). They knew themselves that they had exceedingly poor crops in some parts, indeed not half a crop during the present year (a voice, 'Not a crop'), and he knew there were people at present subsisting on Indian meal, and not even enough of that. This was the centenary year of '98, and surely it was an unfortunate state of affairs that they should have the spectre of absolute famine staring them in the face. However, it proved once again that this country was misgoverned; it proved that the Government was callous to their wants (a voice, 'It is too true'). He would not stand between them and the distinguished speakers who were to follow him, but he wished to say just one word as to this great year of '98 (cheers). The men of Mayo were not afraid to speak of '98 (loud and prolonged cheers). Indeed it would be a great shame if any Irishman worthy of the name were afraid or ashamed to speak of '98 (cheers), for in that remarkable year it was a dark and evil time, and they had Irishmen as good and patriotic as any that ever lived, who were not afraid to shed their blood for the cause of Ireland (cheers). (A voice — We have men who would do so to-day (cheers). Yes, thank God, we have. In those days they had Wolfe Tone, Robert Emmet, Father Murphy of Vinegar Hill, Father Manus Sweeny, all giving their lives for the cause of their country (prolonged cheers). Would they not be ungrateful and unworthy if they forgot the memories of those days of '98, and of the good and noble and patriotic men whose names clustered around it (cheers). They were assembled in their thousands at that great meeting to prove that they still cherished the memories of those days and those men, that they would keep their memory green, and practice the lessons which they taught (loud cheers). . . .

The Very Rev. Canon Greally, who was greeted with loud and prolonged cheers, said he had great pleasure in proposing the following resolutions: —

1. That we the Nationalists of West Mayo in monster meeting assembled to celebrate with reverence and pride the memories of Ireland's glorious struggle for liberty in 1798, and we trust that in the centennial year our countrymen will do honour to the memory of the United Irishmen by sinking personal and sectional differences and uniting in one solid mass to organise a series of demonstrations worthy of the immortal principles of the United Irishmen, and of our exile[s] and kindred who are coming across to join in the celebrations (cheers), and we hereby pledge ourselves to take immediate action for the formation of United Irish clubs on a basis that will secure the fullest representation of every section of Irish Nationalists and of their elected representatives, party and local. (Cheers.)

2. That the population of large districts of the Westport Union are already reduced to the direst condition of destitution and starvation, and have absolutely no means of their own of averting a widespread famine for the next three months. That we condemn in the strongest terms the tardy and cruelly made — quote relief proposals made by the Government, which proposals throw all the responsibility and a great part of the pecuniary bur[th]en of relief upon the unfortunate ratepayers, the majority of whom are themselves crushed with merciless rack-renters, debts, and rates, and we appeal to the public opinion of the world and of our exiled countrymen against this barbarous neglect of the Government to afford adequate relief out of the millions unjustly wrung by England annually out of this impoverished country. (Cheers.)

3. The most effective means of preventing the frequent cries of distress and famine in this so-called congested district would be the breaking up of large grazing ranches with which the district is cursed, and the partition of them amongst the small landholders, who were driven into the bogs and mountains to make room for the sheep and bullocks of English and Scotch adventurers and Irish grabbers. (Cheers.)

4. That in this time of great distress, owing to the almost total failure of the potato crop, we denounce as legalised robbery the exactions of full rents by landlords, and we denounce as cruel the evictions of widows and orphans for the non-payment of impossible rents. (Cheers.)

5. That in union with our fellow-countrymen throughout the length and breadth of Ireland we denounce the nefarious system of land grabbing, the most effective prop of evicting landlordism, and we hereby

solemnly pledge ourselves to use every legitimate means to crush out the detestable practice and to bring the grabber to a full sense of his misdeeds. (Cheers.)

6. That for the purpose of carrying out the resolutions of this meeting an organisation be hereby established, to be called the West Mayo United Irish League, open to all sections of Irish Nationalists and consisting of parish branches to be governed by a central committee meeting from time to time in Westport, and composed of the clergy of all the parishes of West Mayo, all Nationalist town commissioners and poor law guardians and six representatives of each parish to be elected by the parish branches. A provisional organising committee with power to add to their numbers, to meet on Thursday next and make arrangements for the formation of the parish branches of the league. (Cheers.). . . .

44. Salisbury on the state of the empire
Address to the Primrose League, London, 4 May 1898, reported in *The Times*, 5 May 1898

. . . If we could simply look upon the world as it presents itself to us, if we could merely count our colonies and our possessions and our growing and enormous trade, we might indeed look forward to the future without disquietude. We know we shall maintain against all comers that which we possess, and we know, that in spite of the jargon about isolation, we are amply competent to do so. (cheers) But that will not secure the peace of the world.

LIVING AND DYING NATIONS

You may roughly divide the nations of the world as the living and the dying. On the one side you have the great countries of enormous power growing in power every year, growing in wealth, growing in dominion, growing in the perfection of their organisation. Railways have given them the power to concentrate upon any one point the whole military forces of their population and to assemble armies of a magnitude and power never dreamed of in the generations that have gone by. Science has placed in the hands of these armies weapons ever growing in the efficacy of destruction, and, therefore, adding to the power — fearfully to the power — of those who have an opportunity of using them. By the side of these splendid organisations of which nothing seems to diminish the forces and which present rival claims which the future may only be able by a bloody arbitrament to adjust — by the side of these there are a number of communities which I can only describe as dying, though the epithet applies to them, of course, in very different degree and with a very different amount of application. They are mainly communities that are not Christian, but I regret to say that it is not exclusively the case, and in these States disorganisation and decay are advancing almost as fast as concentration and increasing power are advancing in the living nations that stand beside them. Decade after decade they are weaker, poorer, and less provided with leading men or institutions in which they can trust, apparently drawing nearer and nearer to their fate and yet clinging with a strange tenacity to the life which they have got. In them misgovernment is not only not cured, but is constantly on the increase. . . . How long this state of things is likely to go on I do not attempt to prophesy. All I can indicate is that the process is proceeding — the weak States are becoming weaker and the strong States are becoming stronger. It needs no speciality of prophecy to point out to you what the inevitable result of the combined process must be. For one reason or for another — from the necessities of politics — or under the pretence of philanthropy the living nations will gradually encroach upon the territory of the dying, and the seeds and cause of conflict amongst civilised nations will speedily appear. Of course, it is not to be supposed that any one nation of the living nations will be allowed to have the profitable monopoly of curing or cutting off these unfortunate patients (laughter) and the controversy is as to who shall have the privilege of doing so, and in what measure he shall do it. These things may introduce causes of fatal difference between the great nations whose mighty armies stand opposite threatening each other. These are the dangers, I think, which will threaten us in the period that is coming on. It is a period that will tax our resolution, our tenacity, and Imperial instincts to the utmost. Undoubtedly we shall not allow England to be at a disadvantage in any re-arrangement that may take place. (Cheers). On the other hand, we shall not be jealous if desolation and sterility are removed by the aggrandisement of a rival power in regions to which our army cannot extend. But be that how it may, it is only another ground for me to implore you not to imagine that because we have settled the affairs of Ireland, because our own internal politics seem calm, because we seem capable of dealing with any problem that may arise — not to imagine that the time has gone by when the spirit of the lesson preached by the Primrose League is less necessary to the health and security of this country. Do not abate your efforts because you think your task is done. Your task is ever living and it never was more important than now, as is indicated by the threatening circumstances of the world outside. . . .

45. The republican theme

United Irishman, 29 April 1899

We print to-day an article suggesting the formation of a National Republican Association which we commend to the earnest consideration of our readers. Whether they will coincide as fully in the news expressed by its author and as thoroughly of the proposal as we do, we leave them in their own calm judgment to determine. For our part, we believe the Nationalists of Ireland have too long suffered the exploitation of their name by men whose concept of Irish Nationality had, in mercy to them, better be left undefined. So long, in our opinion, as the most intelligent and most patriotic section of the nation submits to its persistent negation, in a mistaken belief that some material interest of the country may be served by such submission or through a dislike to assert itself in days when reviling passes current as criticism and denunciation takes the place of argument — so long will the cause it cherishes continue to lose vital force. Beyond this, we will say no further, until we have learned the views of our readers on the proposal contained in the article to which we have referred.

46. John Redmond on nationalist unity, in a speech to the United Irish League Convention in the Rotunda, Dublin

Irish Independent, 12 December 1900

The Chairman (Mr. J. Redmond) said — Gentlemen, I propose now to take a vote upon the question. Before doing so I claim from the Convention their indulgence to state my own view in two or three brief sentences (cheers). . . . I decline altogether, so far as I am personally concerned, to enter into any question affecting causes of dispute which arose in what I may without offence call the Anti-Parnellite Party before the reunion and the Convention of last June (cheers). From the moment of that reunion, when I was by unanimous vote of all sections of that Party selected as Chairman, my one great and overpowering desire has been to use all my best abilities and my most strenuous efforts to UNITE ALL IRISH NATIONALISTS in the ranks of the National Organisation. When the Convention of last June was coming on I advised — nay, gentlemen, I entreated — Mr. Healy to attend it (cheers). After the Convention had been held I again, on my own responsibility, as chairman of the Irish Party, urged strongly upon Mr. Healy and his friends to bow to the authority of the Convention and to accept the National organisation which it had founded; and, furthermore, not to thwart, but rather to support the collection of the General Election Fund, which was a vital necessity of the National situation. I am sorry to say that my advice fell upon deaf ears. . . .

47. 'Come back to Erin'; poem written to commemorate Victoria's visit to Ireland in April 1900

Published by McGowan and Ingram Ltd., Belfast. Poster collection of National Library of Ireland

Come back to Erin, Victoria Regina,
Come back to Erin, our dear Empress-Queen;
Come in the springtime, Victoria *mavourneen,*
Come when our meadows with shamrocks are green.

Come back to Erin, Victoria Regina,
Come back to Erin, the land we adore;
Come back and cheer us, Victoria the Noble,
Come! for we love thee, Victoria *asthore.*

Come back to Erin, Victoria Regina,
'Come!' will re-echo o'er mountain and glen;
Come with the shamrocks, Victoria the Peerless,
Come, and our thunders will greet thee again.

Come back to Erin, Victoria Regina,
Cead Mile Failte awaits thee alway;
Come! we'll be lonely, Victoria, beloved,
Come, and we'll meet thee in fair Dublin Bay.

Come back to Erin, Victoria Regina,
Come! we'll be counting the days till you come!
Come, for we know that you share in our sorrows;
Come back, *bainriogan,* to our green Island-home.

Come back to Erin, Victoria Regina,
Come for the sake of our soldiers who bled;
Come, for they fought for the flag of Britannia;
Come for their sakes who bewail for the dead.

Come back to Erin, Victoria Regina,
Come! may that coming be calm and serene;
Come! we'll be sighing to see thee, *mavourneen,*
Come back to Erin, our own Gracious Queen!

J.R.SCOTT

Dublin, *April, 1900.*

101

48. George Wyndham's initial impressions of Ireland upon his appointment as chief secretary

J.W.Mackail and Guy Wyndham, *Life and letters of George Wyndham* (London, n.d.[1925]), vol. II, 408-12

To his Mother

Chief Secretary's Lodge
Phoenix Park, Dublin, *November* 25, 1900

I loved your letter and I believe in its ideal. We are the children of the Past, England, Ireland, Scotland and Wales, and we have younger brothers and sisters by a second marriage, Canada, Australasia, South Africa. Ireland is the daughter about whom the parents quarrelled. She has been Cinderella and is poor and hurt. But now invited back to her seat on the dais she may take a common pride in being one of the first family. But all this is far away and not ready as yet even to be spoken of. She is still too poor.

We will have a long talk in London. I am not only reconciled to being here. I see it was inevitable. A Chief Secretary is like a Ghibelline Duke of the 13th century representing Empire and a larger organic conception in a Guelf republic. Many have failed here because they did not realize that they were not in the 19th century. I always have a difficulty in persuading myself that I am. I really love the Irish and they have been very kind and courteous to me during the last fortnight.

I went round the North of Connaught to Mallaranny by Achill from Tuesday to Saturday. It was of the greatest service to me and a brilliant tragi-comedy all the time. We drove and drove — such a party! Self, Hanson; Wrench, a Unionist, loyal, sensible land commissioner. Father O'Hara, Father O'Flyn who was 'advanced' and is enchanting. Mr. Doran, the other type, a slow pragmatical Irishman, whose eye only gleams when he points out arterial drainage. And so we bumped round, going into the cottiers' wretched hovels. No one knows in England what 'Hell or Connaught' means. And all the Nationalist remedies of confiscation and compulsory sale would only stereotype an intolerable existence. I wish you and Pamela could have seen Srah, a heap of hovels huddled on to one soppy knoll above the bog level — in effect a simple piggery. One house had a family of five in one room 11 feet by 7 feet. In the other room a family of seven. It was complete and picturesque, stooping to get under the lintel and waiting till your eyes could pierce the peat-haze there slowly emerged to sight — a hand loom; the pig; the cow and her manger; the donkey; the bed; a rocking-cradle with child; the hearth; the spinning-wheel.

Yesterday morning at Mallaranny with its wild fuchsia hedges we had the full rain-laden blast from the Atlantic. Took a special at 12.20 to Westport and caught the mail passing Athlone to Broadstone at 7.15. I drove off and dressed at the Shelbourne Hotel and on to a Public Dinner to the Irish Hospital. His Excellency, the Lord Chancellor, Attorney General, Lord Iveagh and many swells and officials were present. I did not speak till twenty to twelve, and then luckily made quite a hit. I am very thankful as I feared, after the long drives and preoccupation in economic problems and long railway journey, that my brains would not work. I, however, followed my new prescription for oratory, viz.: to sleep like a log all the afternoon. I am glad I did not 'jolly' the fence which was likely with such a take off. I found Sibell on getting here and have spent the morning expatiating on the possibilities of the garden. We dine at the Vice-regal to-night. I am your own son on these occasions and all Ireland knows that you were reared at Athlone! . . .

To the Rt. Hon. A.J.Balfour

Chief Secretary's Office

Confidential.   Dublin Castle, *Nov.*, 26th, 1900

Instead of the reasoned account of first impressions which I hoped to write I find myself driven to jot down a midnight scrawl.

1. *The United Irish League,* started 2 and more years ago by O'Brien in Mayo, has spread over the country. Redmond discouraged it; Healy stabbed it, the Priests fought it at the election. It won 'hands down'. Redmond acquiesces. The Bishop of Raphoe, Father O'Hara, and a few more of the abler Priests, are sailing with it in the hope of getting a hand on the tiller. The so-called 'National Convention' to meet whilst our December Parliament is sitting will be composed of delegates from the League and will — see Dillon's speech at Tullamore of yesterday — construct a Parliamentary Party to the exclusion of Healy and his remnant.

They mean to avoid open breaches of the Law, taught by experience that a 'Ponsonby Estate' sort of fight exhausts their treasury. But they neither can, nor care to, control the action of extremists. These however meet in secret conclave and know the Law of Criminal Conspiracy at least as well as our Law Officers, so that whilst nine-tenths of the League's operations are political and legitimate, the remaining tenth is inscrutable.

2. *Police.* This is due, in my opinion, to (a) the fact that the Police — R.I.C. — and Crimes branch has grown rusty during years of division and consequent peace, (b) to the fact that the County and District

Inspectors have evidently got it into their heads that the Government would be glad to receive pleasant reports. There was no true basis for such an inference. But you remember that they expect one thing or the other. Sir Andrew Reed was useless, with Col. Chamberlain and Considine a gradual screwing up of efficiency is going on.

What has happened is this. The local police, to keep up the appearance of zeal, have smothered the Castle with reports by one man who overheard something at a window, and by information accepted on the distinct understanding that it was not to be used. They know as well as the Attorney General that such evidence is worthless. And they add to it a pious opinion that the speech made 'would (?) have no effect'. I have discussed this with Harrel, in whom I have complete confidence, and he, in consultation with Chamberlain, is taking the necessary steps to bring home to the Police that their duty is to be efficient detectives and guardians of the Peace and to leave questions of Law to the Law Officers and questions of Policy to the Government. The three things have become somewhat confused.

3. *Agrarian Agitation.* The League began by an attack upon 'Graziers'. Thanks to T.W. Russell they are now doubling this policy with 'Compulsory Land Purchase'. All the 103 Irish Members with exception of Col. Saunderson 'sans phrase' and McCartney, with a minimum of hedging, have committed themselves to that policy. The only material difference between the Unionists and Nationalists is that the former wish to give a fair, the latter an unfair, price to the Landlord.

All, friends and foes, are strangely cut off from British sentiment. They believe that in spite of War taxation and Imperial Politics, Ireland is going to bathe once more in the limelight. The Nationalist Party, armed with a mandate from the Convention and assisted by Russell, mean, if they can, to imitate Parnell's Parliamentary tactics.

4. *The Ardilaunites.* I hope and believe that when the Parliamentary storm bursts the Ardilaunites will rally for salvation. They are disposed, at present, to run amuck not only against Horace Plunkett and the Agricultural Department but also against the Congested Districts Board.

The C.D. Board in order to do *anything* has bought properties; amalgamated the scattered patches held in 'run-dale' by cottiers, relet at a higher — £15 or £20 instead of 30/- or £3 rent and then sold at 15 to 20 years.

The Ardilaunites are disposed to claim this as a countenance of the League's principles. My opinion, subject to reflection, is that the question of principle lies between free and economic and practical methods and those which are forced, illegal, unsound and illusory. I can hardly develop this in a letter. Briefly, Compulsion apart from all other and prior objections would stereotype the existing and intolerable situation. The family of seven, inhabiting a hovel, and reclaiming 4 acres scattered in from 10 to 15 patches, would be made owners (!) of that 'hereditas'. The rich grazier an owner of a valuable property. The grazier with 200 or 300 acres of poor grass, owner of a mill-stone round his neck.

In a few years the small shopkeeper, the money-lender, the village solicitor would buy out the cottiers and the weary round would begin again.

Are we then to do nothing? In my opinion, subject to reflection, two things must be done, not now, but in the course of the next 3 years.

A. *Land Commission.* This is in a poor state and justifies many of the attacks. Judge Meredith has lost his nerve. Murrough O'Brien is a crank. So long as he can come in *after agreement with Landlord and Tenant*, and cut down the purchase money, the Landlord will not sell. Who would risk going to the workhouse on the decision of one eccentric gentleman with disloyal proclivities? Therefore the Land Commission and procedure must be reformed.

B. *Congested Districts Board.* This Body, or another, must interpose 2 or 3 years of *paternal administration* between the sale *from* the Landlord and the sale *to* the tenanats.

A. and B. are speculative and for the *future.* For the present we must enforce the Law and beat the Parliamentary move. But Purchase will remain a farce and become a dead letter unless (a) some security is given to the Landlord that he will not be ruined and (b) some provision made so that the tenant may buy a holding in which he can live instead of scattered patches of soppy bog. . . .

49. The end of the Victorian era: a republican view
Irish People, 26 January 1901

A REIGN OF BLOOD

We have seen it stated very often latterly that Queen Victoria was deeply affected by the continuance of the War in South Africa. She dearly wished to end her reign in peace. But, leaving Ireland out of consideration for a moment, we cannot help feeling that the hope was a delusive one. For her late Majesty's reign, almost from the very outset, was a reign of War and Bloodshed.

A War with Afghanistan was begun before she was two years on the throne. At the same period British troops were suppressing an insurrection in Canada. China was attacked by Great Britain in 1841, and again in 1849, 1856, and 1860 — while the 'Chinese Question' is yet as dangerous as the South African. The Sikh tribes were victims in 1845 and 1848. War was waged against the Kaffirs in 1846, 1851 and 1877; while only a few years have passed away since Rhodes and Jameson won a 'Rhodesia' drenched in Native blood. The Burmans and the English fought in 1850, 1852, and 1855.

Beginning with the 'Indian Mutiny' of 1857 no less than nine wars against the tribes of Hindustan lie to the discredit of the 'Victorian Era'. In West Africa, yet unsettled, four bloody wars were fought out between 1864 and 1890. Tens of thousands of Englishmen perished in the Crimean struggle with Russia. In New Zealand the Maoris were plundered and almost exterminated. Persia was attacked in 1852; Abyssinia in 1857; the Zulu tribes in 1878; the Basutos in 1879; Egypt in 1862 and again in 1884; the Soudanese in 1894, 1896 and finally in 1899 when Kitchener's dread holocaust of wounded at Omdurman horrified the world; Zanzibar was invaded in 1890; and after having failed to conquer the Boers in 1881, England's statesmen planned as vile a plot against human liberty as ever was recorded and exposed, and had already sacrificed 70,000 men and £100,000,000 of money in the vain effort to subdue the unconquerable peasants of the Transvaal and Orange Free State when the last summons reached the Sovereign who ruled the British Empire while the bearers of that Empire's flag were planting it on the ground fertilised by the blood of the native races in every part of the world during the long cycle of years intervening between the rise of Akhbar Khan as a champion of patriotism in the Himalayan passes, and the addition of the names of Kruger, Joubert, Cronje, Botha, and De Wet to the list of those defenders of liberty against British aggression whose memory the world will ever cherish while the passion for freedom burns in the human breast.

And this was 'the great and glorious reign' which saw
'Freedom slowly broadening out
From precedent to precedent'
in England, but which was marked by freedom-loving England with blood and rapine year in, year out, and all the world over. We are not discussing a 'Personality'. We are reviewing an Era, and, rightly considered, it was not an Era of Glory for England, but of indelible disgrace.

50. George Wyndham on Ireland
Mackail and Wyndham, *George Wyndham*, II, 424-25,428-30

To the Rt. Hon. A.J.Balfour

Confidential   Clouds, Salisbury
September 20*th*, 1901

I have come to England for a week and the enforced idleness affords an opportunity for a conversation on paper that needs no reply.

1. I have travelled round the West Coast and visited all the fishing centres, considering them in relation to (a) the aptitudes of the population, (b) the natural facilities, (c) the artificial facilities, whether of piers or of means of transit by railways or steamers.

I am deeply impressed by the amount of money which has been wasted, notably in 1883, and by the results which could be obtained for a modest expenditure of some £40,000.

Let me now 'block in' a few general observations.

1. The Irish believe that we only spend money on reproductive works under compulsion of lawlessness and agitation.

2. This is not the case. The error arises from the fact that we have usually spent money only when Ireland was, for the time being, sensational and interesting to the public. For example you find traces of expenditure on marine works which fall into 3 categories.

(x) Money spent in '30, 31, 32, after emancipation excitement, guided by the report of a Commission of that date. It was the best report, and the works were generally built in the right places. But many of them have perished or even disappeared.

(y) Money spent in 1883 — £250,000 — after the 80-81 trouble. This was almost uniformly wasted.

(z) Money spent by you and Gerald to the best purpose under the C.D.B. and later, the New Department. This is the only effort that has outlived a 'succès de scandale' of Ireland on the stage of Westminster. But it needs a little fresh capital at certain points.

The pity of it is that at typical spots, such as Teeling, you find the submerged ruins of the '30-32 pier in the right place; the £8000 1883 pier in the wrong place, 7 miles further from the market and some small, though useful, patchings. . . .

To the Rt. Hon. A.J. Balfour

Confidential   Chief Secretary's Lodge,
                                                 November 2nd, 1901.

It may interest you to know how I am getting on. I saw Cadogan in London on Thursday and am returning next Wed. night to see Beach on Thursday or Friday 7th or 8th. I cannot say too earnestly how necessary I feel it to be that the Cabinet should decide on a comprehensive Land Policy and place me in a position to speak early in the Session or sooner. Every day that I give to studying the question convinces me that we must accept the 'in globo' principle and announce it soon. It would be a great calamity not to come out with our policy until the agitation has gone further. I am keeping the lawless parts wedged off from the rest of Ireland. But the strain is increasing. On the whole I am satisfied with the working out of the plan submitted to the Cabinet for dealing with lawlessness. I have scheduled for administrative guidance certain 'disturbed' areas (which include the farms around which the agitation is fermented, of which there is a list No. 1) and filled them up with Police charged to the extent of one-half on the district, under selected officers.

Next I have a list No. 2 of notorious agitators who have attacked individuals. My instructions to the Police are that, whenever an 'agitator' on the list attempts a surprise meeting near the house or holding of a person held up to odium in a 'disturbed' district, the Police are to warn him that he cannot be allowed to hold a meeting and, if he persists, to 'move him on' and break up the meeting.

The manoeuvring of the agitators has become more refined since the old days. They do not advertise their meetings so that 'proclamation' on my part rarely becomes possible. The Police cannot be left to decide when a meeting becomes an 'unlawful assembly'. But, by the plan sketched above, they have not to decide that point on their own discretion. They obey my instructions, and when a speaker on List No. 2 attempts a meeting near a holding on List No. 1 act on the opinion formed in anticipation by the Government that any such collocation would constitute an 'unlawful assembly'. Now, assume that their action is challenged — as it will be — I can reply on the particular case by turning up the 'dossier' of the 'agitator' and the 'dossier' of the farm and its occupier. Putting the two together I say that the Government formed the opinion on these facts, that the meeting would be an unlawful assembly and, therefore, had instructed the Police to prevent it.

The agitators are puzzled for the moment. John O'Donnell has left to 'fire the heather' in England, at least so one of the informants tells us. But Dillon seems disposed to 'try a fall' and force my hand. There is no sympathy with them in the east and south and not very much, so far, in the west. For example, last Sunday they prepared two big surprise Field-days. At Mullinabreenah they attempted them over an area 10 miles by 8 and were everywhere forestalled by the Police, whose strategic dispositions and communications by bicycle were an admirable piece of work. The agitators did not get in a word anywhere and the people in general who watch the game think small beer of them. At Kilmaine they tried to bring about a crisis. On the 2 previous Sundays, the Police, acting on the plan I have sketched, had stopped John O'Donnell and Regan from speaking. So last Sunday, a Fair-day which brought 6000 people together, these two reappeared suddenly accompanied by Willy Redmond. About 600 people only supported them; the balance went on quietly with their Fairing. The Police did very well: stopped O'Donnell and Regan who are on the List No. 2 and let W. Redmond speak. He failed to 'toe the line' and made a moderate speech. When O'Donnell tried to follow him the Police charged and sent the crowd flying. They then must have told Willy Redmond that he had shown the 'white feather'. So they carted him off to the house of another boycotted man some miles off. But the Police anticipated them on cars and broke them up again.

I understand that Dillon will now have a shot. All the above is only the small change of Irish Government. My heart is set on the Land Bill. In case it may interest you I enclose an early sort of essay on small holdings and grass farms. Now is the time to come on with a constructive policy. Nine-tenths of the people are hanging back from the agitation. The Graziers have had a very bad year and prices for stock are very low. If we can get in with a reasonable constructive policy before the agitation develops and whilst the 'grass' interest is still suffering from past inflation and present low prices, I believe we shall win.

I came across a curious case illustrating the merits of 'in globo'. It could not be used in public as it turned up during researches in the Registration of Titles office. An eminent Peer, Lord Morley in fact, has sold his estate 'in globo' for £40,000 to two persons who borrowed the money in the market in order to buy and expect to make £5000 or £6000 by resale to the tenants.

Cadogan, Wrench and Franks have a new idea for dealing with Judicial Rents. I proposed the bold treatment of saying we would have no third revision, if the State came forward to assist 'in globo'. I admit the danger that the Landlords who *never* know their interests would, if that were done, stop selling and wait for the next collapse or spoliation by the other Party. (That is *bound* to come unless we can help the small-holders to buy, or hire some grass on leases, to be held for their common benefit.)

Their suggestion on which they are very sweet is to say that, in future, when any tenant takes his landlord into court the Landlord may have a price for sale fixed and compel the tenant to buy. They instance the analogy of Free Farms Grants and True Value. But it won't do as it stands. Cadogan means in any case to submit it to the Cabinet. I object, somewhat on the general ground that it will confirm the present vicious view of a contest between the two parties over single existing holdings, but, more strongly, because it is naked compulsion. The Tenant must pay a price to which he has not agreed, or forego his expectation of revision.

It might be made less objectionable with this amendment which

109

occurred to me last night. When either party brings the other into court (it is the Tenant 99 times out of a hundred) the other may demand that a price shall be fixed. Take the usual case of the Tenant bringing the Landlord into Court. The Landlord then has a price fixed. Then if (a) the Tenant refuses to buy at that price, he must go on at the current rent for another 15 years, but if (b) the Landlord refuses to take the price the Tenant gets a revision and the right to another in 15 years.

There is a good deal to be said for this. I know that some of the Landlords' champions would accept it. They fear, with good reason, the revisions every 15 years. And it is a danger that if they were let off them generally they would just drift on to their doom, which is only to be avoided by purchase *including* provisions for bringing some of the grass into the market. . . .

51. Cumann na nGaedheal appeal to the Ancient Order of Hibernians in the United States

William O'Brien(of Dublin) collection, National Library of Ireland

TO THE ANCIENT ORDER OF HIBERNIANS

Cumann na nGaedheal,
196 Great Brunswick Street
Dublin, 1*st November*,1902

Descendants of Irishmen —

You know Ireland's wrongs. You know how England has worked, and is working, for her ruin. In Elizabeth's and in Cromwell's time it was by the sword England tried to exterminate the Irish race. She found the sword too dangerous and too slow; she invented the famine policy, and, during Queen Victoria's reign over one million Irish people died of hunger in a land of plenty.

The famine policy is carried out by the continual draining of Ireland's wealth to England by over-taxation, by checks on industry, and by absentee landlordism.

The uselessness of the talk of 80 Irishmen in England's Parliament of 670 Members, to prevent England continuing to rob and destroy Ireland, is proved by the fact that taxation has been continually raised in Ireland during the last 20 years, till to-day Irishmen pay in taxation per head four times what they paid at the beginning of Victoria's reign, and between forty and fifty thousand Irish people are obliged each year to emigrate.

In fifty years our population has been reduced almost by one-half; in less than fifty more years, if things go on as at present, there will no longer be a Catholic or Nationalist majority in Ireland.

In face of these facts, it is terrible for us to know that if Irishmen had been taught never to enter the English Army, THERE WOULD PROBABLY BE NO BRITISH EMPIRE TO OPPRESS US TO-DAY.

If you read the history of England's great wars, you will see that it was Irishmen — driven by starvation into the English Army — who won nearly all the battles which made England powerful. Painful as it is, it is necessary for us to realise this, so as to understand the importance of putting down recruiting in Ireland.

The worthlessness, as soldiers, of the modern Englishman, reared amid the smoke and corruption of England's great factory towns, has been clearly shown in the South African War.

England knows her Army, shattered by the Boers, is incapable of protecting her vast possessions; she knows she cannot get men fit to be soldiers in England. Again she turns to Ireland for recruits. She wants 100,000 men, and the recruiting sergeants have orders to try every town and village in Ireland; and the so-called Irish Guards are to arrive in Dublin this month on a recruiting campaign.

Here is a practical opportunity of striking our oppressor — and we appeal to you, members of the A.O.H., to assist us in this work: —

Cumann na nGaedheal has done much during the last three years to stop recruiting, but much remains to be done. Poverty is great; the inducements in the way of pay and bounties to those who enlist have been increased. The Society has carried on the work single-handed, assisted only by 'The United Irishman'. We want to send lecturers this winter into every town and village where the recruiting sergeants go, who will fearlessly proclaim that it is treason to Ireland for any Irishman to put on England's uniform; we want to keep watch round the barracks; we want to distribute anti-recruiting literature in all the taverns and meeting-places where the recruiting sergeant finds his victims. Our funds are limited; we appeal to you to help us by subscribing to the fund for carrying on this work.

It is the most practical way we have for the moment of weakening England; and, by keeping Irishmen out of the English Army and Navy, we shall be removing a stain from Ireland's name.

Yours fraternally,

JOHN O'LEARY, *President.*

ROBERT JOHNSTON, MAUD GONNE,⎱
JOHN MacBRIDE, JAMES P. EGAN ⎰ *Vice-Presidents*

SHAWN O'SULLIVAN, *Hon. Treasurer .*

PETER WHITE, JOSEPH KENN, *Hon. Secretaries.*

52. The Irish land conference
Return of the resolutions and statement of the Irish landowners convention. . . and report of the Irish land conference, dated 3rd day of January 1903. . . ., *Parliamentary papers*, 1903, lvii, 326-29

THE IRISH LAND CONFERENCE

Whereas it is expedient that the Land Question in Ireland be settled so far as it is practicable and without delay;

And whereas the existing position of the Land Question is adverse to the improvement of the soil of Ireland, leads to unending controversies and lawsuits between owners and occupiers, retards progress in the country, and constitutes a grave danger to the State;

And whereas an opportunity of settling once for all the differences between owners and occupiers in Ireland is very desirable;

And whereas such settlement can only be effected upon the basis mutually satisfactory to the owners and occupiers of the land;

And whereas certain representatives of owners and occupiers have been desirous of endeavouring to find such basis and for that purpose have met in conference together;

And whereas certain particulars of agreement have been formulated, discussed, and passed at the Conference, and it is desirable that the same should be put into writing and submitted to His Majesty's Government.

After consideration and discussion of various schemes submitted to the Conference we are agreed: —

I. That the only satisfactory settlement of the Land Question is to be effected by the substitution of an occupying proprietary in lieu of the existing system of dual ownership.

II. That the process of direct interference by the State in purchase and re-sale is, in general, tedious and unsatisfactory, and that therefore, except in cases where at least half the occupiers or the owner so desire, and except in districts included in the operations of the Congested Districts Board, the settlement should be made between owner and occupier, subject to the necessary investigation by the State as to title, rental and security.

III. That it is desirable in the interests of Ireland, that the present owners of land should not as a result of any settlement be expatriated, or having received payment for their land, should find no object for remaining in Ireland, and that, as the effect of a far-reaching settlement must necessarily be to cause the sale of tenancies throughout the whole of Ireland, inducements should, wherever practicable, be afforded to selling owners to continue to reside in that country.

IV. That for the purpose of obtaining such a result an equitable price ought to be paid to the owners, which should be based upon income.

Income as it appears to us is second-term rents, including all rents fixed subsequent to the passing of the Act of 1896, or their fair equivalent.

V. That the purchase price should be based upon income as indicated above, and should be either the assurance by the State of such income or the payment of a capital sum producing such income at 3 per cent., or at 3¼ per cent., if guaranteed by the State, or if the existing powers of trustees be sufficiently enlarged.

Costs of collection, where such exist, not exceeding 10 per cent., are not included for the purpose of these paragraphs in the word 'income'.

VI. That such income or capital sum should be obtainable by the owners —

(*a*.) Without the requirement of capital outlay upon their part, such as would be involved by charges for proving title to sell, six years' possession as proposed in the Bill brought forward in the Session of 1902 appears to us a satisfactory method of dealing with the matter;

(*b*.) Without the requirement of outlay to prove title to receive the purchase money;

(*c*.) Without unreasonable delay;

(*d*.) Without loss of income pending re-investment;

(*e*.) And without leaving portion of the capital sum as a guarantee deposit.

VII. That as a necessary inducement to selling owners to continue to reside in Ireland, the provision in the Bill introduced by the Chief Secretary for Ireland in the Session of 1902 with regard to the purchase of mansion houses, demesne lands, and home farms by the State, and resale by it to the owners, ought to be extended.

VIII. We suggest that in certain cases it would be to the advantage of the State as ensuring more adequate security, and also an advantage to owners in such cases if, upon the purchase by the State of the mansion house and demesne land, and re-sale to the owner, the house and demesne land should not be considered a security to the mortagees.

IX. That owners wishing to sell portions of grazing land in their own hands for the purpose of enlarging neighbouring tenancies should be entitled to make an agreement with the tenants, and that in the event of proposed purchase by the tenants such grazing land may be considered as part of the tenancies for the purpose of purchase.

X. That in addition to the income, or capital sum producing the income, the sum due for rent from the last rent day till the date of the agreement for purchase and the hanging gale should be paid by the State to the owner.

XI. That all liabilities by the owner which run with the land, such as head rents, quit rents, and tithe rent-charge, should be redeemed, and the capital sum paid for such redemption deducted from the purchase-money payable to the owner. Provided always that the price of redemption should be calculated on a basis not higher as regards annual value than is used in calculating the purchase price of the estate. In any special cases where it may have to be calculated upon a different basis the owner should not suffer thereby.

Owners liable to drainage charges should be entitled to redeem same upon equitable terms, having regard to the varying rates of interest at which such loans were made.

XII. That the amount of the purchase-money payable by the tenants should be extended over a series of years, and be at such a rate in respect of principal and interest as will at once secure a reduction of not less than 15 per cent., or more than 25 per cent. on second term rents or their fair equivalent, with further periodical reductions as under exisiting Land Purchase Acts, until such time as the Treasury is satisfied that the loan has been repaid. This may involve some assistance from the State beyond the use of its credit, which, under circumstances hereinafter mentioned, we consider may reasonably be granted. Facilities should be provided for the redemption at any time of the purchase-money, or part thereof, by payment of the capital, or any part thereof.

XIII. That the hanging gale, where such custom exists, should be included in the loan, and paid off in the instalments to be paid by the purchasing occupier, and should not be a debt immediately recoverable from the occupier, but the amount of rent ordinarily payable for the period between the date when the last payment fell due, and the date of agreement for sale should be payable as part of the first instalment.

XIV. That counties wholly or partly under the operations of the Congested Districts Board or other districts of a similar character (as defined by the Congested Districts Board Acts and by Section 4 Clause 1 of Mr. Wyndham's Land Purchase Amendment Bill of last Session) will require separate and exceptional treatment with a view to the better distribution of the population and of the land, as well as for the acceleration and extension of these projects for migration and enlargement of holdings which the Congested Districts Board, as at present constituted, and with its limited powers, has hitherto found it impossible to carry out upon an adequate scale.

XV. That any project for the solution of the Irish Land Question should be accompanied by a settlement of the evicted tenants question upon an equitable basis.

XVI. That sporting and riparian rights should remain as they are, subject to any provisions of existing Land Purchase Acts.

XVII. That the failure to enforce the Labourers Acts in certain portions of the country constitutes a serious grievance, and that in districts where, in the opinion of the Local Government Board, sufficient accommodation has not been made for the hosuing of the labouring classes, power should be given to the Local Government Board, in conjunction with the local authorities, to acquire sites for houses and allotments.

XVIII. That the principle of restriction upon sub-letting might be extended to such control as may be practicable over resales of purchasers' interest and mortgages, with a view to maintaining unimpaired the value of the State's security for outstanding instalments on loans. . .

We wish to place on record our belief that an unexampled opportunity is at the present moment afforded His Majesty's Government of effecting a reconciliation of classes in Ireland upon terms which, as we believe, involve no permanent increase of Imperial expenditure in Ireland; and that there would be found on all sides an earnest desire to co-operate with the Government in securing the success of a Land Purchase Bill which, by effectively and rapidly carrying out the principles above indicated, would bring peace and prosperity to the country.

Signed at the Mansion House, Dublin this 3rd day of January, 1903.

> DUNRAVEN, *Chairman.*
> MAYO.
> W.H. HUTCHESON POË.
> NUGENT T. EVERARD.
> JOHN REDMOND.
> WILLIAM O'BRIEN.
> T.W. RUSSELL.
> T.C. HARRINGTON.

53. Wyndham on Irish nationalism

Mackail and Wyndham, *George Wyndham*, II, 474-75

To his Father

35 Park Lane, W.,
November 21*st*, 1903.

I am not surprised at your inability to follow the 'exits and entrances' of Irish Leaders. I understand, but it is not easy to explain.

Briefly, there are two fundamental groups in Irish Nationalism: (1) The political descendants of the 'Young Irelander'. They, as a rule, wish to improve the economic and constitutional position of Ireland, in order some day to make what they hold to be better economic and constitutional terms with England. They hate the Union and hate 'British' ideals, but, as a rule, would like to gather up all the personal resources of Ireland, Moderate landlords, the Bar, the Towns, Commerce, etc. into a more harmonious and therefore stronger Ireland, hoping, immediately, to get more generous financial treatment and acquiescence to Irish modes of thought, *e.g.* Protection, State-aid to Industry etc., and ultimately, to get Home Rule, or a large measure of Local Self Government.

(2) The second group are, primarily, Agrarian Socialists and, secondarily, professional agitators who attack property and sow dissension in order to postpone any solution.

Historically, Parnell belonged to group (1) but, for a time, fused with it group (2) in his 'No Rent' agitation, in order to 'kick up a dust' and collect money in America.

Per contra, O'Brien belonged to group (2) but, seeing the misery and futility of Agrarian Agitation, joined Redmond in signing the Land Conference Peace.

They meant to go for Class Reconciliation.

But Dillon, who is a pure Agrarian sore-head; Davitt, who is a pure Revolutionary Socialist; Sexton, Editor of the 'Freeman', who has been left out of Parliamentary life; joined together to 'spike' conciliation. The high-water mark of Class Conciliation is represented by the 'Irish People' — O'Brien's paper — of November 7th.

Immediately after publishing that, with an article in it by Dunraven — praise of myself — the substitution of 'shamrocks' for crossed 'pikes and muskets' between paragraphs, he 'threw in the sponge', resigned and stopped the paper.

This, on the face of it, is bad. But it has frightened the moderates; and I am re-weaving my web.

The Roman Catholic Church wobbles from one side to the other.

Meanwhile the dynamic finance of the Land Act continues to operate and good sense will win, though not quite so soon as I might have hoped.

Redmond went to Limerick — the city — and was well supported.

His fear, and the fear also of the landlords, is that I may resign in disgust. It is all to the good that they should be frightened. But I have not the slightest intention of taking their antics to heart and hope that, in some ways, all the pother will do good.

Just for the moment the Irish Government is the only popular and powerful force in Irish life.

This shows how right I was to stick to Ireland. If I had gone elsewhere O'Brien would have resigned and saddled me with the blame for leaving him and Redmond alone exposed to the 'Freeman' and Davitt, Dillon & Co. . . .

54. Arthur Griffith's Hungarian thesis
United Irishman, 2 January 1904

THE RESURRECTION OF HUNGARY

. . . You may be old enough yourself to remember when Hungary fell and 'Freedom shrieked aloud' — when Kossuth was a fugitive, with the bloodhounds of Austria on his track, when the Austrian dragoon was the Law from Buda-Pesht to the Carpathians, when day after day Hungarian partiots were shot or hanged like dogs by the victorious soldiery of Francis Josef, when in fact 'Peace reigned in Warsaw', and men said — 'Hungary was'. Therefore, when you look around today and see Hungary freer and stronger and more prosperous than Austria, when you know that if Hungary declared herslf a republic tomorrow — which she intends to do when the sad old man who reigns in Vienna dies — Austria would not fight, because she could not — you may well rub your eyes, reflecting that Hungary never once sent a Parliamentary Party to Vienna to 'fight on the floor of the House' for Home Rule, never once admitted the right of Austria to rule over her, never once pretended to be 'loyal' to the Power that had smitten her, never once held monster indignation meetings and resolutioned, and fired strong adjectives — and yet, notwithstanding, forced Austria to her knees and wrung from her unwilling hands the free Constitution which has made Hungary the Power she is to-day. . . .

55. Formation of the Ulster Unionist Council

Resolution adopted at a Belfast meeting on 2 December 1904. Public Record Office of Northern Ireland, D 1327/7/6A

That an Ulster Council be formed, and that its objects shall be to form an Ulster Union for bringing into line all Local Unionist Associations in the Province of Ulster, with a view to consistent and continuous political action; to act as a further connecting link between Ulster Unionists and their Parliamentary representatives; to settle in consultation with them the Parliamentary Policy, and to be the medium of expressing Ulster Unionist opinion, as current events may from time to time require, and generally to advance and defend the interests of Ulster Unionism in the Unionist Party.

56. The Independent Orange Order

Belfast News Letter, 14 July 1905

A manifesto, signed by Brs. R. Lindsay Crawford, Imperial Grand Master; Rev. D.D. Boyle (Grand Chaplain, Ballymoney), T.H. Sloan, M.P., C.G.C.; and Richard Braithwaite, C.G.S., was issued at the meeting yesterday at Magheramorne on behalf of the Independent Orange Order. . . .

TO ALL IRISHMEN WHOSE COUNTRY
STANDS FIRST IN THEIR AFFECTIONS.

FROM

'The Independent Orangemen of Ireland'.

The following are the concluding and most important paragraphs: —

REDISTRIBUTION OF SEATS

As Irishmen, we protest against any reduction in the total number of seats allotted to Ireland. The Act of Union guarantees our country its present representation, and we cannot conceive any Protestant supporting the reduction of Ireland's forces in the British House of Commons, and the transfer of twenty-one seats to the sacerdotalists of England. Justice, however, demands representation to the loyal minority more fairly proportionate to its numbers and wealth.

A PLEA FOR NATIONALITY

Castle Government stands self-condemned. All parties are agreed as to the necessity for sweeping reforms in the government and administration of Ireland. Bureaucratic government, it is everywhere recognised, must be superseded by the rule of the people. It only remains to determine on what lines reform is to proceed, and what part Irishmen are to play in bringing it about. *On the willingness and ability of Irishmen to co-operate in carrying out reasonable reforms in their own country will rest their claim to a more extended form of self-government.* We do not hide from ourselves the dangers that have to be faced in the further extension of the elective principle in the government of Ireland, but the principle having been already conceded by the Unionists, under the Local Government Act, cannot now be seriously disputed, and must proceed to its logical conclusion. Government by the people for the people is a democratic principle, limited only in its application by the ability of the people to govern. *The weakness of the Devolution proposals lay in their reactionary tendencies — in their attempt to set aside the elective principle, and to substitute for non-representative departments an unrepresentative council.* Unionism is likewise a discredited creed. The effect of the Unionist policy in Ireland has been to weaken the secular forces of the country and to increase the power and influence of clericalism in every department of secular life. The combined intelligence of the Ulster party has not even succeeded in evolving a constructive policy capable of effecting the drainage of the Bann. If we review the recent Castle revelations it will be found that the deal was between the present Government and the Roman Catholic hierarchy, and that in return for a sectarian college the full national demand was to be watered down to a scheme of Devolution, in which the elective principle was to be neutralised by co- option. National ideals were once more to be sacrificed on the altar of sectariansim, and Home Rulers and Unionists alike duped by their leaders. It was not the representatives of the people that the Government consulted, but the hierarchy. It was not Mr. Redmond, the leader of the Nationalist party, whom Mr. Wyndham approached as to the proposed settlement of the university education — the question which, we are assured, more nearly concerns the laity — but representatives of the Roman Catholic hierarchy. On the other hand, the Irish Unionist representatives, including members of the Government, were kept completely in the dark regarding the policy of the Government in Ireland. Surely the facts suggest to the Nationalists and Unionists alike the unwisdom of perpetuating a suicidal strife, in which both parties are ever sacrificed to the demands of clericalism and to the exigencies of English parties. We do not trust either of the English parties on any of the questions that divide Ireland, and we are satisfied that both Liberals and Tories will continue in the future, as they have done in the past, to play off Irish Protestants and Nationalists against each other, to the prejudice of our country. This being so, we consider it is high time that Irish Protestants should consider their position as Irish citizens and their attitude towards their Roman Catholic countrymen, and that the latter should choose once for all between nationality and sectarianism. *In an Ireland in which Protestant and Roman Catholic stand sullen and discontented it is not too much to hope that they will reconsider their positions, and, in their common trials, unite on a true basis of nationality.* The higher claims of our distracted country have been too long neglected in the strife of party and of creed. The man who cannot rise above the trammels of party and of sect on a national issue is a foe to nationality and to human freedom. There is room in Ireland for a patriotic party, with a sound constructive policy such as we have outlined — a party that will devote itself to the task of freeing the country from the domination of impracticable creeds and organised tyrannies, and to securing the urgent and legitimate redress of her many grievances. We foresee a time in Irish history when thoughtful men on both sides will come to realise that the Irish question is not made up of Union and repeal; that not in Acts of Parliament nor in their repeal lies the hope and salvation of our country, so much as in the mutual inclination of Irish hearts and minds along the common plane of nationality — a nationality that binds the people together in the school, in the workshop, and in the senate in the promotion of what has been too long neglected — the material interests of our native land, and the increased wealth and happiness of her people.

57. The Sinn Féin position
Resolutions passed at a public meeting following the first annual party ard fheis, 28 November 1905 reported in the *United Irishman,* 9 December 1905

That the people of Ireland are a free people, and that no law made without their authority or consent is or can ever be binding on their conscience. That the General Council of County Councils presents the nucleus of a National authority, and we urge upon it to extend the scope of its deliberation and action; to take within its purview every question of National interest and to formulate lines of procedure for the nation.

That National self-development through the recognition of the duties and rights of citizenship on the part of the individual, and by the aid and support of all movements originating from within Ireland, instinct with National tradition, and not looking outside Ireland for the accomplishment of their aims, is vital to Ireland.

58. Arthur Griffith's speech to 1905 Sinn Féin ard fheis
United Irishman, 9 December 1905

The Anglicisation of the Irish mind is best exhibited in its attitude towards economics. . . . I am in economics largely a follower of the man who thwarted England's dream of the commercial conquest of the world, and who made the mighty confederation before which England has fallen commercially and is falling politically — Germany. His name is a famous one in the outside world, his works are the text books of economic science in other countries — in Ireland his name is unknown and his works unheard of — I refer to Frederick List, the real founder of the German Zollverein. . . .

Brushing aside the fallacies of Adam Smith and his tribe, List points out that between the individual and humanity stands, and must continue to stand, a great fact — the Nation. The Nation, with its special language and literature, with its peculiar origin and history, with its special manners and customs, laws and institutions, with the claims of all these for existence, independence, perfection, and continuance for the future, with its separate territory, a society which, united by a thousand ties of minds and interests combines itself into one independent whole, which recognises the law of right for and within itself, and in its united character is still opposed to other societies of a similar kind in their national liberty, and consequently can, only under the existing conditions of the world, maintain self-existence and independence by its own power and resources. As the individual chiefly obtains by means of the nation and in the nation, mental culture, power of production, security and prosperity, so is the civilisation of the human race only conceivable and possible by means of the civilisation and development of individual nations. But as there are amongst men infinite differences in condition and circumstances, so there are in nations — some are strong, some are weak, some are highly civilised, some are half civilised, but in all exists as in the unit the impulse of self-preservation and the desire for improvement. It is the task of national politics to ensure existence and continuance to the nation to make the weak strong, the half civilised more civilised. It is the task of national economics to accomplish the economical development of the nation and fit it for admission into the universal society of the future. . . .

We in Ireland have been taught by our British lords lieutenant, our British Educational Boards, and our Barrington Lecturers, that our destiny is to be the fruitful mother of flocks and herds — that it is not necessary for us to pay attention to our manufacturing arm, since our agricultural arm is all sufficient. The fallacy is apparent to the man who thinks — but it is a fallacy which has passed for truth in Ireland. With List I reply: a nation cannot promote and further its civilisation, its prosperity, and its social progress equally as well by exchanging agricultural products for manufactured goods as by establishing a manufacturing power of its own. A merely agricultural nation can never develop to any extent a home or foreign commerce, with inland means of transport, and its foreign navigation, increase its population in due proportion to their well-being or make notable progress in its moral, intellectual, social and political development: it will never acquire important political power or be placed in a position to influence less advanced nations and to form colonies of its own. A mere agricultural state is infinitely less powerful than an agricultural- manufacturing state. The former is always economically and politically dependent on those foreign nations who take from it agriculture in exchange for manufactured goods. . . . An agricultural nation is a man with one arm who makes use of an arm belonging to another person, but cannot, of course, be sure of having it always available. An agricultural-manufacturing nation is a man who has both arms of his own at his own disposal. . . . We must offer our producers protection where protection is necessary; and let it be clearly understood what Protection is. Protection does not mean the exclusion of foreign competition — it means the enabling of the native manufacturer to meet foreign competition on an equal footing. It does not mean that we shall pay a higher profit to any Irish manufacturer but that we shall not stand by and see him crushed by mere weight of foreign capital. If an Irish manufacturer cannot produce an article as cheaply as an English or other foreigner, solely because his foreign competitor has had larger resources at his disposal, then it is the first duty of the Irish nation to accord protection to the Irish manufacturer. If, on the other hand, an Irish manufacturer can produce as cheaply, but charges an enhanced price, such a man deserves no support — he is in plain words a swindler. It is the duty of our public bodies in whose hands the expenditure of £4,000,000 annually is placed to pay where necessary an enhanced price for Irish manufactured articles, when the manufacturers show them they cannot produce them at the lesser price — this is Protection. . . . With the development of her manufacturing arm will proceed the rise of a national middle-class in Ireland and a trained national democracy — and — I here again quote List against the charlatans who profess to see in a nation's language and tradition things of no economic value — 'in every nation will the authority of national language and national literature, the civilising arts and the perfection of municipal institutions keep pace with the development of the manufacturing arm'. How are we to accord Protection to and procure the development of our manufacturing arm? First, by ourselves individually; secondly, through our County, Urban, and District Councils, and Poor Law Guardians; thirdly, by taking over control of those inefficient bodies known as Harbour Commissioners; fourthly, by stimulating our manufacturers and our people to industrial enterprise; and fifthly, by inviting to aid in our development, on commercial lines, Irish-American capital. In the first case, every individual knows his duty, whether he practises it or not — it is, unless where fraud is attempted, to pay if necessary an enhanced price for Irish goods, and to use whenever possible none but Irish goods. As to our public elective bodies which annually control the expenditure of our local taxation, their duty is the same. The duty of our harbour bodies is to arrange the incidence of port dues so that they shall fall most heavily on manufactured goods coming into the country, and to keep and publish a table of all goods imported and to whom consigned. . . .

We propose the formation of a Council of Three Hundred, composed of members of the General Council of County Councils and representatives of the Urban Councils, Rural Councils, Poor Law Boards, and Harbour Boards of the country to sit in Dublin and form a *de facto* Irish Parliament. Associated and sitting and voting with this body, which might assemble in Dublin in the spring and in the autumn, could be the persons elected for Irish constituencies, who decline to confer on the affairs of Ireland with foreigners in a foreign city. On its assembly in Dublin this National Assembly should appoint committees to especially consider and report to the general assembly on all subjects appertaining to the country. On the reports of these committees the Council should deliberate and formulate workable schemes, which, once formulated, it would be the duty of all County and Urban Councils, Rural Councils, Poor Law Boards, and other bodies to give legal effect to so far as their powers permit, and where their legal powers fall short, to give it the moral force of law by inducing and instructing those whom they represent to honour and obey the recommendations of the Council of Three Hundred individually and collectively. . . .

59. A northern republican voice
The Republic, Belfast, 20 December 1906

DUNGANNON CLUB, BELFAST

On Friday last, a well-attended Debate was held at the Dungannon Club, 114 Royal Avenue, Belfast, The point of issue being: 'Should the Sinn Féin men base their demands on the Constitution of 1782?' A large majority based their demands on the right of Irishmen to govern Ireland without any interference whatsoever.

A lecture will be delivered by Seamus Murphy on 'Republican Government and its application to Ireland'. All Irishmen will be welcome.

60. Labour conflict in Belfast
Irish News, Belfast, 12 July 1907

At a meeting of carters held last evening in the Exhibition Hall Mr. Larkin created a sensation by announcing the terms of the circular from the coal employers. . . . The following is a copy of the circular referred to, and read out by Mr. Larkin in his speech: —

TO THE EMPLOYEES IN THE BELFAST COAL TRADE

We have unanimously decided:

1. That no person representing any union or combination will, after this date, be recognised by any of us.

2. That we will exercise our right to employ and dismiss whom we choose, and on whatever terms we choose, and that all persons while employed by us shall work together harmoniously.

3. That, in the event of a strike, whether general or confined to one or more firms, taking place, due to dissatisfaction with the terms or conditions of employment prevailing in the trade without at least three days written notice having been given by the men to the employers, specifying the grievance complained of, we will immediately lock out all our men.

To enable the men to carefully consider these conditions, work will not be resumed until Monday, the 15th inst., at 10 o'clock a.m. and then only if there shall have been previously shown a general unanimity amongst the men to accept our terms.

61. C.J. Dolan's election address, 1908 by-election
Sinn Féin, 22 February 1908

TO THE ELECTORS OF NORTH LEITRIM

Fellow-Countrymen,

Two years ago you sent me to be your representative in the British House of Commons. You sent me to voice your demand for Self-Government, and you also gave me a mandate to strive for whatever remedial measures lay within our reach, and I went to the House of Commons determined to serve your interests and the interests of our country to the best of my ability. But I was not long there before I realised the truth of Michael Davitt's statement — that no Irish grievance, however genuine would ever be remedied in that Assembly unless the Government had to choose between reform and martial law in Ireland. . . . The day of Parnell, Davitt, and the Land League is over, and the voice of Ireland is drowned amidst contending English factions.

Although I felt that the Irish members were wasting their time in the British House of Commons, I waited to see what the Liberals would do to redeem their pledges regarding Home Rule. These pledges had raised high hopes in the breasts of Irishmen and many looked forward with confidence to the Council Bill. . . . The publication of the Bill destroyed whatever lingering belief I had in the sincerity of the Liberals. Henceforth I felt that if I continued to attend Westminster I would be deceiving my constituents and betraying the cause of Irish Nationalism.

I have come home to tell you the truth, and to abide by the consequences; I have come home to tell you that the Irish Members are helpless in the House of Commons, where they are outnumbered six to one, and their speeches unheeded; that the proper place for the representatives of Ireland to meet is Dublin, not London; that the true field of action is Ireland, not England; that it is only by our efforts that Ireland can be raised to a position of prosperity and started on the path of national development; and that in appealing to Englishmen we are wasting our energies and demoralising our people. . . .

I stand for Ireland, Free, Self-reliant, and Prosperous. . . . Sinn Féin means the end of empty talk and humbug, and the beginning of genuine National work; it means more wealth, more employment, and better wages for the people; it heralds the dawn of a new era rich with promise for our long suffering country, and as a believer in the policy of Sinn Féin, a believer in a self-reliant, self-supporting Ireland, I confidently solicit your support.

C.J.Dolan

62. Formation of the Irish Transport and General Workers Union

Preface, *Rules of the Irish Transport and General Workers Union*, dated 1 January 1909 (Dublin, 1911), 3-4

Trades Unionism in Ireland has arrived at a certain stage of growth when this question confronts us — What is to be our next step in fostering its future development? Are we going to continue the policy of grafting ourselves on the English Trades Union movement, losing our own identity as a nation, in the great world of organised labour? We say, emphatically no. Ireland has politically reached her manhood. Industrially she is in swaddling clothes, and it is our purpose, come weal or woe, to cherish the infant with the milk of economic truth, clothe her in the school of experience, educate her in the solidarity of the workers of Ireland, with their fellows, the world over; in the hope that in the near future she may become sensible of her dignity, powerful enough to voice her own demands. The workers of Ireland must realise that society is changing rapidly, the capitalist class in Ireland is being reinforced by the influx of foreign capitalists, with their soulless, sordid, money-grubbing propensities. It behoves the Irish workers to realise the power of the employing class, who are not only well organised industrially but practically monopolise the political power in this country as they do in all other countries at present. The old system of sectional union amongst unskilled workers is practically useless for modern conditions (this also applies to the skilled workers). Less that 50,000 unskilled workers are organised in Ireland, and when you consider that there is at least 800,000 so-called unskilled workers unorganised, surely it must be recognised that the necessity for such an organisation as this we invite to enrol in is self-evident. The Irish Transport and General Workers Union offer to you a medium whereby you may combine with your fellows to adjust wages, regulate hours and conditions of labour, wherever and whenever possible and desirable by negotiation, arbitration, and if the conditions demand it, by withholding our labour until amelioration is granted. Further, we demand political recognition for the enforcement of our demands. Our immediate programme being legal eight hours' day, provision of work for all unemployed, and pensions for all workers at 60 years of age. Compulsory Arbitration Courts, adult suffrage, nationalisation of canals, railways and all means of transport. The land of Ireland for the people of Ireland. Our ultimate ideal, the realisation of an Industrial Commonwealth.

By the advocacy of such principles and carrying out of such a policy, we believe we shall be ultimately enabled to obliterate poverty, and help to realise the glorious time spoken of and sung by the Thinkers, Prophets, and the Poets, when all children, all women, and all men shall work and rejoice in the deeds of their hand, and thereby become entitled to the fulness of the earth and the abundance thereof.

63. Maynooth and the Irish language
Sinn Féin, 26 June 1909

The Rev. Dr. O'Hickey, D.D., Professor of Irish in Maynooth, has been dismissed by the Trustees of that Establishment for publishing a series of letters and articles in favour of the inclusion of Irish as an essential subject in the curriculum of the National University in Dublin. The Trustees of Maynooth are Catholic Bishops — some of the same Catholic bishops who publicly declared some time ago that the question of Irish or no Irish in the University was one for fair discussion. Let their words and their actions be considered and contrasted by the Catholics of Ireland and judgement formed upon them. Any further comment is needless. The naked fact that a professor of Maynnoth has been dismissed from his office for advocating the Irish language as an essential for Irish education is all the people of Ireland and the Irish people abroad need to know. . . .

64. The National University and Irish
Sinn Féin, 2 July 1910

Two-thirds of the members of the Senate of the National University were opposed to the recognition of the language of the country as its national language, but a substantial majority of the Senate has voted to make the Irish language an essential subject for entrance from the year 1913. . . . The Senate of the University has declared for essential Irish not because it is anxious to have essential Irish but because it cannot get the rate-in-aid levied by the County Councils without essential Irish. . . .

In August 1908 when the matter first arose and when the bulk of the Senators and the Senators' friends were engaged in contemptuously treating the demand for essential Irish, we searched for the weak point in the West-British armour and found it in a study of the Act. The English Government in drafting the Bill had not prohibited the making of Irish an essential subject. . . . Once again England could blandly say to the complaining Irish: 'Well I did not prevent you having Irish in your University. I gave you Home Rule in your University — it is you yourselves who have decided that the Irish language is of no importance['']. The refusal of a Home-Ruled Irish University, largely supported out of the rates, to regard Irish as essential would have done more to throw back the Irish language movement than if the Liberal Government had continued its repressive policy of prosecuting men for using the Irish form of their names. Mr. Birrell was clever enough to see this and believed that no one in Ireland would understand his game. In this *he* was mistaken. The Bill was drafted to throw the burden of support on the County Councils. . . . On August 13th, 1908 we first pointed out to the County Councils how they could utilise their powers under the Act in the contrary direction to that which the schemers who drafted it had contemplated. We had faith in the County Councils and we made the County Councils the fulcrums of the fight. The County Councils have won. The Castle, the Catholic hierarchy, the leaders of the Parliamentary Party, the so-called National Daily Press of Ireland, and the social influences of West-Britain were arrayed against them, and they have won. . . .

65. The Irish demand as seen by John Redmond
J.E. Redmond, *What Ireland wants* (Dublin, 1910), 14-15

. . . Here, then is 'what Ireland wants': 'Legislative and executive control of all purely Irish affairs, subject to the supreme authority of the Imperial Parliament'.

In other words, we want an Irish Parliament, with an Executive responsible to it, created by act of the Imperial Parliament, and charged with the management of purely Irish affairs (land, education, local government, transit, labour, industries, taxation for local purposes, law and justice, police, etc.), leaving to the Imperial Parliament, in which Ireland would probably continue to be represented, but in smaller numbers, the management, just as at present, of all Imperial affairs — army, navy, foreign relations, customs, Imperial taxation, matters pertaining to the Crown, the colonies, and all those other questions which are Imperial and not local in their nature, the Imperial Parliament also retaining an overriding supreme authority over the new Irish legislature, such as it possesses to-day over the various legislatures in Canada, Australia, South Africa, and other portions of the Empire.

This is 'what Ireland wants'. When she has obtained it, a new era of prosperity and contentment will arise. As happened when Lord Durham's policy was carried out in Canada, men of different races and creeds will join hands to promote the well-being of their common country. Responsibility, thrown for the first time for over a century upon the people, will have the same effect in Ireland as elsewhere. Trust in the people will effect as startling and dramatic a transformation of feeling and sentiment in Ireland as in South Africa. Those of us who have been struggling in this cause for thirty years are thankful to feel that at last the fighting is practically over, and that all that remains is to settle the exact terms on which the Treaty of Peace is to be drawn up.

66. Terence MacSwiney on the principles of freedom
Irish Freedom, June 1911

Brothers and Enemies

i

Our enemies are brothers from who we are estranged. Here is the fundamental truth that explains and justifies our hope of re-establishing a real patriotism among all parties in Ireland, and a final peace with our ancient enemy of England. It is the view of prejudice that makes of the various sections of our people hopelessly hostile divisions, and raises up a barrier of hate between Ireland and England that can never be surmounted. If Ireland is to be regenerated, we must have internal unity; if the world is to be regenerated, we must have world-wide unity — not of government, but of brotherhood. To this great end every individual, every nation has a duty; and that the end may not be missed we must continually turn for the correction of our philosophy to reflecting on the common origin of the human race, on the beauty of the world that is the heritage of all, our common hopes and fears, and in the greatest sense the mutual interests of the peoples of the earth. If, unheeding this, any people make their part of the earth ugly with acts of tyranny and baseness, they threaten the security of all; if inconscious of it, a people always high-spirited are plunged into war with a neighbour, now a foe, and yet fight, as their nature compels them, bravely and magnanimously, they but drive their enemy back to the field of a purer life, and, perhaps, to the realisation of a more beautiful existence, a dream to which his stagnant soul steeped in ugliness could never rise.

ii

On the road to freedom every alliance will be sternly tried. Internal friendship will not be made in a day, nor external friendship for many a day, and there will be how many temptations to hold it all a delusion and scatter the few still standing loyally to the flag. We must understand, then, the bond that holds us together on the line of march, and in the teeth of every opposition. Nothing but a genuine bond of brotherhood can so unite men, but we hardly seem to realise its truth. When a deep and ardent patriotism requires men of different creeds to come together frankly and in a spirit of comradeship, and when the most earnest of all creeds do so, others who are colder and less earnest regard this union as a somewhat suspicious alliance; and if they join in, do so reluctantly. Others come not at all; these think our friends labour in a delusion, that it needs but an occasion to start an old fear and drive them apart, to attack one another with ancient bitterness fired with fresh venom. We must combat that idea. Let us consider the attitude to one another of three units of the band, who represent the best of the company and should be typical of the whole; one who is Catholic, one who is Protestant, and one who may happen to be neither. The complete philosophy of any one of the three may not be accepted by the other two; the horizon of his hopes may be more or less distant, but that complete philosophy stretches beyond the limit of the sphere, within which they are drawn together to mutual understanding and comradeship moved by a common hope, a brave purpose and a beautiful dream. The significance of their work may be deeper for one than for another, the origin of the dream and its ultimate aim may be points not held in common; but the beautiful tangible thing that they all now fight for, the purer public and private life, the more honourable dealings between men, the higher ideals for the community and the nation, the grander forbearance, courage, and freedom, in all these they are at one. The instinctive recognition of an attack on the ideal is alive and vigilant in all three. The sympathy that binds them is ardent, deep and enduring. Observe them come together. Note the warm hand grasp, the drawn face of one, a hard-worker; of another, the eye anxious for a brother hard pressed; of the third, the eye glistening for the ideal triumphant; of all, the intimate confidence, the mutual encouragement and self-sacrifice, never a note of despair, but always the exultation of the Great Fight, and the promise of a great victory. This is a finer company than a mere casual alliance; yet it makes the uninspired pause, wondering and questioning. These men are earnest men of different creeds; still they are as intimately bound to one another as if they knelt at the one altar. In the narrow view the creeds should be at one another's throats; here they are marching shoulder to shoulder. How is this? And the one whose creed is the most exacting could, perhaps, give the best reply. He would reply that within the sphere in which they work together the true thing that unites them can be done only the one right way; that instinctively seizing this right way they come together; that this is the line of advance to wider and deeper things that

130

are his inspiration and his life; that if a comrade is roused to action by the nearer task, and labours bravely and rightly for it, he is on the road to widening vistas in his dream that now he may not see. That is what he would say whose vision of life is the widest. All objectors he may not satisfy. That what is life to him may leave his comrade cold is a difficulty; but against the difficulty stand the depth and reality of their comradeship, proven by mutual sacrifice, endurance and faith, and he never doubts that their bond union will sometime prove to have a wise and beautiful meaning in the Annals of God.

iii

But the men of different creeds who stand firmly and loyally together are a minority. We are faced with the great difficulty of uniting as a whole North and South; and we are faced with the grim fact that many whom we desire to unite are angrily repudiating a like desire, that many are sarcastically noting this, that many are coldly refusing to believe; while through it all the most bitter are emphasising enmity and glorifying it. All these unbelievers keep insisting North and South are natural enemies and must so remain. The situation is further embittered by acts of enmity being practised by both sides to the extreme provocation of the faithful few. Their forbearance will be sorely tried, and this is the final test of men. By those who cling to prejudice and abandon self-restraint, extol enmity, and always proceed to the further step — the plea to wipe the enemy out: the counter plea for forbearance is always scorned as the enervating gospel of weakness and despair. Though we like to call ourselves Christian, we have no desire for — nay even make a jest of — that outstanding Christian virtue; yet men not held by Christian dogma have joyously surrendered to the sublimity of that divine idea. Hear Shelley speak: 'What nation has the example of the desolation of Attica by Mardonius and Xerxes, or the extinction of the Persian Empire by Alexander of Macedon restrained from outrage? Was not the pretext for this latter system of spoliation derived immediately from the former? Had revenge in this instance any other effect than to increase, instead of diminishing, the mass of malice and evil already existing in the world? The emptiness and folly of retaliation are apparent from every example which can be brought forward.' Shelley writes much further on retaliation, which he denounces as 'futile superstition'. Simple violence repels every high and generous thinker. Hear one other, Mazzini: 'What we have to do is not to establish a new order of things by violence. An order of things so established is always tyrannical even when it is better than the old.' Let us bear this in mind when there is an act of aggression on either side of the Boyne. There will not be wanting on the other side a cry for retaliation and 'a lesson'. We shall receive every provocation to give up and acknowledge ancient bitterness, but then is the time to stand firm, then we shall need to practise the divine forbearance that is the secret of strength.

iv

But with only a minority standing to the flag we cry out for some hope of final success. Men will not fight without result for ever; they ask for some sign of progress, some gleam of the light of victory. Happily, searching the skies, our eyes can have their reward. We shall, no doubt, see outstanding, dark evidence of old animosity; we shall hear fierce war-cries and see raging crowds, but the crowds are less numerous and the wrath has lost its sting. Men who raged twenty years ago rage now, but their fury is less real; and young men growing up around them, quite indifferent to the ideal, are also indifferent to the counter cries: they are passive, unimpressed by either side. Rightly approached, they may understand and feel the glow of a fine enthusiasm; they are numbed by prejudice, they will become warm, active and daring under an inspiring appeal. Remember, and have done with despair. Think how you and I found our path step by step of the way: political life was full of conventions that suited our fathers' time, but have faded in the light of our day. We found these conventions unreal and put them by. This was no reflection on our fathers; what they fought for truly is our heritage, and we pay them a tribute in offering it in turn our loyalty inspired by their devotion. But their errors we must rectify; what they left undone we must take up and fulfil. That is the task of every generation, to take up the uncompleted work of the former one, and hand on to their successors an achievement and a heritage. Youth recognises this instinctively, and every generation will take a step in advance of its predecessor, putting by its prejudices and developing its truth. Every individual may know this from his own experience, and from it he knows that those who are now voicing old bitter cries are aging, and will soon pass and leave no successors. Not that prejudice will die for ever. Each new day will have its own, but that which is now dividing and hampering us will pass. Let the memory of its bitterness be an incentive to checking new animosities and keeping the future safe; but in the present let us grasp and keep in our mind that the barrier that sundered our nation must crumble, if only we have faith and persist, undeterred by old bitter cries, for they are dying cries, undepressed by millions apathetic, for it is the great recurring sign of the ideal, that one hour its light will flash through quivering multitudes, and millions will have vision and rouse to regenerate the land.

67. Southern unionists on home rule

Declaration adopted by a meeting in Dublin, 10 October 1911, reported in *The Times*, 11 October 1911

We, Irishmen belonging to the three southern provinces, being of all creeds and classes, representing many separate interests, and sharing a common desire for the honour and welfare of our country, hereby declare our unalterable determination to uphold the legislative union between Great Britain and Ireland.

We protest against the creation of a separate parliament for Ireland whether independent or subordinate. We protest against the creation of an Executive dependent for its existence upon the pleasure of such a Parliament. We do so upon the following grounds: — Because any measure for the creation of a separate Irish Parliament and a separate Irish Executive would produce most dangerous social confusion, involving a disastrous conflict of interests and classes, and a serious risk of civil war;

Because such a measure would endanger the commercial relations between Ireland and Great Britain and would cause in Ireland widespread financial distrust, followed by a complete paralysis of enterprise;

Because such a measure would imperil personal liberty, freedom of opinion, and the spirit of tolerance in Ireland;

Because such a measure, instead of effecting a settlement, would inevitably pave the way for further efforts towards the complete separation of Ireland and Great Britain;

Because no statutory limitations restricting the authority of an Irish Legislative Assembly or the power of an Irish Executive could protect the freedom and the rights of minorities in this country;

Because such a measure would hand over Ireland to the government of a party which, notwithstanding professions the political purpose of which is obvious, had proved itself during the long course of action unworthy of the exercise of power by its repeated defiance of the law and disregard of the elementary principles of honesty and justice;

Because the great measures enacted in recent years by the Imperial Parliament have resulted in such industrial, agricultural, social and educational progress that our country has been steadily advancing in prosperity, and we view with the greatest alarm an experiment which must in large measure destroy the good work already done and hinder the progress now in operation.

Finally, regarding the question from a wider point of view than that which concerns alone the internal government of Ireland, highly prizing as we do the advantages we derive from our present imperial position, and being justly proud of the place we Irishmen have long held amongst those to whom the Empire owes its prosperity and fame, having been always faithful in our allegiance to our Sovereigns and upholders of the Constitution, we protest against any change that will deprive us of our birthright, by which we stand on equal ground with our fellow-countrymen of Great Britain as subjects of our King and citizens of the British Empire.

68. Two poems of 1912

1.

Mise Éire

Mise Éire
Sine mé ioná an Chailleach Béarra.
Mór mo ghlóir:
Mé do rug Cú Chulainn cródha.
Mór mo náir:
Mo chlann féin do dhíol a máthair.
Mór mo phian:
Bith-náimhde dom' shíor-chiapadh.
Mór mo bhrón:
D'éag an dream 'nar chuireas dóchas.
Mise Éire:
Uaignighe mé ioná an Chailleach Béarra.

Pádraic Mac Piarais

An Barr Buadh, 30 Márta 1912

2.

Ulster, 1912

The dark eleventh hour
Draws on and sees us sold
To every evil power
We fought against of old.
Rebellion, rapine, hate,
Oppression, wrong and greed
Are loosed to rule our fate,
By England's act and deed.

The faith in which we stand
The laws we made and guard,
Our honour, lives and land
Are given for reward
To murder done at night,
To treason taught by day,
To folly, sloth, and spite,
And we are thrust away.

The blood our fathers spilt
Our love, our toils, our pains,
Are counted us for guilt,
And only bind our chains.
Before an Empire's eyes,
The traitor claims his price.
What need of further lies?
We are the sacrifice.

We know the war prepared
On every peaceful home,
We know the hells declared
For such as serve not Rome —
The terror, threats, and dread
In market, hearth, and field —
We know, when all is said,
We perish if we yield.

Believe, we dare not boast,
Believe, we do not fear —
We stand to pay the cost
In all that men hold dear.
What answer from the North?
One Law, one Land, one Throne.
If England drives us forth
We shall not fall alone.

Rudyard Kipling

Morning Post, 9 April 1912

69. Ulster covenant opposing home rule,
From a copy in National Museum of Ireland

ULSTER'S
SOLEMN LEAGUE AND COVENANT

Being convinced in our consciences that Home Rule would be disastrous to the material well-being of Ulster as well as to the whole of Ireland, subversive of our civil and religious freedom, destructive of our citizenship and perilous to the unity of the Empire, we, whose names are under written, men of Ulster, loyal subjects of His Gracious Majesty King George V, humbly relying on the God whom our fathers in days of stress and trial confidently trusted, do hereby pledge ourselves in solemn Covenant throughout this our time of threatened calamity to stand by one another in defending for ourselves and our children our cherished position of equal citizenship in the United Kingdom and in using all means which may be found necessary to defeat the present conspiracy to set up a Home Rule Parliament in Ireland. And in the event of such a Parliament being forced upon us we further solemnly and mutually pledge ourselves to refuse to recognize its authority. In sure confidence that God will defend the right we hereto subscribe our names. And further, we individually declare that we have not already signed this Covenant.

The above was signed by me at _____
'Ulster Day', Saturday, 28th September, 1912
God Save the King.

70. Concluding section of MacSwiney's 'Principles of Freedom'
Irish Freedom, December 1912

The Bearna Baoghail — Conclusion

i

But when principles have been proved and objections answered, there are still some last words to say for some who stand apart — the men who held the breach. For, they do stand apart, not in error but in constancy: not in doubt of the truth but its incarnation; not average men of the multitude for whom human laws are made, who must have moral certainty of success, who must have the immediate allegiance of the people. For it is the distinguishing glory of our prophets and our soldiers of the forlorn hope, that the defeats of common men were for them but incentives to further battle; and when they held out against the prejudices of their time, they were not standing in some new conceit, but most often by prophetic insight fighting for a forgotten truth of yesterday, catching in their souls to light them forward, the hidden glory of tomorrow. They knew to be theirs by anticipation the general allegiance without which lesser men cannot proceed. They knew they stood for the Truth, against which nothing can prevail, and if they had to endure struggle, suffering and pain, they had the finer knowledge born of these things, a knowledge to which the best of men ever win — that if it is a good thing to live, it is a good thing also to die. Not that they despised life or lightly threw it away; for none better than they knew its grandeur, none more than they gloried in its beauty, none were so happily full as they of its music; but they knew, too, the value of this deep truth, with the final loss of which Earth must perish: the man who is afraid to die is not fit to live. And the knowledge for them stamped out Earth's oldest fear, winning for life its highest ecstasy. Yes, and when one or more of them had to stand in the darkest generation and endure all penalties to the extreme penalty, they knew for all that, they had had the best of life and did not count it a terrible thing if called by a little to anticipate death. They had still the finest appreciation of the finer attributes of comradeship and love; but it is part of the mystery of their happiness and success, that they were ready to go on to the end, not looking for the suffrage of the living nor the monuments of the dead. Yes, and when finally the re-awakened people by their better instincts, their discipline, patriotism and fervour, will have massed into armies, and marched to freedom, they will know in the greatest hour of triumph that the success of their conquering arms was made possible by those who held the breach.

ii

When, happily, we can fall back on the eloquence of the world's greatest orator, we turn with gratitude to the greatest tribute ever spoken to the memory of those men to whom the world owes most. Demosthenes, in the finest height of his finest oration, vindicates the men of every age and nation who fight the forlorn hope. He was arraigned by his rival, Aeschines, for having counselled the Athenians to pursue a course that ended in defeat, and he replies thus: 'If, then, the results had been foreknown to all — not even then should the Commonwealth have abandoned her design, if she had any regard for glory, or ancestry, or futurity. As it is, she appears to have failed in her enterprise, a thing to which all mankind are liable, if the Deity so wills it.' And he asks the Athenians: 'Why, had we resigned without a struggle that which our ancesters encountered every danger to win, who would not have spit upon you?' And he asks them further to consider strangers, visiting their City, sunk in such degradation, 'especially when in former times our country had never preferred an ignominious security to the battle for honour'. And he rises from the thought to this proud boast: 'None could at any period of time persuade the Commonwealth to attach herself in secure subjection to the powerful and unjust; through every age has she persevered in a perilous struggle for precedency and honour and glory.' And he tells them, appealing to the memory of Themistocles, how they honoured most their ancestors who acted in such a spirit: 'Yes, the Athenians of that day looked not for an orator or a general, who might help them to a pleasant servitude: they scorned to live if it could not be with freedom.' And he pays them, his listeners, a tribute: 'What I declare is, that such principles are your own; I show that before my time such was the spirit of the Commonwealth.' From one eloquent height to another he proceeds, till, challenging Aeschines for arraigning him, thus counselling the people, he rises to this great level: 'But, never, never can you have done wrong, O Athenians, in undertaking the battle for freedom and safety of all: I swear it by your forefathers — those who met the peril at Marathon, those that took the field at Plataea, those in the sea-fight at Salamis, and those at Artimesium, and many other brave men who repose in the public monuments, all of whom alike, as being worthy of the same honour, the country buried, Aeschines, not only the successful and victorious.' We did not need this fine eloquence to assure us of the greatness of our O'Neills and our Tones, our O'Donnells and our Mitchels, but it so quickens the spirit and warms the blood to read it, it so touches — by the admiration won from ancient and modern times — an enduring principle of the human heart — the capacity to appreciate a great deed and rise over every physical defeat — that we know in the persistence of the spirit we shall come to a veritable triumph. Yes; and in such light we turn to read what Ruskin called the greatest inscription ever written, that which Herodotus tells us was raised over the Spartans, who fell at Thermopylae, and which Mitchel's biographer quotes as most fitting to epitomise Mitchel's life: 'Stranger, tell thou the Lacedemonians that we are lying here, having obeyed their words.' And the biographer of Mitchel is right in holding that he who reads into the significance of these brave lines, reads a message not of defeat but of victory.

iii

Yes; and in paying a fitting tribute to these great men who are examplars, it would be fitting also, in conclusion, to remember ourselves as the inheritors of a great tradition; and it would well become us not only to show the splendour of the banner that is handed on to us, but to show that this banner we, too, are worthy to bear. For, how often it shall be victorious and how high it shall be planted, will depend on the conception we have of its supreme greatness, the knowledge that it can be fought for in all times and places, the conviction that we may, when least we expect, be challenged to deny it; and that by our bearing we may bring it new credit and glory or drag it low in repute. We do well, I say, to remember these things. For in our time it has grown the fashion to praise the men of former times but to deny their ideal of Independence; and we who live in that ideal, and in it breathe the old spirit, and preach it and fight for it and prophesy for it an ultimate and complete victory — we are young men, foolish and unpractical. And what should be our reply? A reply in keeping with the flag, its history and its destiny. Let them, who deride or pity us, see we despise or pity their standards, and let them know by our works — lest by our election they misunderstand — that we are not without ability in a freer time to contest with them the highest places — avoiding the boast, not for an affected sense of modesty but for a saving sense of humour. For in all the vanities of this time that make life and Literature choke with absurdities, pretensions and humbug, let us have no new folly. Let us with the old high confidence blend the old high courtesy of the Gaedheal. Let us grow big with our cause. Shall we honour the flag we bear by a mean, apologetic front? No! Wherever it is down, lift it; wherever it is challenged, wave it; wherever it is high, salute it; wherever it is victorious, glorify and exult in it. At all times and forever be for it proud, passionate, persistent, jubilant, defiant; stirring hidden memories, kindling old fires, wakening the finer instincts of men, till all are one in the old spirit, the spirit that will not admit defeat, that has been voiced by thousands, that is noblest in Emmet's one line, setting the time for his epitaph: 'When my country' — not if — but 'when my country takes her place among the nations of the earth.' It is no hypothesis; it is a certainty. There have been in every generation, and are in our own, men dull of apprehension and cold of heart, who could not believe this, but we believe it, we live in it; we know it. Yes, we know it, as Emmet knew it, and as it shall be seen to-morrow; and when the historian of to-morrow, seeing it accomplished, will write its history, he will not note the end with surprise. Rather will he marvel at the soul in constancy, rivalling the best traditions of undegenerate Greece and Rome, holding through disasters, persecutions, suffering, and not less through the seductions of milder but meaner times, seeing through all shining clearly the goal; he will record it all, and still marvelling, come to the issue that dauntless spirit has reached, proud and happy; but he will write of that issue — Liberty;

Inevitable: in two words to epitomise the history of a people that is without a parallel in the Annals of the World.

71. Resolutions presented at the 1913 Labour Day meeting in Dublin
Poster collection, National Library of Ireland

1. That this Mass Meeting of the workers of the City and County of Dublin extends fraternal greetings to the workers of every country who are striving for the emancipation of their class; urges upon all organized workers the necessity of a closer federation of labour; declares that the complete control by the people of the internal affairs and resources of this country is essential to the satisfaction of the demands of Irish labour; and calls upon all Irish workingmen to support the Irish Industrial Revival by buying Irish goods, produced under fair conditions of labour, and so support their fellow-Trade Unionist.

2. That we affirm the right of every human being to work and live, and demand that the Labour Party's Right to Work Bill should be passed into Law in the present Session of Parliament; we demand the recognition of a universal 48-hour week, and the payment of a minimum wage at least sufficient to maintain an adult and his family; we call for the immediate introduction of a Bill to carry out the recommendations of the Vice-Regal Commission on Poor Law; that we demand the abolition of the anomaly which exists by having the medical benefits of the Insurance Act applied to Ireland; and we condemn the system by which an excessive number of boys are introduced to some branches of industry; and we further call for the Nationalisation of the Irish Railways, as recommended by the Majority Report of the Vice-Regal Commission.

3. That we consider it to be the duty of the State to provide proper food and clothing for children whose parents are unable or unwilling to maintain them; to deal with the unemployed question by re-adjusting the relations between capital and labour, abolishing excessive overtime, and providing work for all who are able to undertake it.

4. That we pledge ourselves to use every effort to give effect to the foregoing resolutions, to maintain an annual Labour Day Demonstration, and to return direct labour representatives on all public boards.

72. Proclamation banning a mass meeting during the Dublin labour conflict
Poster collection, National Museum of Ireland

A PROCLAMATION

Whereas it has been represented to me, being a Justice of the Peace in and for the County of the City of Dublin by an information duly sworn, that a number of persons will meet or assemble at

SACKVILLE STREET
OR ITS NEIGHBOURHOOD

in the said County of the City of Dublin, on or about the

31st day of August, 1913

and that the object of such Meeting or Assemblage is seditious, and that said Meeting or Assemblage would cause terror and alarm to, and dissension between, His Majesty's subjects, and would be an unlawful assembly.

NOW I do hereby prohibit such Meeting or Assemblage, and do strictly caution and forewarn all Persons whomsoever, that they do abstain from taking part in or encouraging or inciting to the same.

AND I do hereby give notice that if in defiance of this Proclamation any such Meeting or Assemblage at Sackville Street or its neighbourhood shall be attempted or take place, the same will be prevented and all Persons attempting to take part in or encouraging the same, or inciting thereto, will be proceeded against according to law.

AND I do hereby enjoin all Magistrates and Officers instrusted with the preservation of the Public Peace, and all others whom it may concern, to aid and assist in the due and proper execution of the Law in preventing any such Meeting or Assemblage as aforesaid, and in the effectual dispersion and suppression of the same, and in the detection and prosecution of those who after this Notice, shall offend in the respect aforesaid.

Given under my hand this 29th day of August, 1913

E.G. SWIFTE,
Chief Divisional Magistrate,
Dublin Metropolitan Police District

GOD SAVE THE KING

73. Report of a labour meeting during the 1913 conflict
Irish Times, 7 October 1913

MEETING OF WORKERS

CONTINUANCE OF THE FIGHT

Men to be consulted

The labour leaders addressed a large meeting in Beresford place last night. There was no excitement.

Mr. O'Brien, who presided, said that an impartial inquiry had proved that the workers were in the right. In the opinion of a discriminating public their case was already won.

Mr. James Connolly declared that the workers were prepared to negotiate, and they were also prepared to fight. The employers had put forward men to talk of broken agreements. But the workers could have brought forward men and women and children to talk of broken lives. They could have brought forward the children from the sweating dens of Dublin.

Mr. P.T. Daly said that Timothy Healy, whom the employers had engaged as their counsel, had been so long delving in law books that he forgot the problems of life, and the only thing that presented itself to him was the problem of taking dividends. A letter from His Grace Archbishop Walsh appeared in the Dublin Press that day. The suggestion contained in that letter had been flouted by the employers of Dublin. How many of their Catholic priests had come out in the evening papers to condemn the employers for flouting His Grace's letter? None. Mr. Daly next criticised the Dublin members of Parliament for their inactivity during the present dispute, and also Mr. David Sheehy for a speech which he recently delivered. He added that when the Transport Union men went down to organise the agricultural labourers of Meath Mr. Sheehy would not have his £400 a year after the next election.

James Larkin said that in his time he had kept strange company, and had slept in the same room with strange people, but he had never sat with men who represented such a low order of intelligence or who had so little sense of decency or of common honesty as the men with whom the workers' representatives had been compelled to sit during the last week. When, contrary to their expectations, the Court of Inquiry stated that there might be a reason for the sympathetic strike, they decided to withdraw from the Conference. The Commissioners had said definitely in plain English that in their opinion the conduct of the employers deserved condemnation. Why did the Evening Telegraph omit the most important part of the document issued by the Court? Because this was part of the foul, insidious campaign that had been carried on against him for the last six years. The employers said that men like himself had no right to interfere in the carrying on of their industry. Why, then, had the employers accepted help in stating their case from men outside their own industries? The employers had stated in the face of the Court — 'We will not play the game any longer; we will sulk'. They had acted foolishly; they had acted vindictively, because they were getting the worst of the fight. What the employers wanted to do was to make the workers fettered slaves. Were the workers willing to sacrifice their liberty? (Cries of 'No!') Were they willing to carry on the fight? ('Yes'). Within the next few hours every man would have the opportunity of answering the question for himself whether he was satisfied to fight this matter to a finish. It was the fight of a century. It was a fight, not for themselves, but for their hungry children and wives. The part the women workers took in the procession on Sunday showed that their women were worth fighting for. The best way for the employers to kill men like Larkin would be by kindness. Let them give the men and women of Dublin a fair chance of life; let them give them a fair share of the wealth they created; and then he would have to seek another sphere of activity. He did not want to be always guilty of agitation, always fighting. He would much sooner read a book or paint a picture if he could. It was the employers who made men what he had become — what they called a demagogue. . . .

74. Open letter from George Russell (AE) 'to the masters of Dublin'
Irish Times, 7 October 1913

Sirs — I address this warning to you, the aristocracy of industry in this city, because, like all aristocracies, you tend to grow blind in long authority, and to be unaware that you and your class and its every action are being considered and judged day by day by those who have power to shake or overturn the whole social order, and whose relentlessness in poverty to-day is making our industrial civilisation stir like a quaking bog. You do not seem to realise that your assumption that you are answerable to yourselves alone for your actions in the industries you control is one that becomes less and less tolerable in a world so crowded with necessitous life. Some of you have helped Irish farmers to upset a landed aristocracy in this island, an aristocracy richer and more powerful in its sphere than you are in yours, with its roots deep in history. They, too, as a class, though not all of them, were scornful or neglectful of the workers in the industry by which they profited; and to many who knew them in their pride of place and thought them all-powerful they are

143

already becoming a memory, the good disappearing together with the bad. If they had done their duty by those from whose labour came their wealth they might have continued unquestioned in power and prestige for centuries to come. The relation of landlord and tenant is not an ideal one, but any relations in a social order will endure if there is infused into them some of that spirit of human sympathy which qualifies life for immortality. Despotisms endure while they are benevolent, and aristocracies while *noblesse oblige* is not a phrase to be referred to with a cynical smile. Even an oligarchy might be permanent if the spirit of human kindness, which harmonises all things otherwise incompatible, is present.

You do not seem to read history so as to learn its lessons. That you are an uncultivated class was obvious from recent utterances of some of you upon art. That you are incompetent men in the sphere in which you arrogate imperial powers is certain, because for many years, long before the present uprising of labour, your enterprises have been dwindling in the regard of investors, and this while you carried them on in the cheapest labour market in these islands, with a labour reserve always hungry and ready to accept any pittance. You are bad citizens, for we rarely, if ever, hear of the wealthy among you endowing your city with the munificent gifts which it is the pride of merchant princes in other cities to offer, and Irishmen not of your city who offer to supply the wants left by your lack of generosity are met with derision and abuse. Those who have economic power have civic powers also, yet you have not used the power that was yours to right what was wrong in the evil administration of this city. You have allowed the poor to be herded together so that one thinks of certain places in Dublin as of a pestilence. There are twenty thousand rooms, in each of which live entire families, and sometimes more, where no functions of the body can be concealed and delicacy and modesty are creatures that are stifled ere they are born. The obvious duty of you in regard to these things you might have left undone, and it be imputed to ignorance or forgetfulness; but your collective and conscious action as a class in the present labour dispute has revealed you to the world in so malign an aspect that the mirror must be held up to you, so that you may see yourself as every humane person sees you.

The conception of yourselves as altogether virtuous and wronged is, I assure you, not at all the one which onlookers hold of you. No doubt, you have rights on your side. No doubt, some of you suffered without just cause. But nothing which has been done to you cries aloud to Heaven for condemnation as your own actions. Let me show you how it seems to those who have followed critically the dispute, trying to weigh in a balance the rights and wrongs. You were within the rights society allows you when you locked out your men and insisted on the fixing of some principle to adjust your future relations with labour when the policy of labour made it impossible for some of you to carry on your enterprises. Labour desired the fixing of some such principle as much as you did. But, having once decided on such a step, knowing how many thousands of men, women and children, nearly one-third of the population of this city, would be affected, you should not have let one day to have passed without unremitting endeavours to find a solution of the problem.

What did you do? The representatives of labour unions in Great Britain met you, and you made of them a preposterous, an impossible demand, and because they would not accede to it you closed the Conference: you refused to meet them further: you assumed that no other guarantees than those you asked were possible, and you determined deliberately in cold anger, to starve out one-third of the population of this city, to break the manhood of the men by the sight of the suffering of their wives and the hunger of their children. We read in the Dark Ages of the rack and thumb screw. But these iniquities were hidden and concealed from the knowledge of man in dungeons and torture chambers. Even in the Dark Ages humanity could not endure the sight of such suffering, and it learnt of such misuses of power by slow degrees, through rumour, and when it was certain it razed its Bastilles to their foundations. It remained for the twentieth century and the capital city of Ireland to see an oligarchy of four hundred masters deciding openly upon starving one hundred thousand people, and refusing to consider any solution except that fixed by their pride. You, masters, asked men to do that which masters of labour in any other city in these islands had not dared to do. You insolently demanded of those men who were members of a trade union that they should resign from that union; and from those who were not members you insisted on a vow that they would never join it.

Your insolence and ignorance of the rights conceded to workers universally in the modern world were incredible, and as great as your inhumanity. If you had between you collectively a portion of human soul as large as a threepenny bit, you would have sat night and day with the representatives of labour, trying this or that solution of the trouble, mindful of the women and children, who at least were innocent of wrong against you. But no! You reminded labour you could always have your three square meals a day while it went hungry. You went into conference again with representatives of the State, because dull as you are, you know public opinion would not stand your holding out. You chose as your spokesman the bitterest tongue that ever wagged in this island, and then, when an award was made by men who have an experience in industrial matters a thousand times transcending yours, who have settled disputes in industries so great that the sum of your petty enterprises would not equal them, you withdraw again, and will not agree to accept their solution, and fall back again upon your devilish policy of starvation. Cry aloud to Heaven for new souls! The souls you have got cast upon the screen of publicity appear like the horrid and writhing creatures enlarged from the insect world, and revealed to us by the cinematograph.

You may succeed in your policy and ensure your own damnation by your victory. The men whose manhood you have broken will loathe you, and will always be brooding and scheming to strike a fresh blow. The children will be taught to curse you. The infant being moulded in the womb will have breathed into its starved body the vitality of hate. It is not they — it is you who are blind Samsons pulling down the pillars of the social order. You are sounding the death knell of autocracy in industry. There was autocracy in political life, and it was superseded by democracy. So surely will democratic power wrest from you the control of industry. The fate of you, the aristocracy of industry, will be the fate of the aristocracy of land if you do not show that you have some humanity still among you. Humanity abhors, above all things, a vacuum in itself, and your class will be cut off from humanity as the surgeon cuts the cancer and alien growth from the body. Be warned ere it is too late. — Yours, etc.,

'AE'.

Dublin, October 6th, 1913.

75. Constitution of the Irish Citizen Army
This body was founded in October 1913, during the industrial conflict; the constitution was adopted in March 1914. *Irish Worker*, 22 August 1914

1. That the first and last principle of the Irish Citizen Army is the avowal that the ownership of Ireland, moral and material, is vested in the people of Ireland.
2. That its principal objects shall be:
   a. To arm and train all Irishmen capable of bearing arms to enforce and defend its first principle.
   b. To sink all differences of birth, privilege and creed under the common name of the Irish People.
3. That the Citizen Army shall stand for the absolute unity of Irish Nationhood and recognition of the rights and liberties of the World's Democracies.

4. That the Citizen Army shall be open to all who are prepared to accept the principles of equal rights and opportunities for the People of Ireland and to work in harmony with organized Labour towards that end.

5. Every enrolled member must be, if possible, a member of a Trades Union recognized by the Irish Trade Union Congress.

76. Formation of the Irish Volunteers, 1913

Announcement of meeting for formation of the organization. Poster collection, National Library of Ireland

Ógláigh na hÉireann — The Irish Volunteers

In view of the present situation in National Affairs, a voluntary provisional conference has been held for the formation of a National Volunteer Force. The undersigned have been deputed to act as Provisional Secretaries and to communicate with the various large organisations having National aims. It is not asked that any existing organisation should officially adopt the Volunteer movement. We only request that the movement should be brought to the knowledge of the members of each organisation and an opportunity given to them to act as they think right.

The following points have been agreed upon: —

Immediate steps to be taken to enable Volunteers to be enrolled in Dublin and to promote the enrolment of Volunteers throughout Ireland.

The purpose of the Irish Volunteers will be to secure and maintain the rights and liberties common to all the people of Ireland.

Volunteers to be enrolled according to locality and not according to any other classification (except where young men live under a special discipline and authority).

Those who act in initiating the Volunteer movement do not assume direction or authority over the subsequent conduct of the movement.

Persons desirous of furthering the movement will obtain the fullest information and assistance at our disposal.

A public meeting to commence the enrolment of Irish Volunteers will be held in the Large Concert Hall, Rotunda, on Tuesday, 25 November, at 8 p.m.

EOIN MacNEILL
LAURENCE J. KETTLE } *Provisional Secretaries.*

It is requested that this communication may be displayed where it can be read by the members of the various bodies that receive it.

77. Manifesto of the Irish Volunteers
Volunteer Gazette, December 1913

At a time when legislative proposals, universally confessed to be of vital concern for the future of Ireland, have been put forward, and are awaiting decision, a plan has been deliberated by one of the great English political parties, advocated by the leaders of that party and by its numerous organs in the Press, and brought systematically to bear on English public opinion, to make the display of military force and the menace of armed violence the determining factor in the future relations between this country and Great Britain.

The party which has thus substituted open force for the semblance of civic government is seeking by this means not merely to decide an immediate political issue of grave concern to this Nation, but also to obtain for itself the future control of all our national affairs. It is plain to every man that the people of Ireland, if they acquiesce in this new policy by their reaction, will consent to the surrender, not only of their rights as a nation, but of their civic rights as men.

The Act of Union deprived the Irish Nation of the power to direct its own course and to develop and use its own resources for its own benefit. It gave us instead the meagre and seldom effective right of throwing our votes into the vast and complicated movement of British politics. Since the Act of Union, a long series of repressive statutes has endeavoured to deal with the incessant discontent of the Irish people by depriving them of various rights common to all who live under the British Constitution. The new policy goes further than the Act of Union, and further than all subsequent Coercion Acts taken together. It proposes to leave us the political franchise in name and to annihilate it in fact. If we fail to take such measures as will effectually defeat this policy, we become politically the most degraded population in Europe, and no longer worthy of the name of nation.

Are we to rest inactive, in the hope that the course of politics in Great Britain may save us from the degradation openly threatened against us? British politics are controlled by British interests, and are complicated by problems of great importance to the people of Great Britain. In a crisis of this kind, the duty of safeguarding our rights is our duty first and foremost. If we remain quiescent, by what title can we expect the people of Great Britain to turn aside from their own pressing concerns to defend us. Will not such an attitude of itself mark us out as a people unworthy of defence?

Such is the occasion, not altogether unfortunate, which has brought about the inception of the Irish Volunteer movement. But the Volunteers, once they have been enrolled, will form a prominent element in the National life under a National Government. The Nation will maintain its Volunteer organisation as a guarantee of the liberties which the Irish people shall have secured.

If ever in history a people could say that an opportunity was given to them by God's will to make an honest and manly stand for their rights, that opportunity is given us to-day. The stress of industrial effort, the relative peace and prosperity of recent years, may have dulled the sense of the full demands of civic duty. We may forget that the powers of the platform, the Press and the polling booth are derived from the conscious resolve of the people to maintain their rights and liberties. From time immemorial it has been held by every race of mankind to be the right and duty of a freeman to defend his freedom with all his resources and with his life itself. The exercise of that right distinguishes the freeman from the serf, the discharge of that duty distinguishes him from the coward.

To drill, to learn the use of arms, to acquire the habit of concerted and disciplined action, to form a citizen army from a population now at the mercy of almost any organised aggression — this, beyond all doubt, is a programme that appeals to all Ireland, but especially to young Ireland. We begin at once in Dublin, and we are confident that the movement will be taken up without delay all over the country. Public opinion has already and quite spontaneously formed itself into an eager desire for the establishment of the Irish Volunteers.

The object proposed for the Irish Volunteers is to secure and maintain the rights and liberties common to all the people of Ireland. Their duties will be defensive and protective, and they will not contemplate either ag[g]ression or domination. Their ranks are open to all able-bodied Irishmen, without distinction of creed, politics, or social grade. Means will be found whereby Irishmen unable to serve as ordinary Volunteers will be enabled to aid the Volunteer forces in various capacities. There will also be work for women to do, and there are signs that the women of Ireland, true to their record, are especially enthusiastic for the success of the Irish Volunteers.

We propose for the Volunteers' organisation the widest possible basis. Without any other association or classification the Volunteers will be enrolled according to the district in which they live. As soon as it is found feasible, the district sections will be called upon to join in making provision for the general administration and discipline and for united co-operation. The Provisional Committee which has acted up to the present will continue to offer its services until an elective body is formed to replace it.

A proportion of time spared, not from work, but from pleasure and recreation, a voluntary adoption of discipline, a purpose firmly and steadily carried through, will renew the vitality of the nation. Even that degree of self-discipline will bring back to every town, village and countryside a consciousness that has long been forbidden them — the sense of freemen who have fitted themselves to defend the cause of freedom.

In the name of National Unity, of National dignity, of National and individual Liberty, of manly citizenship, we appeal to our countrymen to recognise and accept without hesitation the opportunity that has been granted to them to join the ranks of the Irish Volunteers, and to make the movement now begun not unworthy of the historic title which it has adopted.

78. Asquith proposes temporary exclusion of unionist Ulster
Hansard 5 (Commons), lix, 906-08, 9 March 1914

. . . The Question, Sir, that you are about to put from the Chair is that this Bill be read a second time. But I do not conceive that I should be making an appropriate use of the occasion if I were to take advantage of it to restate the case so often presented in favour of a Bill which in successive Sessions has twice passed through the House of Commons. This, however, I will say: Those who have supported it in all its stages are as convinced to-day as they ever were of the soundness, both of its principles and its machinery. They regard it as an attempt at once sincere and considerate to base upon a solid foundation the fabric of Irish self-government, and they do not believe — none of them believe — if it were placed as it stands on the Statute Book to-morrow that its practical operation would involve injustice or oppression either to classes or to individuals in Ireland. I am obliged, in this respect, to repeat to-day with clearness and with emphasis at the outset of what I have to say to the House, what I have said many times before, both inside and outside its walls. If then, I come here to-day, as I do, with suggestions to make, which, if accepted, would require substantial modifications in, or to speak with greater accuracy, substantial additions and supplementary provisions to our plan, it is not because we are running away from it, but because we are, above all things, anxious that the changes which we believe to be inevitable in the government of Ireland should start under conditions which will secure for them, from the first, the best chance of ultimate success.

What are the dangers which lie ahead, and which, in my opinion, at any rate, it is the duty of statesmanship, if it be possible, to avert? On the one hand, if Home Rule as embodied in this Bill is carried now, there is, I regret to say it, but nobody can deny it, in Ulster the prospect of acute dissension and even of civil strife. On the other hand, if at this stage Home Rule were to be shipwrecked, or permanently mutilated, or indefinitely postponed, there is in Ireland, as a whole, at least an equally formidable outlook. The hazards in either event are such as to warrant in all quarters, I think, not indeed a surrender of principles, but any practical form of accommodation and approach which would lead to an agreed settlement. It is obvious — it is no use blinking the facts — that such a settlement must involve, in the first place, on the side of our opponents the acceptance of a Home Rule Legislature and Executive in Dublin, and, on the other hand, on the side of our supporters, some form of special treatment for the Ulster minority over and above any of the safeguards which are contained in this Bill. . . .

With that preface, let me now come to describe to the House the various ways in which we. . . . try to meet them. By far the most serious of them, of course, is that which is presented by what is compendiously and conveniently called the question of Ulster. I have tried, and my colleagues have tried, honestly and seriously, to meet that difficulty by three different roads. In the first place — and this was the solution, or, at any rate, an expedient which I confess commended itself very much to my own judgement — we tried the road which goes by a name I think first invented by my right hon. Friend (Sir E. Grey) — what is called 'Home Rule within Home Rule'. . . . Without for a moment defining the part of Ulster to which the suggestion was to apply, leaving that over for further consideration, calling the part to which it was to apply by the name of statutory Ulster, which means that it does not include the whole province, I had first in view with a vivid memory, in all the Debates which have taken place in this House and upon this Bill, statements made from that bench by the Ulster Members, by no one, I think, with more emphasis than by the right hon. Gentleman (Sir E. Carson), that what they were really afraid of as the consequence of Home Rule was not so much the legislation of an Irish Parliament as the administration of an Irish Executive. That, as the House knows, has been frequently stated. It was of the essence of my proposal — what is called 'Home Rule within Home Rule' — that as regards administration, Ulster . . . should be, until the Imperial Parliament otherwise decided, entirely exempt from the executive and administrative authority of the Irish Parliament in Dublin. It is not such a difficult problem as it seems. The police and everything connected with land purchase are, under the Bill as it stands, reserved services, which do not pass within the ambit or province of the Irish

Executive; and as regards what was left — education and local government — it seemed to me it might very well be in the excluded area, or the protected area, because it was not to be excluded, administered by some local authority; while as regards the important province of factory and workshop administration that would remain, as it is at present, under the Secretary of State here at Whitehall. . . .

Then, as regards legislation, my proposal was this — and I am still rather wedded to it, though I am afraid I met with very little support in any quarter — that Ulster should return, like all the rest of Ireland, representatives to both the Upper and the Lower Houses of the Irish Legislature, but then when any law was passed by those two Houses to which in respect of its application to Ulster the majority of the representatives of Ulster were opposed, it should not come into force *quoad* Ulster, if they protested, until it received the sanction of the Imperial Parliament. . . .

I now come to the second. The second was this, a suggestion that the whole of Ireland should be, in the first instance, included, both for legislative and executive purposes, in the Bill as it stands, but that an option should be given, after the lapse of a certain time, for the Ulster counties . . . to remove themselves from the jurisdiction of the Irish Legislature and Executive, and to revert to the position in which they at present stand. That is a proposal which we had considered even before it was put forward, as it has been put forward by a high authority, a very distinguished Irishman, to whom Ireland is under a very great debt of gratitude for many public services — I mean Sir Horace Plunkett. Here, again, the proposal has the great merit that it starts from the beginning with a fully representative and fully developed Irish Legislature, with no adjustments of a very complicated kind, such as are incident to any form of exclusion, to embarrass them — a practical working Irish Parliament, a Parliament for all Ireland which would in a very few years show whether the apprehensions were or were not well founded. If they were not, things would go on as they are. If they were well founded, the minority had a constitutional door of escape. I think there is a great deal to be said for that plan. There again, I must add that it would be an excellent thing if it could be made acceptable to those whom it is proposed to include, but I am afraid it cannot — or cannot, at any rate, for the moment — and compulsory inclusion at the outset, even with the option of exclusion as time goes on, has, of course, all the drawbacks and all the dangers incident to any scheme that has to be coercively enforced. Therefore, I am afraid it cannot be regarded as giving a practical answer to the demand for an agreed road to settlement.

Both these roads being blocked — I hope not permanently — for the time being, we then proceeded to explore the third. I do not say that we had not had it in view throughout, because we did not proceed in this logical manner step by step. We had to explore in detail the third road, which goes popularly by the name of 'exclusion'. There are obvious and formidable objections to exclusion in whatever guise they may be clothed, and I believe they are felt quite as much by men of all parties and opinions in Ireland as they are by more detached critics outside. What are they? You start, whatever form exclusion takes, with an Irish Legislature which — in the first instance, at any rate — is not fully representative of and responsible to the whole of the Irish people. You recognise whatever form exclusion may take — and in recognising you run the risk of stereotyping and perpetuating — traditions which are inherited from the past, which we all hope, and many of us believe, the future will soften and in time obliterate. It has the further drawback that it necessarily keeps the controversy alive, and finally it involves a number of more or less complicated and difficult administrative and financial adjustments. No one is more alive than I am to the force and seriousness of these objections. The Unionists, of course, can get rid of the difficulties of exclusion by a simple denial of Home Rule. Home Rulers can get rid of them if they are ready to start Home Rule in an atmosphere of discord and of tumult. But it appears to me that each, Unionist and Home Ruler alike, can find, in some form, provisional exclusion by a media between the surrender of principle and the application of force. Exclusion in any form must be put forward, and can only be put forward, not as a solution, but as an expedient which may pave the way in time for a final settlement. . . .

. . . We have come to the conclusion that the best, and, indeed, the only practical, way — at any rate far the simplest and the fairest plan — is to allow the Ulster counties themselves to determine, in the first instance, whether or not they desire to be excluded. I will say something in a moment about two crucial points of difficulty which arise — the points of area and of time — but I would first, very briefly, describe to the House what is the plan we are putting forward. It is that any county in the province of Ulster is to be excluded for a certain period, if on a poll being taken of the Parliamentary electors in the county before the Bill comes into operation, a majority — a bare majority — vote in favour of exclusion. The poll will be taken in a county if a requisition is presented signed by , say, one-tenth of the electors, and presented, say, within three months of the date of the passing of the Bill. The poll will be taken for the county as a whole, without regard to its Parliamentary Divisions. . .

. . . The House will observe that I have used the term 'county', and when I speak of the county I include as separate counties for this purpose the two great county boroughs in Ulster — Belfast and Londonderry. . . .

. . . Then arises the question what ought to be the term of exclusion for a county, if it pleases it to vote for its own exclusion. We have, after much consideration, thought it ought to be a term of six years, and six years, not from the taking of the poll, but six years from the first meeting of the Irish Legislature in Dublin. Why have we adopted that period?

Sir EDWARD CARSON: Will the right hon. Gentleman say what happens at the end of six years?

The PRIME MINISTER: I am coming to that. We have taken the term of six years to ensure that before the period of exclusion comes to an end there shall be, first, ample time — six years — to test by experience the actual working of the Irish Parliament. That is why we take the beginning of the six years, not from the taking of the poll, but from the first assembling of the new legislature, and, in the second place, to ensure, also, that before that period of exclusion comes to an end there shall be a full and certain opportunity for the electors of the whole of the United Kingdom, both Great Britain and Ireland, with that experience to pronounce whether or not the exclusion shall come to an end. . . .

. . . We believe that that is a fair and equitable arrangement. It gives to these counties, it gives to the whole of Ulster, in the first instance, the option to say whether they will come within the Bill, and if they vote for exclusion they cannot be brought back into it unless with the assent, at a General Election, of a majority of the electorate of the whole of the United Kingdom.

Mr. BONAR LAW: I think that it is quite clear, but I am sure it would be better that it should be absolutely unquestioned; does the right hon. Gentleman mean that at the end of the six years the counties which have the option now are not to have it for themselves?

The PRIME MINISTER: Yes. They would come in at the end of the six years unless the Imperial Parliament otherwise decides. . . .

79. Bonar Law on the Curragh mutiny

Hansard 5 (Commons), lx, 72-74, 23 March 1914

The PRIME MINISTER: I beg to move, 'That this House do now adjourn'.

Mr. BONAR LAW: The right hon. Gentleman has made a statement which, in view of the gravity of the situation as we all know, and as he best of all knows, seems to me one of the most amazing instances of paltering with the House of Commons and the country which we have ever had. The position is far more serious than the statement would lead us to suppose. A new danger has arisen, a danger which, I think, anyone might have foreseen, but which has apparently come upon the Government as a bolt from the blue, the danger, that is — and I shall show that I am not exaggerating — that our Army should be destroyed before our eyes. In the face of such a danger, it is the duty of everyone — and I shall try to fulfil it — not to do or say anything which will aggravate a position which is already disastrous, and which must soon lead to a disaster that cannot be repaired. The right hon. Gentleman spoke as if there had been only a suggestion of resignation on the part of the officers. As a matter of fact he knows, and everyone who has followed the subject knows, that a very large number of officers have intimated their intention to resign. That is not confined by any means to the Cavalry brigade, which has been chiefly referred to. I have received proof that is absolutely unquestionable, that the same thing has happened to many other than Cavalry regiments. In proof of that statement, and of the gravity of the situation, I shall read one letter only, or part of it, which has been received by an hon. Friend behind me from an officer in a Line regiment now at the Curragh, in Ireland. This is what the letter says: —

> 'I wonder whether the people in England are aware of the way in which we are being treated over this Ulster business. At 12:30 p.m. to-day the commanding officer came back from a conference with the brigadier with orders to hold a conference of officers, and to put the following proposal before them: "Any officer whose home is Ulster can be given leave. Officers who object to fighting against Ulster are to say so, and they will be at once dismissed from service".'

[Interruption.] I do really regard the position as so serious that I hope the House on both sides will listen.

> 'To decide this, we were given half-an-hour. Everyone objects to going, and nine or ten refused under any condition to go.'

Mr. JOHN WARD: What is the date of that?

Mr. BONAR LAW: The 20th March. Nine or ten in a single Line

regiment refused under any conditions to go! The right hon. Gentleman the Secretary for War, in repeating, indeed, what was said by the Prime Minister in the published statement issued last night, makes the statement that this movement of troops was a purely precautionary measure, with no other object than to defend arsenals and other property of that kind belonging to the Government. If that be the case, then I cannot imagine any action more utterly foolish than that which has been taken by the Government. There was no new position in Ulster at all, there was no outbreak of disorder, there was no threatened outbreak of disorder — I am not going to exaggerate in any way — there was no threatened outbreak of disorder in any sense of which the same thing could not have been said during the last two years. If the Government had chosen to take these precautionary measures two or three months ago, they could have been taken without any suggestion that their action was provocative, or that they intended to begin coercing Ulster. But what are the facts? I ask hon. Members on both sides carefully to weigh them. The First Lord of the Admiralty went down to Bradford and made a speech, which he intimated was made in order to express the declared policy of the Government. In that speech he told the country that we, the Government, were going to put these grave matters to the proof. Then, and not till then, the order was given to move troops into Ulster. But that does not stand alone. I am going to read — I have permission to read — a statement taken down by one who heard it of what was said by the General Officer Commanding the troops in Ireland to his commanding officers. This is what he said: —

'Sir Arthur Paget said that active operations were to be begun against Ulster, that he expected the country to be in a blaze by Saturday, that he had been in close communication with the War Office, and that he had the following instructions from the War Office to convey to the officers. "Officers domiciled in Ulster would be allowed to disappear, and would be reinstated in their position, but they must give their word of honour that they would not fight for Ulster"' —

A perfectly fair proposal.

'Officers who are not prepared to undertake active operations against Ulster for conscientious or other scruples were to send in their resignations, and would be dismissed the Army. It was to be fully understood that the officers, brigadiers and any officers who avoided service on an incorrect plea of domicile in Ulster would be tried by Court Martial'....

80. Irish Trade Union Congress executive opposes Ulster exclusion
Irish Worker, 28 March 1914

Manifesto To the Workers of Ireland
From Irish Trade Union Congress Parliamentary Committee

FELLOW WORKERS,

AROUSE! AWAKE! ARISE! We are in the midst of a National Crisis. The workers of Ireland have been kept asunder and divided in regard to political action during the past thirty years. They have been utilised and humbugged by the various political parties. And after that long period of waiting we find that the workers are the only class in the community whose interests are not consulted. For some years we have been endeavouring to remedy this, but we have been put off with promises of consideration which have not been carried out.

We have been informed — although the industrial workers' possible representation in the Home Rule Parliament is but 34 as against 128 for the landed and other interests — that no amendment can be made in our favour of the Schedule of the Home Rule Bill. Of these 34 seats 14 are in Belfast. And yet, while no consideration will be given to the workers, it is now proposed, in response to what has been called 'Carson's Bluff', to exclude portion of the Province of Ulster, including Belfast, from the operations of the Bill, whilst a Military Oligarchy have set themselves up as censors as to what laws shall or shall not be enacted or enforced.

To us of the Irish working class the division of Ireland into two parts is unthinkable. To us as Irishmen the cutting off of that Province or any part thereof, which gave our country such men as Shane O'Neill, Hugh Roe O'Donnell, Aodh Ruadh O'Neill, McCracken, Orr, Francis Davis, 'The Belfast Man', and the host of Northern men who battled for freedom, and which from a labour, as well as from a National, point of view, is of so much importance, is an act of pure suicide and should not be persisted in. We claim Ulster in its entirety; her sons are our brothers, and we are opposed to any attempt to divide us.

As Irish workers we are not concerned with the Officers of the British Army taking the line they have, nor are we concerned because of the effect their action may have upon Britain's Army, but we claim that what the Officer may do in pursuance of his political and sectarian convictions so, too, may the Private in pursuance of his; and if to-day British Generals and other Staff Officers refuse to fight against the privileged class to which they belong so, too, must the Private Soldier be allowed to exercise his convictions against shooting down his brothers and sisters of the working class when they are fighting for their rights.

If it is lawful for Carson to arm, it is lawful for us — the workers — to arm; if it is lawful for Carson to drill, it is lawful for us to drill; if it is right and legal for Carson to fight, then it is right and legal for us to fight for economic freedom.

A duty has been thrust upon us, and in furtherance of that duty we hereby convene a National Labour Demonstration to be held in Dublin on Sunday, April 5th, 1914, to which every city and town in Ireland is invited to send delegates to deal with this important crisis in our history, viz., the suggested amputation of Ireland's right hand, the exclusion of Ulster, and the criminal and traitorous conduct of a privileged class-conscious group masquerading as Army Officers, who have set themselves up as a military junta evidently determined to thwart the Will of the people.

THE WILL OF THE PEOPLE MUST PREVAIL. GOD SAVE THE PEOPLE!

(Signed)

James Larkin, Chairman.	M.J. Egan, T.C., J.P.
Thomas Johnson, Vice Chairman.	John O'Sullivan
D.R. Campbell, Treasurer	William O'Brien
Thomas McPartlin	M.J. O'Lehane
R. O'Carroll, T.C., P.L.G.	P.T. Daly, Secretary
W.E. Hill	

Trades Hall, Dublin, 27th March, 1914

80. A republican view of exclusion
Irish Freedom, April 1914

THE LOWEST DEPTH

Parliamentarianism in Ireland has reached its lowest depth, and not alone that, but the lowest depth ever reached by any Irish political movement with any popular support. It has calmly listened to a proposal for the dismemberment of Ireland and declared its willingness to accept it. In these columns last month we wrote: 'The probabilities are that the English will take advantage of the crisis in order to make a new settlement which will emphasize the division of the nation, will bring forward some scheme the operation of which will tend towards making a permanent estrangement possible.' And the English have done precisely that, have brought forward a proposal which is intended to place in their hands the means of maintaining a permanent division in this nation, of maintaining a permanent grip upon Irish soil, of still maintaining within our body politic a foreign solidity which would nullify all efforts to rebuild the nation. The subserviency and incapacity of Mr. Redmond and his Party have emboldened the English to paralyse even the petty Bill which the Government of Ireland Bill was, and to make a proposal which, if accepted, will split the Irish nation effectively, and, if not accepted, will smash the Bill and enable the Liberal Party to act the role of the injured innocent. Never in any responsible assembly was so shamefully corrupt a proposal made, and never was it so shamelessly listened to by the representatives of a nation it proposed to dismember, and never did an alleged National press so shamelessly lie about it.

The new proposal, in Mr. Asquith's own words, is as follows:

> **It is that any county in the Province of Ulster is to be excluded for a certain period, if upon a poll being taken of the Parliamentary electors of the County before the Bill comes into operation a bare majority votes in favour of exclusion.**
>
> **If the majority in any County should vote in favour of exclusion that County will be automatically excluded for the prescribed period of years.**

That is two-thirds of the proposal, and the term of years is given as six years: and the other third, the vital thing in the proposal, is altogether ignored by the Irish press, which trumpets this proposal as a TEMPORARY exclusion. Here, in Mr. Asquith's own words, is the third part of this precious proposal: —

> **If they decide upon exclusion they cannot be brought back within the Bill without the assent of the majority of the electors of the whole United Kingdom.** (Ministerial cheers).

We know that some of the Ulster counties would vote themselves out, and this proposal means that they could NOT vote themselves in again, that only a majority vote of the English House of Commons could vote them in; thereby giving to England the power to maintain a divided nation here for generations to come.

Mr. Redmond has declared in the English House of Commons his willingness to accept this proposal, and Mr. Devlin, whose constituency would, by it, become part of England, has raised no voice of dissent: from the Irish Parliamentary Party comes nothing but the old cry that the day is not far distant, that we must trust Mr. Redmond and his Party. And this abbreviation of Irish territory, this dismemberment of the Irish nation, and dismemberment with the consent, mark you, of the Irish people, is to be the price of peace. Peace, forsooth! By the Lord, no! Rather let the rivers of Ireland run red with blood, and her harvests remain ungathered, and her homesteads lie burnt and desolate! Yea, oh Lord, give us war, and famine, and pestilence, and the scourging road of adversity: anything rather than that disgraceful peace. If this nation is to go down, let it go down gallantly as becomes its history, let it go down fighting, but let it not sink into the abjectness of carving a slice out of itself and handing it over to England. Better no will at all, than this.

It is a fundamental principle of all national effort, and national polity, in Ireland that the nation is one and indivisible, from Fair Head to Cape Clear, and from Beann Edair to Gaillimh, Gael, Dane, Norman, Scot, Cromwellian, Williamite, all have been taken to Ireland's bosom, and all are of her children. We deny the right of any Party in Ireland to give allegiance to any power outside Ireland, we deny the right of any Party in Ireland to alienate itself or any of the Irish soil it holds from the main body of the nation, and we deny the right of any Party in Ireland to consider any dismemberment proposal, much less accept it. And if any Party in Ireland does accept such a proposal, the young men of Ireland will make it hot for that Party.

The Irish Parliamentary Party have long ago lost all conception of Irish nationality. They have become merely the obedient tail of the English Liberal Party, and their complete abandonment of any thought of a virile policy, of any thought of doing any more for Ireland in Ireland, their utter reliance upon votings and speeches, have brought them to a mental paralysis in which they can no longer recognise the oneness of Ireland, or the oneness of England in its determination to keep Ireland down. Mr. Dillon and Mr. Redmond and Mr. Devlin have sullied the Irish national cause by tacking it on to every sentimental platitude the English Liberals have thought fit to utter about democracy, and all the other plausibilities that mean nothing, and now the Irish nation seems less to them than Lloyd George. Their utility now consists in preventing one English Party from passing votes of censure on Lloyd George. They could vote against that, but they could only look on, palsied, when the dismemberment of Ireland was proposed. They have steadily preached that the Englishman had at last turned honest and could be trusted, that the way to salvation lay through harmlessness and slavish obedience, that we must pretend to an enthusiasm for the Empire, give up for the nonce the idea of a separate Irish nation, and be content with local autonomy. And they have brought Ireland to this! We tell them that WE will save Ireland yet, in spite of them, and that it is time for them to step aside and leave the leadership of the people to men and women who do not fear to speak of Ninety-eight, who know how to treat a proposal for the dismemberment of Ireland.

As for Ulster, Ulster is Ireland's and shall remain Ireland's. Though the Irish nation, in its political and corporate capacity, were gall and wormwood to every Unionist in Ulster, yet shall they swallow it. We will fight them, if they want fighting, but we shall never let them go, never.

Whatever Mr. Redmond and his Party may do now, Nationalist Ireland has had enough of weak policies and weak men. The time has come to move on other lines, to gird up our loins and lead the nation on the toilsome path it must travel before it finds salvation. There will come, soon, a definite outcome to all this and then we who believe in the Irish nation, believe in its capacity to free itself without ever recording a vote in any assembly outside Ireland, must give Ireland a lead. It is a time when all the virility, all the national feeling, all the manhood in Ireland must stand together upon a common platform and raise up again the old glory of a totally independent Ireland.

IN THE MEANTIME, VOLUNTEER.

82. The Ulster Volunteer Force in action
Capt. F. Hall, U.V.F. military secretary, 'Narrative of events connected with the "Ulster coup" Friday April 24th 1914'. Public Record Office, Northern Ireland, PRB 1559

Prior to the passing of the second Reading (for the 3rd time) of the H.R. Bill it was decided that it w[oul]d be necessary to fully arm the U.V.F. This decision had been in abeyance for a considerable time — although plans were formulated — but it was felt by many that it was inadvisable to bring in arms or to spend money on them if there was still a chance of a peaceful settlement or the resignation of the Cabinet.

Accordingly (1) was sent over to the Continent to buy a full cargo of arms and amm[unitio]n and to arrange shipment. This he did: the full detail of his movements are known only to a few but his plans were watched by the German authorities & he was searched by Danish Customs after loading out of barges which passed through the Kiel Canal. . . . After clearing without his papers he cruised according to orders for some time in the Baltic and finally worked round to the N. coast of Scotland. On some date between April 1st and 15th unknown to me he transhipped his whole cargo at sea from the 'Fanny' to the S.S. Balmerino, which remained off the N. coast of Scotland. (1) returned incog[nito] to Belfast — I did not see him — just at the time of the 'Army

Crisis' & interviewed (2), (3), (4) at Craigavon. In the meantime (5) had been sent to the N. of Scotland to intercept the ship & had actually sold her and her cargo back to German dealers. (1) was not told this (I believe) as (5) did not return until he had left. (1) & (3) arranged that the whole cargo must be brought into Belfast and (2) & (4) concurred. The whole matter was kept absolutely in the hands of a small committee consisting principally of (3), (4), (5), (6), (7) & no details were given out.

I personally was told of the scheme by 5 at 6 p.m. on Friday 17th April — A meeting was held that evening at the O[ld] T[own] H[all] at which (2) told us that he desired that the job be done without conflict with the authorities & that a row at that time must be fatal to our interests. Prior to this meeting others had been told & the feeling quickly spread that any attempt to land the cargo in Belfast must lead to trouble. Orders had already been prepared for Belfast Div[isio]n U.V.F. to man the streets, barricade bridges, wire entanglements, etc. The proceedings of the meeting were secret & everyone present was sworn not to divulge what took place at it: I therefore cannot say what took place then.

After the meeting I took strong exception to the way in which the arrangements had been made, without consulting any of those who really knew the local conditions & stated my views openly that such proceedings could only end in a furious riot. I also went dead against the proposed plan of handing out rifles and amm[unition]n direct to the men in Belfast, or of storing them in bulk under armed guard in Belfast drill halls: also to a scheme whereby men were to be brought up from country towns & sent home by special trains with arms. (An earlier suggestion that a Great Protest Demonstration be held the same night in the Ulster Hall was dropped even before the above meeting.) In these views I found myself absolutely backed up by 8, 9, 10, 11, 12 and others.

A further meeting was held next morning and before it the plans as arranged were put before the 'Commission' 3,4,10,11,12. I was not present. It was then decided to abandon the 'military' move and make it a purely 'smuggling' move but still to adhere to the plan of bringing the ship into the Musgrave Channel. This relieved tension to a certain extent but the 'moderate' element still held that it was unwise to attempt anything in Belfast. & the opinion was freely expressed that no attempts should be made to bring in arms in bulk in view of the then state of the political situation. (3) left for London after the meeting on Friday evening 17th April.

Considerable friction arose between the 'Military' side & the 'local political' with regard to the abandonment of the militant policy & on Monday 20th relations were distinctly strained.

13, 14, 5 (all strangers) were keen on the bold militant policy & 13 was distinctly annoyed at the orders given to him that force was not to be used.

Constant Committees were held on 20th & 21st mostly attended by men who had never taken any part in previous organisation work in Belfast. All arrangements were proceeded with in connection with the 'smuggling' scheme — the vessel to berth in Musgrave Channel at 9 p.m. on Friday night 24th.

It appeared that (1) had left saying he w[oul]d bring the vessel in at that hour: & that he w[oul]d be stopped by nothing except a written order signed by (2). He had gone to sea in the S.S Clyde Valley alias Mountjoy, which met the Balmerino somewhere off the Bristol Channel & transhipped her whole cargo at sea on the nights of 27th and 28th.

On Tuesday morning 21st (4) & (15) evidently realised that the scheme was not feasible & that local opinion was against it. An alternative scheme of landing at Larne and Bangor was proposed but not discussed — (it had been the intention all along that small ships should be loaded alongside the Clyde Valley while she was landing the bulk of her cargo in the Musgrave channel & that they sh[oul]d then proceed to Larne & Bangor & land their lots there.) I spoke very strongly to (4) & (15) & placed my objections before them. I stated openly that the scheme was forced upon us by (1) & (3) & that I did not believe that (2) realised the strength of feeling against it, the danger of not, or the difficulty of getting the men out for a 'test mobliization' on a Friday night — (being pay night in the yards & mills.) I urged the advisability of laying the matter before (2).

At 4.30 p.m. I was told that I was to go over to London & see (2). I left by Larne. (Incidentally: in the Stranraer-Euston Sleeping car, I got into conversation with a total stranger evidently an English visitor who did not know who I was & who told me that the Bangor Batt[alio]n U.V.F. were to be mobilized 'for some big thing' on Friday night! So much for the secrecy of our plans!!!)

Wed[nesda]y 22nd. I saw (2) at 10.15 a.m. (in bed.) (3) was staying with him & was sent for as soon as I arrived. I told them the state of feeling in Belfast. (3) was much annoyed & keen for the whole 'military' scheme. We discussed matters for 2 hours. (2) said little but was distinctly worried. I told them the suggested alternative scheme: i.e. the one which was eventually carried out. (2) seemed to approve of it (3) seemed to accept it *'faute de mieux'*. I made one statement which I now regret. I said I did not expect that more than 5 or 10% of the men w[oul]d turn out for a sudden 'test mobilization' on a Friday night. (Subsequent events proved that — stimulated by all sorts of wild rumours which were about — nearly 50% turned out.) I left (2) & (3) at 12.15 with orders to meet them again at the House at 4 p,m.

At 4 I met (2) alone at the House & went up with him to the Carlton: I told him exactly what I had told (4) & (15) with regard to the hot-headed policy of (1) & (3). He said he knew it & knew the feelings on the subject but that he took responsibility himself. He gave me verbal orders to ask (4) to act entirely for him & to do what he considered advisable:he also gave me 3 letters in his own handwriting & signed to (1).

(A) Proceed to Sea again — report a rendezvous to G.O.C. & dont land anything.

(B) Plans altered. You will proceed to Larne. Act under orders of G.O.C. and C was also written at my suggestion. 'In my absence act absolutely under the orders of G.O.C. & obey his directions explicitly. This is essential.'

I returned via Greenore. . . .

Thursday 23rd. I saw (4) & (15) at the O.T.H. 7 gave (4) the verbal orders rec[eive]d from (2) also the 3 letters. He then informed me that plans had been definitely changed & that the 'Larne' scheme that [was] actually carried out was substituted. . . .

The actual details for the work which was carried out on the night of the 24th/25th were not taken in hand until midday on the 23rd. A fairly accurate account has now got into the papers.

Head Quarters U.V.F. moved from the O.T.H. to 'Maryville'. The O.T.H. being considered (rightly) untenable if a row started or if police interfered.

Orders were issued to mobilize <u>Belfast, Down, Antrim, Derry & Armagh</u> & such roads as were to be used in <u>Tyrone</u> to be picketted by local Batt[alio]ns.

All Motor Sections were mobilized & placed under orders of local Commanders. Cars for Larne assembled at <u>Antrim</u>. Those for Bangor at various places.

Arrangements were made to 'short circuit' (<u>not</u> to cut or damage) all telegraph & 'phone wires to Larne at Magheramorne, at 9.15 p.m. after last train had gone down. All lines on Bangor Road & rail to be 'shorted' at midnight except the Glasgow Trunk Lines.

The private telephone connecting H'[oly]wood Barracks to Exchange was tapped & a man sat at it from 10 p.m. till 3 a.m.

G.P.O. exchange was watched carefully — all operators being special men — also night telegraph staff!

The Staff were distributed: McCammon at Bangor, Spender at Larne, G.O.C. C.S.O. Davis and self at Head Q[uarte]rs. also Lloyd Campbell. — Craig at Donaghadee. 10 Motor Cyclists at Larne — 10 at Bangor 12 at Head Q[uarte]rs. 5 @ Donaghadee.

I dined with the Ropers, having arranged a code message with H[ea]d Q[uarte]rs in case R was called up to go to Barracks.

At 10 p.m. I went round all districts in the City. Batt[alio]ns were mobilizing everywhere no excitement — no disturbance anywhere. I visited the Guard at O.T.H. & walked down to Musgrave Channel. Found about 1000 men E. Belfast Reg[imen]t U.V.F. fallen in on roadway about 20 yards from wharf. Steam up on two cranes ordered for the S.S. Balmerino. (Bates & X.X. had gone out in S.S. Milewater to intercept the Clyde Valley — alias Mountjoy — off the head.)

At 11 p.m. a vessel came dead slow up the Channel & took about 25 minutes to get alongside. By this time 15 Customs officers under Mr. Jones, Chief Customs Surveyor Belfast, had collected. As the vessel came alongside the Customs hailed her 'Whats your cargo'. Skipper replied 'I am instructed to tell you its coal'. Having made sure it was the Balmerino — (we were desperately afraid of the Clyde Valley refusing to obey orders & that she w[oul]d come straight in — I motored up to Maryville. The City was absolutely deserted, except for our pickets.

Communications between Larne, Bangor, Donaghadee & Head Q[uarte]rs was kept up by signallers & cyclists. Both worked without a hitch.

At 1 a.m. we rec[eive]d word by cyclist from Larne that the 'Mountjoy' was short of coal water and engine room stores. She had only just enough coal to take her to Bangor. We secured a motor lorry & loaded it in an hour with the oil & other engine room stores she wanted. We told Bangor to have 30 tons of coal ready for her. They did so. When she arrived there all was put on board while she was unloading — the hose on the pier was not long enough so they called out the fire brigade & watered her with their hose!! When she had finished un-loading 5 of her crew refused to go to sea so Volunteers were called for from the U.V.F. & they took her out!

At 3.30 a.m. I rec[eive]d orders from G.O.C. to allow the Customs to inspect the Balmerino & went down again to Musgrave Channel. I wouldn't have missed that job for £1000. 4 a.m., just day light, I got down to her, found 1500 U.V.F. fallen in, 15 Customs men, 2 Harbour Police, Commissioner Smith, D.I. Dunlop, (Detection Staff) probably 6 detectives & a few R.I.C. men not more than 4.

We fell in the U.V.F., ordered them to march home, telling them that their work had been eminently successful — just before they marched off I went up to the ship — with Smith on one side of me, Dunlop on the other & ordered the mate to remove hatches for the Customs. The 15 Customs men stood round like mutes round a grave. Their faces when those hatches were taken off I shall never forget. After hold empty:

165

forward Hold — 40 tons of bunker coal!!

I returned to Head Quarters 4.30 a.m., found reports all correct from Larne. At Larne the 'Mountjoy' burthed at 10.10 p.m. & immediately commenced unloading on to the quay. At the same time two small vessels were brought alongside her. 'Roma' took 30 tons & was to steam straight round to Workman & Clarks Yard. 'Innismurray' took 29 tons to Donaghadee. The Mountjoy herself took 80 tons to Bangor.

The only hitch in the whole proceedings was with the Roma. She had been chartered in a hurry that morning (Friday.) Her crew were 'wrong' & we had to put men on her to bring her round: she made a very bad passage, took 3½ hours instead of 2½, and just as she was berthing at Workmans & Clarke the Customs men whom I had released from the Balmerino came up the river in their motor boat & spotted her. They boarded her, took her papers but could not touch the cargo, which was landed in the yard. She was arrested next day in Ayr, but she had done her work.

At Bangor all worked well, ditto at Donaghadee although they did not start to unload there till 6 a.m. & finished at 8 a.m.

Stories of queer incidents are still coming in: —

1. Dist. Inspector Dunlop sent his car to his brother — a parson on Friday 24th. Its number was taken by the police at Larne & reported to the Castle for gun-running!

2. At Lisburn the signal to mobilize was given on the factory hooters: when they sounded a Sergt. R.I.C. (R.C.) & 4 Constables (Prot) were just having their tea. The 4 Constables dashed upstairs, put on plain clothes & were off! They went to the local Batt[alio]n Com[mande]r & asked if it was 'business' or only a test mobilization. He assured them it was only a test. 'Oh! Well, they said, then we needn't lose our jobs yet!!' & went back & got into uniform.

All the stuff as it was landed was immediately carted away. Larne stuff was sent straight away up country — some as far as Omagh. Bangor & Donaghadee stuff was dumped in depots. They shot some 1300 rifles on to Bob Maxwell at Finnebrogue much to his annoyance, but of course he played up. All this was practically distributed by Thursday 30th.

Throughout the whole proceedings there was not — so far as has been reported up to 7 p.m. Friday May 1st — a single casualty of any sort. Nor have we been interfer[r]ed with in any way whatsoever.

83. Sir Edward Grey on Ireland and the European war
Hansard 5 (Commons), lxv, 1824, 3 August 1914

. . . The one bright spot in the whole of this terrible situation is Ireland. The general feeling throughout Ireland — and I would like this to be clearly understood abroad — does not make the Irish question a consideration which we feel we have now to take into account. . . .

84. Redmond's statement in House of Commons on the threat of war
Hansard 5 (Commons), lxv, 1828-29, 3 August 1914

I hope the House will not consider it improper on my part, in the grave circumstances in which we are assembled, if I intervene for a few moments. I was moved a great deal by that sentence in the speech of the Secretary of State for Foreign Affairs in which he said that the one bright spot in the situation was the changed feeling in Ireland. In past times when this Empire has been engaged in these terrible enterprises, it is true — it would be the utmost affectation and folly on my part to deny it — the sympathy of the Nationalists of Ireland, for reasons to be found deep down in the centuries of history, have been estranged from this country. Allow me to say that what has occurred in recent years has altered the situation completely. I must not touch, and I may be trusted not to touch, on any controversial topic. By [But?] this, I may be allowed to say, that a wider knowledge of the real facts of Irish history have, I think, altered the views of the democracy of this country towards the Irish question, and to-day I honestly believe that the democracy of Ireland will turn with the utmost anxiety and sympathy to this country, in every trial and every danger that may overtake it. There is a possibility, at any rate, of history repeating itself. The House will remember that in 1778, at the end of the disastrous American War, when it might, I think, truly be said that the military power of this country was almost at its lowest ebb, and when the shores of Ireland were threatened with foreign invasion, a body of 100,000 Irish Volunteers sprang into existence for the purpose of defending her shores. At first no Catholic — ah, how sad the reading of the history of those days is! — was allowed to be enrolled in that body of Volunteers, and yet, from the very first day the Catholics of the South and West subscribed money and sent it towards the arming of their Protestant fellow-countrymen. Ideas widened as time went on, and finally the Catholics of the South were armed and enrolled as brothers in arms with their fellow-countrymen of a different creed in the North.

May history repeat itself. Today there are in Ireland two large bodies of Volunteers. One of them sprang into existence in the North. Another has sprung into existence in the South. I say to the Government that they may to-morrow withdraw every one of their troops from Ireland. I say that the coast of Ireland will be defended from foreign invasion by her armed sons, and for this purpose armed Nationalist Catholics in the South will be only too glad to join arms with the armed Protestant Ulstermen in the North. Is it too much to hope that out of this situation there may spring a result which will be good not merely for the Empire, but good for the future welfare and integrity of the Irish nation? I ought to apologise for having intervened, but while Irishmen generally are in favour of peace, and would desire to save the democracy of this country from all the horrors of war, while we would make every possible sacrifice for that purpose, still if the dire necessity is forced upon this country we offer to the Government of the day that they may take their troops away, and that if it is allowed to us, in comradeship with our brethern in the North, we will ourselves defend the coasts of our country.

85. Sinn Féin opposes Irish participation in the war
Sinn Féin, 8 August 1914

IRELAND AND THE WAR

Ireland is not at war with Germany. She has no quarrel with any Continental Power. England is at war with Germany, and Mr. Redmond has offered England the services of the National Volunteers to 'defend Ireland'. What has Ireland to defend and whom has she to defend it against? Has she a native Constitution or a National Government to defend? All know she has not. All know both were wrested from her by the power to whom Mr. Redmond offers the services of Nationalist Ireland. All know that Mr. Redmond has made his offer without receiving a quid pro quo. There is no European Power waging war against the people of Ireland. There are two European Powers at war with the people who dominate Ireland from Dublin castle. The call to the Volunteers to 'defend Ireland' is a call to them to defend the beaurocracy [*sic*] entrenched in that edifice.

Two weeks ago the Irish of Munster, Leinster, and Connacht were, according to the English Unionist Press, persons who dare not be entrusted with the elementary rights of citizenship, since they would invariably use them to oppress, plunder, and even murder any Irishman who believed in the Thirty-Nine Articles or did not subscribe to Transubstantiation. At the same time the Protestant Irish of the North were depicted by the English Liberal Press as bigots on the intellectual plane of the Bosjeman. To-day the Irish are flattered and caressed by their libellers. England wants our aid, and Mr. Redmond, true to his nature, rushes to offer it — for nothing. Maudlin English mobs sing, 'What do you think of the Irish now?' in 1914, as they sang it in 1900 when England was in the grips with the Boers and getting the worst of the grips. When the Irish helped England out of that trouble, Mr. Joseph Chamberlain was able to stand up in the British House of Commons and taunt Mr. John Redmond with the fact that so little did the Irish care about self-government that during the Boer War Mr. Redmond's followers never even attempted a riot, although the island had been denuded of all the regular troops. Mr. Redmond appears eager to give occasion to have the taunt a second time levelled at him by English Ministers. That was what the English thought of the Irish then, and the London 'Globe', 'Standard', 'Morning Post', 'Times', 'Chronicle'. and 'Daily News' of 1912-13 will reward any Protestant or Catholic Irishman with knowledge of what the English think of the Irish — when they can manage without their assistance.

The spectacle of the National Volunteers with English officers at their head, and the Union Jack floating proudly above them, 'defending' Ireland for the **British Government** may appeal to the gushing eyes of Mr. John Redmond, but his eyes are not likely to be blessed with the sight of that apotheosis of slavery. If England wins this war she will be more powerful than she has been at any time since 1864, and she will treat an Ireland which kissed the hand that smote her as such an Ireland ought to be treated. If she loses the war, and Ireland is foolish enough to identify itself with her, Ireland will deservedly share in her punishment.

Our duty is in no doubt. We are Irish Nationalists, and the only duty we can have is to stand for Ireland's interest, irrespective of the interests of England or Germany or any other foreign country. This week the British Government has passed measures through all stages — first reading, second reading, committee, third reading, and report — in the House of Commons in the space of six hours. Let it withdraw the present abortive Home Rule Bill and pass in the same space of time a full measure of Home Rule, and Irishmen will have some reason to mobilise for the defence of their institutions. At present they have none. In the alternative, let a Provisional Government be set up in Dublin by Mr. Redmond and Sir Edward Carson, and we shall give it allegiance. But the confidence trick has been too often played upon us to deceive us again.

86. Irish Labour statement on the war
Irish Worker, 22 August 1914

The Present Situation

Why Should Ireland Starve?

Manifesto to Workers of Ireland

10 August 1914

A European War for the aggrandisement of the capitalist class has been declared. Great Britain is involved. The working-class will, as usual, supply the victims that the crowned heads may stalk in all their panoply of state. Men will die and women and children will be left to weep the loss of husbands and fathers. Ireland is our country, and whilst the signatories to this manifesto may hold different views with regard to politics, we all join in our love of Ireland. The history of Ireland makes a glorious reading for our countrymen. It teaches lessons of endurance and points out mistakes. It shows us what men can do and suffer, and teaches us why they failed in the past. From its pages we can take the good and reject the evil. From its study we can realize things our fathers should have done and which they did not do. In the middle of last century our countrymen died of hunger in thousands, and mothers of Ireland tried to nuture the babe without the sustenance to perform the function that Nature intended they should perform. Children died in the ditches because famine walked the land. In a land of plenty hunger claimed and famine swept the finest peasantry in the world. Our desire is to prevent a recurrence of those horrors.

Our land has been given over to a privileged class. It lies fallow and unfruitful. Our credit was pledged to enable the transfer to be effected. The land our fathers fought for, suffered for, bled for, died for, was brought back with our money — the money of the working-class — from the people to whom it was given when our fathers were betrayed and their heritage stolen. To-day it is in the hands of the profit-mongering crows. It is tilled here and there, but the bullock roams the lands and the people flee the soil. In the 40's the reason of the famine was because the people were slavishly foolish, and they allowed the food that was needed in Ireland to be exported from our shores. And now, although much of our land is not cultivated, there still remains enough foodstuffs to feed our own people. The local authorities should make arrangements immediately for controlling the food supply of the country.

Irish women, it is you who will suffer most by this foreign war. It is the sons you reared at your bosom that will be sent to be mangled by shot and torn by shell; it is your fathers, husbands and brothers whose corpses will pave the way to glory for an Empire that despises you; it is you and your children who will starve at home if the produce of Irish soil is sent out of this country. To you we appeal to aid us in this struggle to save Ireland from the horrors of famine.

Fellow-countrymen, if we allow the farmer to sell his crops for export our people will starve; if we allow the profit-monger to sell the products of our land to be exported to foreign countries our people will die of hunger. Already we are threatened with famine prices; already the gaunt frame of hunger looms large in the outlook because the people think that you will do in 1914 as your fathers did in 1846-47-48. Is it not better to take the risk and responsibility of preventing a repetition of this than to die as our fathers died of hunger and of fever begotten of famine? And you can prevent it. To the men of our class who are armed, we say keep your arms and use them if necessary. If God created the fruits of the earth He created them for you and yours. Do not allow our crops to be gleamed for any other country. They are yours. Keep them at home! Keep them at home we say! Keep them at home by the strength of your right arm.

> 'At last be men, stand forth and clear
> For Freedom's course, a highway.'

God save the People!

Published by the National Executive , Irish Trade Union Congress and Labour Party.

87. Redmond's manifesto on the war
Freeman's Journal, 17 September 1914

The whole-hearted endorsement by the Irish people and the Irish Volunteers of the spirit of my declaration, made on the impulse of the moment, and without seeking for any conditions whatever, that the defence of Ireland might safely be left to the sons of Ireland themselves, shows the profound change which has been brought about in the relations of Ireland to the Empire by the events of the past three years.

The Irish people know, and appreciate the fact fully, that at long last, after centuries of misunderstanding, the democracy of Great Britain has finally and irrevocably decided to trust them, and to give them back their national liberties.

By overwhelming British majorities a Charter of Liberty for Ireland has been three times passed by the House of Commons, and in a few hours will be the law of the land. A new era has opened in the history of the two nations.

During the long discussion of the Irish problem in Parliament and on the platform we promised the British people that the concession of liberty would have the same effect in Ireland as in every other part of the Empire, and notably, in recent years, in South Africa, that disaffection would give way to friendship and goodwill, and that Ireland would become a strength, instead of a weakness, to the Empire.

The democracy of Great Britain listened to our appeal, and have kept faith with Ireland. It is now a duty of honour for Ireland to keep faith with them.

A test to search men's souls has arisen. The Empire is engaged in the most serious war in history. It is a just war, provoked by the intolerable military despotism of Germany. It is a war for the defence of the sacred rights and liberties of small nations, and the respect and enlargement of the great principle of nationality. Involved in it is the fate of France, our kindred country, the chief nation of that powerful Celtic race to which we belong; the fate of Belgium, to whom we are attached by the same great ties of race, and by the common desire of a small nation to assert its freedom; and the fate of Poland, whose sufferings and whose struggle bear so marked a resemblance to our own.

It is a war for high ideals of human government and international relations, and Ireland would be false to her history, and to every consideration of honour, good faith, and self-interest, did she not willingly bear her share in its burdens and its sacrifices.

We have, even when no ties of sympathy bound our country to Great Britain, always given our quota, and more than our quota, to the firing-line, and we shall do so now.

We have a right however to claim that Irish recruits for the Expeditionary Force should be kept together as a unit, officered as far as possible by Irishmen, composed if possible, of county battalions, to form, in fact, an 'Irish Brigade', so that Ireland may gain national credit for their deeds, and feel, like other communities of the Empire, that she too has contributed an army bearing her name in this historic struggle.

Simultaneously with the formation of this Irish Brigade, for service abroad, our Volunteers must be put in a state of efficiency as speedily as practicable, for the defence of the country.

In this way, by the time the war ends, Ireland will possess an army of which she may be proud.

I feel certain that the young men of our country will respond to this appeal with the gallantry of their race.

In conclusion, I would appeal to our countrymen of a different creed, and of opposite political opinions, to accept the friendship we have so consistently offered them to allow this great war, as to which their opinions and ours are the same, and our action will also be the same, to swallow up all the small issues in the domestic government of Ireland which now divide us, that, as our soldiers are going to fight, to shed their blood, and to die at each other's side, in the same army, against the same enemy, and for the same high purpose, their union in the field may lead to a union in their home, and that their blood may be the seal that will bring all Ireland together in one nation, and in liberties equal and common to all.

88. Government of Ireland act, 1914
Acts parl. U.K., 1914, (4 & 5 Geo. V, c. 90)

An Act to amend the provision for the Government of Ireland
[18 September 1914]

. . . . LEGISLATIVE AUTHORITY

1. — (1) On and after the appointed day there shall be in Ireland an Irish Parliament consisting of His Majesty the King and two Houses, namely the Irish Senate and the Irish House of Commons.

(2) Notwithstanding the establishment of the Irish Parliament or anything contained in this Act, the supreme power and authority of the Parliament of the United Kingdom shall remain unaffected and undiminished over all persons, matters, and things in Ireland and every part thereof.

2. Subject to the provisions of this Act, the Irish Parliament shall have power to make laws for the peace, order, and good government of Ireland with the following limitations, namely, that they shall not have power to make laws except in respect of matters exclusively relating to Ireland or some part thereof, and (without prejudice to that general limitation) that they shall not have power to make laws in respect of the following matters in particular, or any of them, namely —

(1) The Crown, or the succession to the Crown, or a Regency. . . .

(2) That making of peace or war or matters arising from a state of war.
. . .

(3) The navy, the army, the territorial force, or any other naval or military force, or the defence of the realm. . . .

(4) Treaties, or any relations, with Foreign States, or relations with other parts of His Majesty's dominions. . . .

(5) Dignities, or titles of honour. . . .

(6) Treason, treason felony, alienage, naturalisation. . . .

(7) Trade with any place out of Ireland (except so far as trade may be affected by the exercise of the powers of taxation given to the Irish Parliament, or by the regulation of importation for the sole purpose of preventing contagious disease, or by steps taken, by means of inquiries or agencies out of Ireland, for the improvement of Irish trade or for the protection of Irish traders from fraud); the granting of bounties on the export of goods; quarantine; or navigation, including merchant shipping (except as respects inland waters, the regulation of harbours, and local health regulations); . . .

(8) Any postal services. . . .

(9) Lighthouses, buoys, or beacons. . . .

(10) Coinage. . . .

(11) Trade marks. . . .

3. In the exercise of their power to make laws under this Act the Irish Parliament shall not make a law so as either directly or indirectly to establish or endow any religion, or prohibit or restrict the free exercise thereof, or give a preference, privilege, or advantage, or impose any disability or disadvantage, on account of religious belief or religious or ecclesiastical status, or make any religious belief or religious ceremony a condition of the validity of any marriage, or affect prejudicially the right of any child to attend a school receiving public money without attending the religious instruction at that school, or alter the constitution of any religious body except where the alteration is approved on behalf of the religious body by the governing body thereof, or divert from any religious denomination the fabric of cathedral churches or, except for the purpose of roads, railways, lighting, water, or drainage works, or other works of public utility upon payment of compensation, any other property. . . .

4. (2) . . . The Lord Lieutenant or other chief executive officer or officers for the time being appointed in his place, on behalf of His Majesty, shall exercise any prerogative or other executive power of His Majesty the exercise of which may be delegated to him by His Majesty.

(3) The powers so delegated shall be exercised through such Irish Departments as may be established by Irish Act or, subject to any alteration by Irish Act, by the Lord Lieutenant, and the Lord Lieutenant may appoint officers to administer those Departments, and those officers shall hold office during the pleasure of the Lord Lieutenant. . . .

5. (1) The public services in connexion with the administration of the

Acts relating to the Royal Irish Constabulary and the management and control of that force, shall be virtue of this Act be transferred from the Government of the United Kingdom to the Irish Government on the expiration of a period of six years from the appointed day. . . .

15. (1) The Irish Parliament shall have power to vary (either by way of addition, reduction, or discontinuance) any Imperial tax so far as respects the levy of the tax in Ireland, and to impose in Ireland any independent tax not being in the opinion of the Joint Exchequer Board substantially the same in character as an Imperial tax, subject to the following limitation: —

(a) The Irish Parliament shall not have power to impose or charge a customs duty, whether an import or an export duty, on any article unless that article is for the time being liable to a customs duty of a like character levied as an Imperial tax. . . .

41. (1) The Irish Parliament shall not have power to repeal or alter any provision of this Act (except as is specially provided by this Act), or of any Act passed by the Parliament of the United Kingdom after the passing of this Act and extending to Ireland, although that provision deals with a matter with respect to which the Irish Parliament have power to make laws.

89. Suspension of the Government of Ireland act
Acts parl. U.K., 1914, (4 & 5 Geo. V, c. 88)

An Act to suspend the operation of the Government of Ireland Act, 1914, and the Welsh Church Act, 1914.

[18 September 1914]

Be it enacted by the King's most Excellent Majesty, by and with the advice and consent of the Lords Spiritual and Temporal, and Commons, in this present Parliament assembled, and by the authority of the same, as follows:

1. — (1) Nothwithstanding anything in the Government of Ireland Act, 1914, no steps shall be taken to put that Act into operation, and nothwithstanding anything in the Welsh Church Act, 1914, the date of disestablishment under that Act shall be postponed, until the expiration of twelve months from the date of the passing of those Acts respectively, or, if at the expiration of those twelve months the present war has not ended, until such later date (not being later than the end of the present war) as may be fixed by His Majesty by Order in Council; and the provisions of those Acts shall have effect accordingly.

(2) In this Act, the Government of Ireland Act, 1914, means any Act

which becomes law during the present session, and which may be cited by that short title; and the Welsh Church Act, 1914, means any Act which becomes law during the present session and which may be cited by that short title.

2. This Act may be cited as the Suspensory Act, 1914.

90. Redmond's speech at Woodenbridge, Co. Wicklow
Freeman's Journal, 21 September 1914

Fellow-countrymen, it was a fortunate chance that enabled me to be present here today. I was motoring past, and I did not know until I arrived here that this gathering of the Volunteers was to take place at Woodenbridge. I could not deny myself the pleasure and honour of waiting to meet you (cheers), to meet so many of those whom I have personally known for many long years, and to see them fulfilling a high duty to their country (cheers). I have no intention of making a speech. All I desire to say to you is that I congratulate you upon the favourable beginning of the work you have made.

A voice — 'Thanks to you.' (cheers)

You have only barely made a beginning. You will yet have hard work before you can call yourselves efficient soldiers, and you will have to have in your hands — every man — as efficient weapons as I am glad to see in the hands of some, at any rate, of your numbers (cheers). Looking back as I naturally do, upon the history of Wicklow, I know that you will make efficient soldiers. Efficient soldiers for what?

Wicklow Volunteers, in spite of the peaceful happiness and beauty of the scene in which we stand, remember this country at this moment is in a state of war, and your duty is a twofold duty. The duty of the manhood of Ireland is twofold. Its duty is, at all costs, to defend the shores of Ireland against foreign invasion. It is a duty more than that of taking care that Irish valour proves itself; on the field of war it has always proved itself in the past (cheers). The interests of Ireland — of the whole of Ireland — are at stake in this war. This war is undertaken in the defence of the highest principles of religion and morality and right, and it would be a disgrace for ever to our country and a reproach to her manhood and a denial of the lessons of her history if young Ireland confined their efforts to remaining at home to defend the shores of Ireland from an unlikely invasion, and to shrinking from the duty of proving on the field of battle that gallantry and courage which has distinguished our race all through its history (cheers). I say to you, therefore, your duty is twofold. I am glad to see such magnificent material for soldiers around me, and I say to you — Go on drilling and make yourselves efficient for the work, and then account yourselves as men, not only for Ireland itself, but wherever the fighting line extends, in defence of right, of freedom and religion in this war (cheers).

91. Irish Volunteers provisional committee breaks with Redmond
Irish Independent, 25 September 1914

Ten months ago a Provisional Committee commenced the Irish Volunteer movement with the sole purpose of securing and defending the rights and liberties of the Irish people. The movement on these lines, though thwarted and opposed for a time, obtained the support of the Irish nation. When the Volunteer movement had become the main factor in the national question, Mr. Redmond decided to acknowledge it, and to endeavour to bring it under his control.

Three months ago he put forward the claim to send 25 nominees to the Provisional Committee of the Irish Volunteers. He threatened, if the claim was not conceded, to proceed to the dismemberment of the Irish Volunteer organization.

It is clear that this proposal to throw the country into turmoil, and to destroy the chances of a Home Rule measure in the near future, must have been forced upon Mr. Redmond. Already ignoring the Irish Volunteers as a factor in the national position, Mr. Redmond has consented to a dismemberment of Ireland, which could be made permanent by the same agencies that forced him to accept it as temporary. He was now prepared to risk another disruption and wreck the cause entrusted to him.

The Provisional Committee, while recognising that the responsibility in that case would be altogether Mr. Redmond's, decided to risk the lesser evil and to admit his nominees to sit and act on the Committee. The Committee made no representations as to the persons to be nominated, and when the nominations were received the Committee raised no question as to how far Mr. Redmond had fulfilled his public undertaking to nominate 'representative men from different parts of the country'. Mr. Redmond's nominees were admitted purely and simply as his nominees, and without co-option.

Mr. Redmond, addressing a body of Irish Volunteers on last Sunday, has now announced for the Irish Volunteers a policy and programme fundamentally at variance with their own published and accepted aims and pledges, but with which his nominees are, of course, identified. He has declared it to be the duty of the Irish Volunteers to take foreign service under a government which is not Irish. He has made this announcement without consulting the Provisional Committee, the Volunteers themselves, or the people of Ireland, to whose service alone they are devoted.

Having thus disregarded the Irish Volunteers and their solemn engagements, Mr. Redmond is no longer entitled, through his nominees, to any place in the administration and guidance of the Irish Volunteers organization. Those who, by virtue of Mr. Redmond's nomination, have, heretofore, been admitted to act on the Provisional Committee, accordingly cease henceforth to belong to that body, and from this date until the holding of an Irish Volunteer Convention the Provisional Committee consists of those only whom it comprised before the admission of Mr. Redmond's nominees.

At the next meeting of the Provisional Committee we shall propose:--

1. To call a Convention of the Irish Volunteers for Wednesday, 25th Nov., 1914, the anniversary of the inaugural meeting of the Irish Volunteers in Dublin.

2. To reaffirm, without qualification, the manifesto proposed and adopted at the inagural meeting.

3. To oppose any diminution of the measure of Irish self-government which now exists as a Statute on paper, and which would not now have reached that stage but for the Irish Volunteers.

4. To repudiate any undertaking, by whomsoever given, to consent to the legislative dismemberment of Ireland, and to protest against the attitude of the present Government, who under the pretence that 'Ulster cannot be coerced' avow themselves prepared to coerce the Nationalists of Ulster.

5. To declare that Ireland cannot, with honour or safety, take part in foreign quarrels otherwise than through the free action of a National Government of her own; and to repudiate the claim of any man to offer up the blood and lives of the sons of Irishmen and Irishwomen to the service of the British Empire while no National Government which could speak and act for the people of Ireland is allowed to exist.

6. To declare that the present system of governing Ireland through Dublin Castle and the British military power, a system responsible for the recent outrages in Dublin, be abolished without delay, and that a National Government be forthwith established in its place.

The signatories to this statement are the great majority of the members of the Provisional Committee of the Irish Volunteers, apart from the nominees of Mr. Redmond who are no longer members of the Committee. We regret that the absence of Sir Roger Casement in America prevents him from being a signatory with us.

(Signed) Eoin MacNeill, Chairman, Provisional Committee; Ua

Rathghaille, Treasurer do.; Thomas MacDonagh, Joseph Plunkett, Piaras Beaslai, Michael J. Judge, Peter Paul Macken, ex.-Ald.; Sean Mac Giobuin, P.H. Pearse, Padraic O'Riain, Bulmer Hobson, Eamonn Martin, Conchubhair O'Colbaird, Eamonn Ceannt, Sean Mac Diarmada, Seamus O'Conchubhair, Liam Mellows, L. Colm O'Lochlainn, Liam Ua Gogan, Peter White.

41 Kildare street, Dublin, September 24, 1914.

92. Statement of Irish Neutrality League
Sinn Féin, 3 October 1914

. . . In the Irish Neutrality League various sections have joined hands, and it may be accepted as a cold fact that henceforth any employer in Ireland who attempts to bring pressure on his workmen to join the British army will have an opportunity of showing his own ability as a first-rate fighting man. Ireland had got to look after herself — got to see that none of her people are bullied into doing what they do not want to do, got to see that no press-ganging under cover of the Militia Ballot act is attempted with impunity. If Ireland remains neutral and Germany wins the war, Ireland will not suffer. Neutrals do not suffer. If England wins, then England is going to treat this country — even though 500,000 Irish dupes died for her — exactly as she pleases. Once Germany goes, England has nothing to fear in Europe except Russia, and so far as the sea is concerned Russia is negligible. The League was formed on Monday night in the Dublin Trades Hall, when Mr. James Connolly was appointed President, Mr. J.T. O'Kelly, T.C., Secretary; Mr. Thomas Farren, Treasurer; and Messrs. W. O'Brien (President of the Trades Council), Arthur Griffith, J. Scollan (A.O.H., American Alliance), Sheehy-Skeffington, J. Milroy, and Countess Markievics chosen as committee.

93. The *Irish Independent* comments on the Irish Neutrality League
Irish Independent, 30 September 1914

Yet Another League

The three tailors of Tooley street have been outdone by a nonsensical body styling itself the 'Irish Neutrality League'. The objects of this new League, as described by its founders, seem to be to direct the whole future policy and conduct of the Irish nation, and more especially to hinder and obstruct as far as possible the recruiting of Irishmen for the army. How any body having such objects in view can call itself a Neutrality League is one of those things which no fellow can understand. It reminds one of the so-called Peace Commission during the labour trouble in Dublin twelve months ago. Composed mainly, if not entirely of partisans, it took on itself the role of peacemaker, but only succeeded in being ridiculous. Its influence was absolutely nil; it produced nothing but resolutions; and it soon died of inanition. A similar fate, in the ordinary course of nature, awaits the Irish Neutrality League.

94. Agreement between Roger Casement and the foreign minister of Germany
Dated 12 November 1914; published in the *Sunday Independent*, 28 December 1924

Article I
With a view of securing the national freedom of Ireland, with the moral and material assistance of the Imperial German Government, an Irish Brigade shall be formed from among the Irish soldiers or other natives of Ireland now prisoners of war in Germany.

Article II
The object of the Irish Brigade shall be to fight solely the cause of Ireland; under no circumstances shall it be employed or directed to any German end.

Article III
The Irish Brigade shall be formed and shall fight under the Irish flag alone. The men shall wear a special distinctively Irish uniform as soon as Irishmen can be got for the purpose either from Ireland or the United States of America. The Brigade shall have only Irish officers. Until such time as Irish officers can be secured German officers will be appointed, with the approval of Sir Roger Casement, to have disciplinary control of the men; but no military operation shall be ordered or conducted by the German officers of the Brigade during such time as the men are under their control.

Article IV
The Irish Brigade shall be clothed, fed, and efficiently equipped with arms and ammunition by the Imperial German Government on the clear understanding that these are furnished as a free gift to aid the cause of Irish independence.

Article V

It is distinctly understood, and is hereby formally declared by the parties to this agreement, that the Irish Brigade shall consist only of volunteers in the cause of Irish national freedom, and as such no member of the Irish Brigade shall receive pay or monetary reward of any kind from the Imperial German Government during the period he shall bear arms in the Irish Brigade.

Article VI

The Imperial German Government undertakes in certain circumstances to send the Irish Brigade to Ireland with efficient military support, and with an ample supply of arms and ammunition to equip the Irish Volunteers in Ireland, who may be willing to join them in the attempt to recover Irish National freedom by force of arms. The certain circumstances hereby understood are the following: —

In the event of a German Naval victory affording the means of reaching the coast of Ireland the Imperial German Government pledges itself to dispatch the Irish Brigade and a supporting body of German officers and men in German transports to attempt and effect a landing on the Irish coast.

Article VII

The opportunity to land in Ireland can only arise if the fortune of war should grant the German Navy a victory that would open with reasonable prospect of success the sea route to Ireland. Should the German Navy not succeed in this effect the Irish Brigade shall be employed in Germany or elsewhere, solely in such a way as Roger Casement may approve as being in strict conformity with Article II. In this event it might be possible to employ the Irish Brigade to assist the Egyptian people to recover their freedom by driving the British out of Egypt.

Article VIII

In the event of the Irish Brigade volunteering for this service, the German Government undertakes to make arrangements with the Austro-Hungarian Government for its transportation through that Empire to Constantinople, and to provide with the Turkish Government for the recognition and acceptance of the Irish Brigade as a Volunteer Corps attached to the Turkish-Egyptian Army in the effort to expel the British from Egypt.

Article IX

In the event of the World War coming to an end without the object of the Irish Brigade having been effected — namely, its landing in Ireland

181

— the German Government undertakes to send each Irishman, members of the Irish Brigade, who may so desire it to the United States of America, with the necessary means to land in that country, in conformity with the United States' Immigration Laws.

Article X

In military operations in that country resulting in the overthrow of British authority and the erection of a National Irish Government, the Imperial German Government will give the Irish Independent Government so established its fullest moral support, and both by public recognition and by general goodwill will contribute with sincerity to the establishment of an Independent Government in Ireland.

95. Patrick Pearse's speech at the burial of O'Donovan Rossa
Diarmuid Ó Donnabháin Rossa, 1831-1915; souvenir of public funeral to Glasnevin cemetery, Dublin, August 1st, 1915 (Dublin, 1915), 2-4

A GHAEDHEALA,

Do hiarradh orm-sa labhairt indiu ar son a bhfuil cruinnuighthe ar an láthair so agus ar son a bhfuil beo de Chlannaibh Gaedheal, ag moladh an leomhain do leagamar i gcré annso agus ag gríosadh meanman na gcarad atá go brónach ina dhiaidh.

A cháirde, ná bíodh brón ar éinne atá ina sheasamh ag an uaigh so, acht bíodh buidheachas againn inar gcroidhthibh do Dhia na ngrás do chruthuigh anam uasal áluinn Dhiarmuda Uí Dhonnabháin Rosa agus thug ré fhada dhó ar an saoghal so.

Ba chalma an fear thú, a Dhiarmuid. Is tréan d'fhearais cath ar son cirt do chine, is ní beag ar fhuilingis; agus ní dhéanfaidh Gaedhil dearmad ort go bráth na breithe.

Acht, a cháirde, na bíodh brón orainn, acht bíodh misneach inar gcroidhthibh agus bíodh neart inar gcuisleannaibh, óir cuimhnighimís nach mbíonn aon bhás ann nach mbíonn aiséirghe ina dhiaidh, agus gurab as an uaigh so agus as na huaghannaibh atá inar dtimcheall éireóchas saoirse Ghaedheal.

It has seemed right, before we turn away from this place in which we have laid the mortal remains of O'Donovan Rossa, that one among us should, in the name of all, speak the praise of that valiant man, and endeavour to formulate the thought and the hope that are in us as we stand around his grave. And if there is anything that makes it fitting that I rather than some other, I rather than one of the grey-haired men who were young with him and shared in his labour and in his suffering, should speak here, it is perhaps that I may be taken as speaking on behalf of a new generation that has been re-baptised in the Fenian faith, and that has accepted the responsibility of carrying out the Fenian programme. I propose to you then that, here by the grave of this unrepentant Fenian, we renew our baptismal vows; that, here by the grave of this un-conquered and unconquerable man, we ask of God, each one for himself, such unshakable purpose, such high and gallant courage, such un-breakable strength of soul as belonged to O'Donovan Rossa.

Deliberately here we avow ourselves, as he avowed himself in the dock, Irishmen of one allegiance only. We of the Irish Volunteers, and you others who are associated with us in to-day's task and duty, are bound together and must stand together henceforth in brotherly union for the achievement of the freedom of Ireland. And we know only one definition of freedom: it is Tone's definition, it is Mitchel's definition, it is Rossa's definition. Let no man blaspheme the cause that the dead generations of Ireland served by giving it any other name and definition than their name and their definition.

We stand at Rossa's grave not in sadness but rather in exaltation of spirit that it has been given to us to come thus into so close a communion with that brave and splendid Gael. Splendid and holy causes are served by men who are themselves splendid and holy. O'Donovan Rossa was splendid in the proud manhood of him, splendid in the heroic grace of him, splendid in the Gaelic strength and clarity and truth of him. And all that splendour and pride and strength was compatible with a humility and a simplicity of devotion to Ireland, to all that was olden and beautiful and Gaelic in Ireland, the holiness and simplicty of patriotism of a Michael O'Cleary or of an Eoghan O'Growney. The clear true eyes of this man almost alone in his day visioned Ireland as we of to-day would surely have her: not free merely, but Gaelic as well; not Gaelic merely but free as well.

In a closer spiritual communion with him now than ever before or perhaps ever again, in spiritual communion with those of his day, living and dead, who suffered with him in English prisons, in communion of spirit too with our own dear comrades who suffer in English prisons to-day, and speaking on their behalf as well as our own, we pledge to Ireland our love, and we pledge to English rule in Ireland our hate. This is a place of peace, sacred to the dead, where men should speak with all charity and with all restraint; but I hold it a Christian thing, as O'Donovan Rossa held it, to hate evil, to hate untruth, to hate oppression, and, hating them, to strive to overthrow them. Our foes are strong and wise and wary; but, strong and wise and wary as they are, they cannot undo the miracles of God who ripens in the hearts of young men the seeds sown by the young men of a former generation. And the seeds sown by the young men of '65 and '67 are coming to their miraculous ripening to-day. Rulers and Defenders of Realms had need to be wary if they would guard against such processes. Life springs from death; and from the graves of patriot men and women spring living nations. The Defenders of this Realm have worked well in secret and in the open. They think that they have pacified Ireland. They think that they have purchased half of us and intimidated the other half. They think that they have foreseen everthing, think that they have provided against everything; but the fools, the fools, the fools! — they have left us our Fenian dead, and while Ireland holds these graves, Ireland unfree shall never be at peace.

96. The Royal Irish Constabulary's view of the political situation in 1915

Chief secretary's office, judicial division, intelligence notes, 1915, State Paper Office, Dublin,

ULSTER

COUNTY ANTRIM

The county was very quiet and peaceable during the year and exceptionally free from serious crime. There was also an entire absence of party and political feeling. As showing the extent to which the truce in party politics was carried out, it may be mentioned that on Easter Sunday a small body of the National Volunteers marched through the streets of Lisburn to the Railway Station, *en route* for Dublin without any notice being taken of them by the Orange Party. The same toleration was extended to them later on in the year when they had route marches through the town. At any other time the appearance of these Volunteers on the streets of Lisburn would probably have led to fierce opposition and serious rioting.

At the beginning of the year the Ulster Volunteer Force in the county had a membership of 9,350 with 9,821 rifles. There was little change in the number of members until November, when the strength of the force was stated to be 7,515. Recruiting for the force was carried on all the time to make good the wastage caused by members joining the Army. At the close of the year the membership was 7,905. In the earlier months of the year some drilling and musketry practice were car[r]ied on, mainly in the towns, and on 26th February, General Sir William Adair held a small review at Ballintoy, but later on there was an almost entire cessation of all active military work.

The National Volunteers at the beginning of the year numbered 2,993 with 380 rifles. About 164 of these Volunteers were reported to be Sinn Feiners. Interest in the movement declined, and the membership fell away to 2,175 at the end of the year. Of these 149 were reported to be Sinn Féiners. The force was quite inactive and military exercises of all kinds practically neglected. There were no branches of the Irish Volunteers in the county.

With the opening of the year there was great anxiety as to the future of the the linen trade, the staple industry of the county. For years flax-growing in the county had been on the decline, and those engaged in the linen trade were relying more and more on Russia and Belgium for supplies of raw material to carry on their business. The closing of the Baltic ports and the invasion of Belgium put a stop to these supplies, and the outlook would have been bad indeed had not special facilities been granted for the transport of flax, tow and flax seed from Russia.

The usual 12th July demonstrations were not held, religious services being substituted for them.

Reporting in October, the County Inspector, in referring to the condition of the people, stated that never within living memory was there so much money in the country. This boom of prosperity he attributed to there being ample employment for all at high wages to a large extent on Government contracts, the high prices obtainable for farm produce and stock, and the payment of separation allowances to soldiers' dependants.

The number of recruits obtained for the Army from the county during the year was 1,990.

COUNTY ARMAGH

During the year the county was very peaceable and free from serious crime and agrarian trouble. Party and sectarian feeling was conspicuous by its absence on both sides. The Ulster Volunteers had a membership of 4,845 at the beginning, and of about 4,490 at the close of the year. In the earlier months of the year some drilling was carried on in the towns, but, apart from this, the force was quite inactive as regards military exercises and operations. They have 5,370 rifles. The National Volunteers started the year with a membership of 4,680 and closed with a membership of 4,126, of whom 192 were reported to be Sinn Feiners. The force was quite inactive during the year. On the 20th June Herbert Pim addressed a meeting at Camlough with the object of furthering the cause of Mr. John McNeill. He met with little support and a good deal of opposition. The Irish Volunteers have no branches in the county.

The Orange Anniversary (12th July) was celebrated very quietly. There was no drumming parties. Some lodges met at Tynan Abbey for a prayer meeting, and Sir James Stronge, Bart., and others delivered recruiting speeches.

Owing to the scarcity of raw material, which was got over to some extent by the use of cotton, a number of linen mills were obliged to work half time; but generally speaking there was plenty of employment during the latter part of the year, when nearly all the mills were able to resume working full time.

The number of men from the country who joined the colours during the year was 1,024.

BELFAST

The city was quiet and peaceable throughout the year. In the early months of the year party feeling, though strong, did not show itself in any overt acts, and as time went on it decreased to a very considerable extent owing to the interest taken in the war. The Ulster and National Volunteers continued to drill and recruit their forces during the early part of the year with considerable vigour; but later on the main activity of the Ulster Volunteers was directed towards recruitment for the Ulster Division of the Army and the care of wounded soldiers. The strength of the Ulster Volunteers at the beginning of the year was 13,420, and at the close 10,967.

The National Volunteers, who began the year with a membership of 1,350, did not vary much in strength, the membership at the end of the year being 1,320. During the spring the National Volunteers were active as regards drilling in preparation for the Review in Dublin on Easter Sunday, at which about 1,000 attended. Later on they became inactive. The Irish Volunteers (Sinn Feiners), numbering about 200, displayed considerable activity right through the year in drilling and keeping up their movement. They do not, however, appear to have been able to increase their membership.

The Orange demonstration on the 12th July was of much smaller dimensions than usual, only about 2,900 taking part in the procession. No drums or banners were carried; and the proceedings at the meeting were of a religious and non-political character.

On the 22nd August a demonstration took place at Milltown Cemetery, where about 2,000 members of the A.O.H. attended with bands and banners. The object of the demonstration was the unveiling of a memorial to the later John Crilly, a prominent member of the Nationalist community in the city. The procession was entirely confined to the Nationalist parts of the city, and there was no disturbance. The unveiling ceremony was performed by Mr. Joseph Devlin, M.P.

The Ulster Covenant Day was observed by the holding of a religious service in the Ulster Hall on the 26th September.

During the early part of the year the female workers in the city suffered considerable privation from want of employment as the mills and factories were only working three-quarter time.

14,463 recruits joined the Army from the city during the year.

COUNTY CAVAN

The county was in a peaceable state during the year and practically free from serious agrarian trouble. In the early part of the year constant protection was afforded to a family named Lynch, who hold an evicted farm, but later on as matters improved protection by patrols was substituted for constant protection. Constant protection was also afforded to a caretaker on a farm in the landlord's hands on the Fay estate, but withdrawn on the departure of the caretaker in February. Some trouble arose on the Tyrrell estate in the Swanlinbar sub-district in February owing to the action of a newly appointed gamekeeper named Thomas King, in strictly carrying out his employer's order to turn off cattle trespassing on his lands. The people of the locality resented his action and made a hostile demonstration against both him and his father, Francis King, by parading with a band on the public road near their house boohing and yelling. For their conduct on the occasion twenty-three persons were arrested on the charge of unlawful assembly and brought before the Resident Magistrate, who adjourned the cases for three months on the parties undertaking to refrain from such conduct in future. The undertaking having been kept, the cases were dismissed at the adjourned hearing in June. No further hostile demonstrations against the Kings took place; but they were subjected to some inconvenience by being boycotted, and the police had to afford them protection by patrols.

Owing to the war, the customary Orange demonstrations on the 12th July were not held.

The Ulster Volunteers began the year with a membership of 2,773, and closed it with a membership of 2,478.

The membership of the National Volunteers fell from 3,739 to 3,334 during the year, of whom 293 were reported to be Sinn Feiners. At the end of the year the Irish Volunteers in the county numbered 153.

453 recruits from the county joined the Army during the year.

The county was peaceable during the year, and free from agrarian trouble and party strife. At the same time old party animosities are not forgotten, and extreme men on both sides say that they will be renewed when the war is over. This applies mainly to the eastern portion of the county, where under the surface the old party and religious feeling is observable now and again, as on St. Patrick's Day when a collision nearly took place at St. Johnston's — an Orange centre — when the A.O.H. attempted to play round the village after having been allowed to play through it. The Ulster and National Volunteer Forces continued to preserve their organisations through the year, but neither force displayed any activity, and drilling and outward displays practically ceased. The Ulster Volunteers numbered 3,000 at the beginning of the year, and 2,580 at its close. The membership of the National Volunteers at the same periods was 9,725 and 7,206 respectively. Of the latter numbers 219 were reported to be Sinn Feiners. There was only one branch of the Irish Volunteers in existence at the end of the year with a membership of five. Though small in numbers they were active in carrying on their propaganda against recruiting, etc. . . . .

97. James Connolly comments on the effect of the war on Ireland
Workers' Republic, 5 February 1916

THE TIES THAT BIND

Recently we have been pondering deeply over the ties that bind this country to England. It is not a new theme for our thoughts; for long years we have carried on propaganda in Ireland pointing out how the strings of self-interest bound the capitalist and landlord classes to the Empire, and how it thus became a waste of time to appeal to those classes in the name of Irish patriotism.

We have said that the Working Class was the only class to whom the word 'Empire', and the things of which it was the symbol did not appeal. That to the propertied classes 'Empire' meant high dividends and financial security, whereas to the Working Class that meant only the things it was in rebellion against.

Therefore from the intelligent working class could alone come the revolutionary impulse.

Recently we have seen the spread of those ties of self-interest binding certain classes and individuals to the Empire — we have seen it spread to a most astonishing degree until its ramifications cover the island, like the spread of a foul disease.

It would be almost impossible to name a single class or section of the population not evilly affected by this social, political, and moral leprosy.

Beginning with our parliamentary representatives, we see men so poisoned by the evil association of parliament and enervated with the unwonted luxury of a salary much greater than they could ever hope to enjoy in private life, that they have instantly and completely abandoned all the traditions of their political party, and become the mouthpieces and defenders of an Imperial system their greatest leaders had never ceased to hold up to the scorn of the world.

We see the ties of self-interest so poisoning those men that they become the foulest slanderers and enemies of all who stand for that unfettered Ireland to which they also once pledged their heartiest allegiance. For the sake of £400 a year they become Imperialists; for the sake of large travelling expenses and luxurious living they become lying recruiters.

Corporation after corporation elected to administer our towns and cities neglect their proper business, and make their city halls and town halls the scene of attempts to stampede the youth and manhood of Ireland out of the country to die inglorious deaths in foreign fields. And while those misguided young and middle-aged men perish afar off the mayors and councillors who sent them to their doom scramble for place and titles at the hands of a foreign tyrant. We hear of a Mayor in a Western city drawing £5 per week as a recruiter, and a Councillor in Dublin prostituting himself for a paltry 17/6 per week for the same dirty cause.

Between those two there are all sorts of grades and steps in infamy. The western Mayor is reckoned by his associates as having got a good price for his soul, whereas the Dublin councillor who sells himself for 17/6 per week is generally despised as having made a sorry trade.

One councillor gets one thing, his colleague gets another. One Dublin city councillor has hired a number of his derelict houses to the Government for munition factories at a tidy sum, another is assured of good contracts, another is promised a reversion of a good salaried position in a few months.

There is nobody in a representative position so mean that the British government will not pay some price for his Irish soul. Newspaper men sell their Irish souls for government advertisements paid for at a lavish rate, Professors sell their souls for salaries and expenses, clergymen sell their's for jobs for their relatives, business men sell their souls and become recruiters lest they lose the custom of government officials. In all the grades of Irish society the only section that has not furnished even one apostate to the cause it had worked for in times of peace is that of the much hated and traduced militant Labour Leaders.

But if the Militant Labour Leaders of Ireland have not apostatised the same can not be said of the working class as a whole. It is with shame and sorrow we say it, but the evil influence upon large sections of the Irish Working Class of the bribes and promises of the enemy cannot be denied.

We know all that can be said in extenuation of their mistakes, all that we ourselves have said and will say in condonation and excuse of their lapses from the path of true patriotism. But when all is said and done the facts remain horrible and shameful to the last degree.

For the sake of a few paltry shillings per week thousands of Irish workers have sold their country in the hour of their country's greatest need and greatest hope. For the sake of a few platry shillings Separation Allowance thousands of Irish women have made life miserable for their husbands with entreaties to join the British Army. For the sake of a few paltry shillings Separation Allowance thousands of young Irish girls have rushed into matrimony with young Irish traitors who in full knowledge of the hopes of Nationalist Ireland had enlisted in the Army that England keeps here to slaughter Irish patriots.

For what is the reason for the presence of the English army in this country? The sole reason for the presence of such soldiers in Dublin, in Ireland, is that they may be used to cut the throats of Irish men and women should we dare demand for Ireland what the British Government is pretending to fight for in Belgium.

For the sake of the Separation Allowance thousands of Irish men, women, and young girls have become accomplices of the British Government in this threatened crime against the true men and women of Ireland.

Like a poisonous ulcer this tie of self-interest has spread over Ireland corrupting and destroying all classes, from the Lord Mayor in his Mansion House to the poor boy and girl in the slum. Corrupting all hearts, destroying all friendships, poisoning all minds.

The British Government stands in the Market Places and streets of Ireland buying, buying, buying, buying *the souls* of the men and women, the boys and girls, whom ambition, or greed, or passion, or vice, or poverty, or ignorance makes weak enough to listen to its seductions.

And yet the great heart of the nation remains true. Some day most of those deluded and misled brothers and sisters of ours will learn the truth, some day we will welcome them back to our arms purified and repentant of their errors.

Perhaps in that day the same evil passions the enemy has stirred up in so many of our Irish people, will play havoc with his own hopes, and make more bitter and deadly the cup of his degradation and defeat.

But deep in the heart of Ireland has sunk the sense of the degradation wrought upon its people — our lost brothers and sisters — so deep and humiliating that no agency less potent than the red tide of war on Irish soil will ever be able to enable the Irish race to recover its self-respect, or establish its national dignity in the face of a world horrified and scandalised by what must seem to them our national apostasy.

Without the slightest trace of irreverence but in all due humility and awe we recognise that of us as of mankind before Calvary it may truly be said:

'Without the Shedding of Blood there is no Redemption.'

98. The Royal Irish Constabulary views the political situation in March 1916

Extract from the confidential report of the inspector general for the month of March 1916. State Paper Office, Dublin

ACTIVITY OF POLITICAL AND SECRET SOCIETIES

The Irish Volunteers still rank foremost among political societies, not by reason of their numerical strength, but on account of their greater activity. Ten branches were formed during the month, and about 500 new members joined, which, taking into consideration the vigorous efforts to spread the movement, must be regarded as a disappointing result. As already suggested in my last report, this slow progress is no doubt due to the exclusion of Ireland from the scope of the Military Service Act, and to the lack of influential patronage. Ten organizers were at work in the counties of Limerick, Galway, Mayo, Cavan, Wexford, Cork, Kerry, Kilkenny, Tyrone, Londonderry, and Antrim. Two of these, Ernest Blythe and William Mellowes, were within the past few days arrested and deported to England in pursuance of orders made last year by the Competent Military Authority under the Defence of the Realm Regulations, and expulsion orders have now been served on two others, viz: — Albert Cotton and Alfred Monaghan. However, with the exception of some priests, nationalists of respectable position in the provinces hold aloof from the Irish Volunteers, and the estimated strength of the Force, excluding the Dublin Metropolitian Police Area, is only 8,179, to which may be added 4,572 mmebers of the National Volunteers (Redmondite) who are reputed Sinn Feiners or otherwise opposed to Mr. Redmond's recruiting policy. They are believed to possess abour 1,886 rifles and 2,579 shotguns, etc.

The Irish Volunteers Headquarters ordered parades throughout the provinces on St. Patrick's Day, and as they seemed likely to afford some indication of the force available for mobilization, the local police carefully supervised them. The total number did not exceed 4,555, of whom only 1,817 were armed, half with rifles and half with shotguns — nor was the attitude of the spectators very encouraging. There was no demonstration of sympathy, and at many places the Volunteers merely marched in the usual processions organized by other public bodies to celebrate the National Festival. Nevertheless the movement is holding its ground firmly, and steadily improving its organization. It has ofter been reported that the Irish Volunteer movement is financed from America, and although there is no absolute proof of this, it is obvious that the expenditure on organization and equipment must be far in excess of the amount realized by local subscriptions. The Volunteers are very short of rifles but a good many single-barrel American shotguns, probably imported some months ago, have lately been served out. There is an evident anxiety to procure as many guns as possible.

In my report last month I referred to the seditious and insurrectionary aims of the Irish Volunteers and their injurious influence on recruiting for the Army, and I drew attention to the possible danger from such a disloyal and hostile body indifferently armed and no doubt also possessed of a quantity of explosives at the present time. I may now state that even in remote places their attitude is becoming more defiant and aggressive. When the house of one of the organizers was being searched last January at Cork a typed circular was found containing instructions to the Irish Volunteers to resist any attempt to seize their arms. The occurrence at Tullamore, on the 20th March, would apparently show how these instructions are understood. A party of Volunteers had discharged revolvers through the windows of their room at a hostile crowd outside and then fired at the police when they entered for the purpose of bringing offenders to justice, seriously wounding a Sergeant. A few days after the occurrence the Council of the Irish Volunteers assembled in Dublin and issued a manifesto warning the public that the Volunteers cannot submit to be disarmed, and that 'the raiding for arms and attempted disarming of men, therefore, in the natural course of things can only be met by resistance and bloodshed'. On April 1st Professor McNeill, President of the Irish Volunteers, in the editorial column of 'The Irish Volunteer', insisting on the right of the Volunteers to be armed, states 'we may be taken unawares here and there, but when we are not taken unawares we shall defend our arms with our lives'. The O'Rahilly, treasurer to the Irish Volunteers, in a letter to 'The Hibernian' on the 8th April, alluding to the Tullamore incident states, 'Thirteen other men are in gaol on a charge of attempted murder because they behaved in the only manner in which it is conceivable for men to behave in pursuance of that Volunteer policy which the whole Irish people so recently endorsed'. A local organizer who gave similar advice to a party of Volunteers at Meelick, County Clare, on March 17th, was prosecuted under the Defence of the Realm Regulations, on the 4th instant, and sent to gaol for three months.

There can be no doubt that the Irish Volunteer leaders are a pack of rebels who would revolt and proclaim their independence, in the event of any favourable opportunity; but with their present resources and without substantial reinforcement it is difficult to imagine that they could make even a brief stand against a small body of troops. These observations however are made with reference to the provinces and not to the Dublin Metropolitan Police Area, which is the centre of the movement.

The Sinn Feiners held very few public meetings during the month; amongst the number were three recruiting meetings for the Irish Volunteers at Belfast, which were a failure. Countess Markievicz delivered a very seditious lecture on Robert Emmet at the City Hall, Cork. Some seditious leaflets were distributed here and there, and disloyal newspapers were in circulation — one of these 'The Gael', a new publication, was seized at places of sale throughout the country by order of the Competent Military Authority. . . .

99. Loyalist attack on Ancient Order of Hibernians hall in County Down, March 1916
Letter of Augustine Birrell, chief secretary for Ireland, to Edward Carson, 31 March 1916. Carson papers, Public Record Office of Northern Ireland, in Patrick Buckland, editor, *Irish unionism*, 1885-1923 (Belfast, 1973), 92-93

My dear Sir Edward — I enclose a telegram just arrived which relates to a curious proceeding near Portadown. It is rather a novelty, & though beyond the demolition of a building & a great deal of gunpowder nothing of great consequence has as yet happened I thought you should be told about it — as so far we have had next to no trouble in the North.

I was very glad to see you in & about the House again, though it is no pleasure to be there. Yours v sincerely

Augustine Birrell

. . . Following telegram received from Dist. Inspector Portadown (begins)

Yesterday between 2.30 & 3 p.m. while men were engaged in building a new A[ncient] O[rder of] H[ibernians] Hall in Breagh S[ub] D[ivision]. Birches, shots were fired from a distance, but no one was injured. At 4.50 a.m. today about 200 men arrived with rifles, revolvers, & swords & bayonets, marched in fours to the site of the hall & after firing about 200 shots demolished the brick wall built yesterday, and smashed all the bricks. These men who are all believed to be neighbouring Orangemen and Unionists were all disguised & none of them were identified by the police patrol which was present. The patrol attempted to follow them when leaving & about 20 rifles were turned on them & ball cartridges fired in their direction without hitting them — in all about 600 or 700 shots were fired. During the demolition of the material about 20 men were posted at a distance round the building with orders to shoot at any person approaching. ends.

100. Loyalist explanation of the attack
Letter from W. Moore, M.P. for North Armagh and officer in the Orange Order, to Carson, 4 April 1916. Carson papers, P.R.O.N.I., in Buckland, *Irish unionism*, 93-94

My dear Carson — I had a deputation of 3 men from Clonmakate yesterday.

You must understand that in that country there are clear demarcations of Protestant and Roman Catholic territory, and processions are not allowed to pass through opposing districts as a well recognised police rule there.

Maghery is the Nationalist head quarters 3 miles away. This townland (of Breagh) contains 12 Protestant & 4 R.C. 2 of whom and the P.P. are opposed to the erection of this Hall. The site chosen is close to an Orange Hall, a Masonic Hall, two churches (C of Ireland & Presbyterian) & in the centre of a triangle with 3 Protestant schools. It is looked upon by the Protestants as a mere act of aggression and boasted of as much by the Nationalists. They began it three years ago & it was levelled. They began it again about 18 months ago & it was again levelled. Nothing more happened until this time they were afforded police protection. Police protection should not be afforded for such an act of aggression. If the police are now withdrawn the Nationalists will never attempt to go on with it & nothing more will be heard of it. James Campbell might speak to Birrell about it. No one was assaulted or hurt & there can hardly be a prosecution. If the police protection is continued & the Nationalists build under it possibly lives will be lost. Our people asked me if <u>they</u> would be given police protection to build an Orange Hall in Maghery? This is not in Portadown District but in Loughgall where the D[istrict] M[aster] has not the same influence. I can do nothing with them. They look on themselves as bound to stop this just as if they were in Derry during the siege.

Yours ever,
W. Moore